SPAIN

Getting to know Spain — 4
Discovering Spain 6–7
Life in Spain 8–9 Yesterday and tomorrow 10–11
People and places 12–13 Getting around 14–17

Don't miss The Top Ten Highlights — 18

Madrid — 20

Old Castile — 46

Castilla-La Mancha and Extremadura — 68

Barcelona — 90

Catalonia and the Pyrenees — 112

The North — 134

The Levant — 162

Sevilla and Western Andalucía — 184

Granada, Córdoba and the Costa del Sol — 204

Lifestyles — 226
Shopping 228–31 Eating out 232–5 Spain with children 236–7 After dark 238–41

Practical information — 242

CONTENTS

Published by Thomas Cook Publishing
A division of Thomas Cook Holdings Ltd
PO Box 227, Thorpe Wood
Peterborough PE3 6PU
United Kingdom

Telephone: 01733 503571
E-mail: books@thomascook.com

Text: © 2000, Thomas Cook Holdings Ltd
Maps prepared by Polly Senior Cartography
Maps © 2000, Thomas Cook Holdings Ltd

ISBN 1 841570 74 5

Distributed in the United States of America by the Globe Pequot Press,
PO Box 480, Guilford, Connecticut 06437, USA.

Distributed in Canada by Whitecap Books, 351 Lynn Avenue,
North Vancouver, British Columbia, Canada V7J 2C4.

Distributed in Australia and New Zealand by Peribo Pty Limited,
58 Beaumont Road, Mt Kuring-Gai, NSW, 2080, Australia.

Publisher: Donald Greig
Commissioning Editor: Deborah Parker
Map Editor: Bernard Horton

Series Editor: Christopher Catling

Written and researched by: Patricia Harris, Nick Inman, David Lyon,
Tony Kelly and Clara Villanueva

All rights reserved. No part of this publication may be reproduced, stored in
a retrieval system or transmitted, in any form or by any means, electronic,
mechanical, recording or otherwise, in any part of the world, without the prior
permission of the publishers. All requests for permission should be made to
the Publisher at the above address.

Although every care has been taken in compiling this publication, and the
contents are believed to be correct at the time of printing, Thomas Cook
Holdings Ltd cannot accept responsibility for errors or omissions, however
caused, or for changes in details given in the guidebook, or for the consequences
of any reliance on the information provided.

The opinions and assessments expressed in this book do not necessarily
represent those of Thomas Cook Holdings Ltd.

Readers are asked to remember that attractions and establishments may open,
close or change owners or circumstances during the lifetime of this edition.
Descriptions and assessments are given in good faith but are based on the
author's views and experience at the time of writing and therefore contain
an element of subjective opinion which may not accord with the reader's
subsequent experience. We would be grateful to be told of any changes or
inaccuracies in order to update future editions. Please notify them to the
Commissioning Editor at the above address.

Cover photograph: Robert Harding Picture Library/Michael Busselle

must-see SPAIN

NICK INMAN

Getting to know Spain

GETTING TO KNOW SPAIN

GETTING TO KNOW SPAIN

Discovering Spain

Spain is the world's second biggest tourist destination (after France), receiving over 50 million visitors annually. For most people, a holiday in Spain means days on the beach and nights eating tapas *and watching flamenco dancing. But Spain is nothing if not diverse: it has* **spectacular countryside** *harbouring an extraordinary array of wildlife and* **historic towns and cities** *packed with great art and architecture.*

Beach bliss

With their seemingly endless sunshine and warm winter temperatures, the Mediterranean coasts are a mecca for package tourists. Spain has Mediterranean and Atlantic coasts, and on both there are still places where you can get away from the crowds. Most of the established resorts are on the **Costa del Sol** (south coast) and the **Costa Brava** and **Costa Blanca** (both on the east). Up and coming are the **Costa Daurada**, **Costa del Azahar** and **Costa Cálida** – all also on the eastern seaboard. Less well known outside Spain, but worth exploring, are the beaches of the Atlantic coasts: the **Costa Verde** (north), **Rías Baixas** (Galicia, in the northwest) and the **Costa de la Luz** (in the southwest, from Tarifa to the Portuguese border).

GETTING TO KNOW SPAIN

> *Foreigners have no right to argue that the effects produced on Spaniards are exactly those which are produced on themselves, or which they imagine would be produced on their readers ... As far as the loss of human life is concerned, more aldermen are killed indirectly by turtles than Spaniards directly by bulls.*

Richard Ford on bullfighting, *A Handbook for Travellers in Spain* **(1845)**

Nature overdose

After Switzerland, Spain is the most mountainous country in Europe, as you will discover if you drive through almost any part of its territory. This makes for some ideal hill-walking country.

But it is not all mountains. Spain stretches from the summits of the Pyrenees to the coast of Africa and is considered to have a greater range of landscapes than any other European country. There are six **national parks** in mainland Spain and around 200 other **nature reserves**, and there is space to spare; some of it is barren but there are still vast areas of countryside bristling with wild flowers and animal life. No wonder *turismo verde* – 'green tourism' – is booming at the moment.

For culture connoisseurs

More than 30 towns, villages and monuments in Spain are classed as **World Heritage Sites** by Unesco – more than any other country in Europe. The Iberian peninsula has been watching civilisations come and go for 800,000 years. The result is a formidable collection of art and architecture, ancient and modern: prehistoric dolmens, Roman amphitheatres, Gothic cathedrals, Christian and Moorish castles, medieval villages, baroque palaces, art-nouveau mansions, striking examples of contemporary architecture and museums stuffed with intriguing historical artefacts and great works of art.

Meet the people

If you can get beyond the stereotypes of flamenco-dancing, bullfighting and siesta-snoozing, the Spanish way of life is an attraction too. This is a land where people know how to enjoy themselves, spending long hours socialising over drinks and *tapas*, or eating leisurely meals out of doors. And nightlife here means just that. When the rest of Europe is ending its day, Spain is just warming up: most people wouldn't start a night on the tiles much before midnight. Spain's bizarre fiestas, meanwhile, exert a fascination all of their own: they are usually visually compelling but can also be hair-raisingly exciting.

GETTING TO KNOW SPAIN

Life in Spain

For a long time Spain was more or less cut off from the rest of Europe behind the Pyrenees and Spanish society developed according to its own rules. With Spain's increasing integration in the European Union and the spread of global culture, things are changing, but there are still many ways in which daily life in Spain is unique.

A different rhythm

Spaniards live according to a clock different from everywhere else in Europe. Lunch is at 1400 or 1500, which makes for a very long morning (the early hours of the morning are so important they are dignified with their own name: ***la madrugada***). The afternoon begins – after a lazy break – at around 1700, and many people will work until 2000 or 2100 at night, eating at 2130 or 2200. It is not uncommon to see the streets swarming with people of all ages around midnight, especially in the summer months when it is too hot to stir out of doors during the day. Newcomers sometimes find these hours hard to cope with. The secret of keeping up with the Spaniards is to go with the flow and pace yourself: rest when everyone else does, and don't rush.

Regional round-up

Modern Spain can only be understood as a country made up of regions. Where you come from has always been of paramount importance in Spain, and the **17 autonomous regions** (including the Balearic and Canary island groups, not covered here) into which the country is divided are keen to emphasise their different characters. Many Basques and Catalans, for instance, claim to have nothing in common with Andalucians or the people of the plains of La Mancha.

Regional differences are seen most clearly when it comes to **language**. You may think Spanish is the language of Spain, but in fact it has four official languages of which Spanish – strictly Castilian, the language of Castile – is only one. The

GETTING TO KNOW SPAIN

Basques, Catalans and Galicians insist their own languages should be given equal importance to Spanish in schools, in official documents and on road signs. Fortunately, Spanish is still used as a lingua franca.

Family, work and religion

If his home town gives a Spaniard one set of personal co-ordinates, it is kin which puts the seal on his identity. The **extended family** survives by and large and many Spaniards are aware they are part of an active network of aunts, cousins, nephews and nieces – although there are pros and cons to having so many people interested in what you are up to. But family life – the pillar of Spanish society – is being squeezed by uncertain job prospects and consumerism as Spain becomes more Europeanised. Old industries are disappearing, agriculture is declining, and isolated villages are being abandoned. Spain now has one of the lowest birth rates in Europe as couples plump for higher standards of living rather than raising numerous offspring. This may weaken extended family ties in years to come.

> " The Spanish have grown up used to secure terms of employment. Now they are having to adapt to the dreaded contrato basura, a 'rubbish contract' which guarantees work for a few months only. "
>
> **Josefina Fernández, writer and translator**

The other bedrock of Spanish life used to be the **Catholic Church**, but no more. Attendance at mass has slumped in recent decades, although Christian traditions – baptisms, confirmations, church weddings – are upheld by the secularised younger generation. Nevertheless, the imagery of Catholicism is everywhere, and an extraordinary number of saints and manifestations of the Virgin Mary are still widely venerated.

GETTING TO KNOW SPAIN

Yesterday and tomorrow

The Iberian peninsula was a prized possession for a succession of ancient civilisations – Tartessans, Phoenicians, Carthaginians, Romans, Visigoths – each driving out its predecessor and leaving behind remnants of its art and architecture.

Moors and Christians

The invasion of Visigothic Spain in 711 by the Islamic people from North Africa, normally called the **Moors**, left an indelible mark on the country, particularly Andalucia. Moorish influence can be seen clearly on innumerable monuments and in living folk traditions. Even the language is a reminder of their presence: Spanish developed out of Latin but is filled with words derived from Arabic (those beginning with *al* are the most obvious).

Moorish Spain – al-Andalus – was a complex society and at times allowed for great tolerance between the three co-existing religions: Islam, Judaism and Christianity. But the Christian chiefs of northern Spain saw it as their holy duty to take back Spain from the infidel. The series of wars that ensued, known as **the Reconquest**, lasted 700 years and left as a legacy castles of every shape and size on every available hill top. The battles fought between Moors and Christians are symbolically re-enacted each year in countless fiestas up and down Spain.

The Golden Age

In 1492, the so-called 'Catholic Monarchs', **Fernando and Isabel**, expelled the last of the Moors, unified Spain and dispatched **Columbus** to America. Over the next two centuries Spain's New World colonies sent back prodigious quantities of gold, and art and architecture flourished, reaching a peak in the so-called Golden Age of the 17th century. This was the time of the painters **Velázquez** and **El Greco**, and the writers **Cervantes** (author of *Don Quixote*) and **Lope de Vega**.

Troubled times

Spain had a chaotic number of rulers and governments between the Golden Age and the early 20th century, briefly becoming a republic but reverting to a monarchy soon after. In 1931 the Second Republic was declared, but in July 1936 **General Francisco Franco** rebelled against the elected government. A civil war ensued, which ended in victory for Franco, and he ruled Spain as a dictator for almost 40 years. No one knew what to expect when he died in 1975, and to many the swift transformation of Spain into a constitutional monarchy, with **King Juan Carlos I** presiding over a democratic government, seemed nothing short of miraculous.

Spain comes into its own

Spain has gone through extraordinary changes since the restoration of democracy, steadily moving into the mainstream of Western countries. In 1986 it joined the then European Community (now the European Union). Its smooth staging in 1992 of the Barcelona Olympic Games and a World Fair in Sevilla impressed the world.

Spain will be one of the first countries in Europe to convert to the **single currency**, and the current right-wing government is set on a policy of privatisation of public companies; Telefónica, the telephone company, has already become an aggressive private concern. The railway monopoly holder, RENFE, may soon follow suit. However, the prosperity brought by joining Europe has created a new problem which will tax Spain over the coming years: **illegal immigration** from North Africa has sparked racial tensions hitherto unseen in a relatively homogenous society.

> *From the earliest times, Spanish Christians, on the whole, had recognized that Muhammadan culture, although not exactly superior to their own, an admission which they might have made had it not been for the Church, was at least something to be valued.*
>
> **Bernard Bevan, *A History of Spanish Architecture* (1938)**

GETTING TO KNOW SPAIN

People and places

Spanish culture is generally not well known in the English-speaking world. Only a few Spaniards have earned international fame, but there are many talented people in Spain who deserve to be better known abroad.

Artists and performers

Idiosyncratic film director **Pedro Almodóvar** has long been the golden boy of the Spanish arts world, and his status as icon was confirmed in 2000 when his *All About My Mother* won the Oscar for best foreign film. Many critics regard his bitter-sweet comedy *Women on the Verge of a Nervous Breakdown* (1987) as his masterpiece. Almodóvar's influence on cinema has been wide reaching; among other things, he was responsible for discovering and promoting two rising Hollywood actors, **Antonio Banderas** and **Penélope Cruz**.

Spain hasn't proved very successful at exporting its pop stars. One of the few international singing stars is **Julio Iglesias**, perhaps because he is willing to record in languages other than Spanish. The music of **Ana Belén** – the woman Spanish women most admire, according to one survey – and the gravel-voiced urban poet **Joaquín Sabina** have never found an audience abroad. Opera singers have done much better, with **José Carreras**, **Montserrat Caballé** and **Plácido Domingo** leading the field.

Neither have Spanish writers won over a readership outside the Hispanic world, with the exception of Nobel Prize-winning novelist **Camilo José Cela**. Spain has a thriving publishing industry and produces some good literature which is not always translated abroad. Popular writers of today include **Antonio Muñoz Molina** and **Arturo Perez-Reverte**.

Spain, however, has been home to many great visual

GETTING TO KNOW SPAIN

artists. The cream of artists working today include **Eduardo Chillida**, **Antoni Tapiès**, **Antonio Lopez** and **Javier Mariscal**, who designed the logo for the 1992 Barcelona Olympics.

Politicians and statesmen

When Franco died it looked unlikely that his chosen successor, **King Juan Carlos I**, would be accepted by the Spanish people. But the king proved himself immediately by setting up a democracy (with the help of **Adolfo Suárez**) and earned the respect of even hardened republicans when he faced down the leaders of a military coup in 1983. His wife, **Queen Sofía**, and their children have similarly endeared themselves to their subjects through their modest lifestyles and hard work.

> *In Spain the dead are more alive than the dead of any other country in the world.*
>
> **Federico García Lorca (1899–1936)**

Post-Franco politics have been dominated by **Felipe González**, the Socialist prime minister through much of the 1980s and 1990s. Remarkably, he escaped unscathed from the corruption scandals which brought down his last government. The present prime minister, **José María Aznar**, who is right of centre, is not perceived to have the same charisma, but he showed bravery when he survived an attempted assassination.

Sports stars

Spain is sports mad, and footballers like **Raúl** and **Guardiola** are much lauded. Two top women's tennis players, **Conchita Martínez** and **Arantxa Sánchez**, come from Spain. The country has also produced great golfers (**Severiano Ballesteros** and **José-Maria Olazábal**) and cyclists (**Miguel Indurain**).

Some people thought that the 20th century would force bullfighting into decline, but it is as popular as ever. Successful *toreros* are invariably men; one woman tried to break in recently but found the taurine world too *machisto* to accept her. Champion bullfighters are treated as celebrities, although because of the nature of their profession – which demands sustained daring and vigour – they come and go, sometimes tragically quickly. One rising star of today is the very young **El Juli.**

GETTING TO KNOW SPAIN

Getting around

Spain's internal communications have been vastly improved in the last 20 years. New motorways have shortened distances and eased the way through once tedious mountain ranges. It is easy to get from city to city by coach or train, and once in any urban area the best way to move around is on foot or by public transport. To explore Spain properly, however, the only option is to hire a car.

Air

The national airline **Iberia** (*tel in UK: 020 7830 0011, tel in Spain: 902 400 500, www.iberia.es*) and its affiliate **Aviaco** operate most domestic air routes. Recently companies such as **Spanair** and **Air Europe** have been offering competition. An air shuttle connects Madrid and Barcelona, and regular flights link all major regional capitals. It's worth asking about flying if you have to travel a long distance within Spain or are in a hurry, but for shorter routes check first whether there is an efficient train or coach service – the time-saving by plane may not justify the larger fare.

Coaches and buses

Most non-car-owning Spaniards prefer coach to train when travelling long distance. This is because main roads are generally good, coach fares are reasonably priced and there is at least one coach company serving any given inter-city route. For more localised transport, coach services radiate out from the provincial capital. Tickets cannot usually be purchased over the phone and you may have to go to a bus station one or two days before travelling to make a reservation. For really localised transport, all large towns and cities in Spain run efficient bus services.

GETTING TO KNOW SPAIN

Rail

The Spanish rail network has about 15,000km (9 300 miles) of track, but trains are only worth using when travelling to or from Madrid, as services between provincial cities are often poor or non-existent (one of the few exceptions being the Barcelona–Valencia line). Most trains are operated by the state-owned company **RENFE** (*tel in UK: Rail Europe on 020 7647 4900, tel in Spain: 902 240 202, www.renfe.es*), which sells three- to ten-day travel passes. The pride of the network is the **AVE high-speed train** which covers the distance between Madrid and Sevilla in under three hours, and which will soon reach Barcelona and the French border.

There are also still a handful of privately run narrow-gauge lines which do not come under the auspices of RENFE. The two most interesting are the north-coast line from San Sebastián to Santiago de Compostela and the east-coast line from Alicante to Denia, both of which are slow to travel on but pass through attractive scenery.

> " *A great thing about Spain – for the traveller – is the Spanish liking for late hours. Arrive at any provincial hotel of the simpler kind – I cannot answer for the grand, international places – and you will be welcomed as if it were noonday.* "
>
> **Kate O'Brien,** *Farewell Spain* **(1937)**

Taxis

Taxis operate in all the major cities. The trademark colour varies from place to place but will always be distinctive enough for you to know

GETTING TO KNOW SPAIN

what kind of vehicle to flag down. A green light means a taxi is available for hire. The fare will be fixed by meter, which may start at a minimum charge.

Cities

Madrid and Barcelona have extensive **metro systems** which are worth getting to know as they are cheap and will get you to almost every corner of the city. Bilbao and Valencia have more limited metros. In smaller towns and cities, walking is usually the best way to get around, with the bus as a back-up.

Car hire

All the major car-hire companies have offices throughout Spain and rates are very competitive. You can often get the best deal by reserving a car from home at the same time as making a flight booking. Local car-hire companies operate at all major and package-holiday airports. When hiring a car you will be asked to show your **passport** and an **EU or international driving licence**. It is worth paying a little extra for a car with air-conditioning if you are travelling between May and September.

Driving

There are 340,000km (211,000 miles) of roads in Spain but they are in a variable state of repair and even the best maps are not up to date with the latest improvements. The best roads are *autopistas*, but using these toll motorways can prove expensive, and while there is always an alternative main road it is likely to be congested with lorries. *Autovías*, on the other hand, are toll-free motorways. Most maps use a colour scheme to indicate which motorway is which.

Spain drives on the left, and its highway code is similar to that of other European countries, with internationally recognisable traffic signs. Warning: the police can issue on-the-spot fines for traffic offences, and being a foreigner does not bring exemption.

GETTING TO KNOW SPAIN

Maps

If you are thinking of driving around rural Spain you will need a good map as road signs are not always adequate. Michelin publishes a reliable 1cm = 10km map of Spain and Portugal which is adequate for general touring. The 1cm = 4km series of maps is a better choice for exploring a particular area. A wide range of Spanish maps are on sale in the UK *(try Stanfords, 12-14 Long Acre, London WC2E 9LP; tel: 020 7836 1321)* and, of course, in Spain *(the best source is the Instituto de Información Geógrafica de España, Calle General Ibañez Ibero 3, Madrid; tel: 91 554 1450)*.

Tourist information

Before travelling, tourist information can be obtained from the **Spanish Tourist Office** *(22–23 Manchester Square, London W1M 5AP; tel: 020 7486 8077, fax: 020 7486 8034, e-mail: londres@tourspain.es, www.tourspain.co.uk* and *www.tourspain.es*). The official websites will answer most general questions.

Tourist information services in Spain are no longer centralised, but are organised region by region, town by town. It is worth calling in at the regional capital's main tourist office, but the best information can always be found in municipal tourist offices.

GETTING TO KNOW SPAIN

Don't miss

1 Barcelona

There are any number of reasons to spend a long weekend in Barcelona, and just as many for a repeat visit. You can see the sights – the extraordinary art-nouveau architecture of **Antoni Gaudí**, the **medieval Gothic Quarter** *et al* – or take in the bars and nightlife. Or just hang out in one of Europe's most stimulating cities. For a break within a break, take a trip to the spectacularly sited **monastery of Montserrat**. Pages 90–111

2 El Escorial

Felipe II claimed to rule the world with paper rather than armies from this **palace-cum-monastery** in the hills north of Madrid. It is normally visited as a day-trip from the capital. If you tire of tramping through its exquisite rooms stuffed with works of art you can always try counting the windows – it is said to have around 2500. Pages 50–1

3 Granada and the Alhambra

Any modern list of the Wonders of the World would have to include the exquisitely decorated fortress-palace of the Alhambra and its adjacent summer residence, the Generalife. Pages 212–15

4 La Mezquita

In the 10th century Córdoba was one of the greatest cities in Europe, if not the world. Its Muslim rulers left behind them this huge mosque complex in which Christians later built a cathedral. Beside the mosque is the **Jewish Quarter**, a warren of narrow streets, tiny squares and white houses, many of them built around secretive Andalucian patios. Page 216

5 Museo del Prado

Madrid's main attraction is its art rather than its architecture. The Prado is one of the world's finest galleries, with outstanding collections of paintings by **Velázquez**, **Goya** and many other great artists. If that's not enough, across the road you have the magnificent art collection assembled by Baron Thyssen-

TOP TEN

Bornemisza. If you prefer modern art, not far away you'll find the **Reina Sofía arts centre**, where Picasso's most famous painting hangs. **Pages 34–7**

6 Picos de Europa

Walk or drive along the **stunning gorges** that cut through Spain's most accessible mountainous national park, or climb steep, zig-zagging paths towards its 2 500-metre (8 200-ft) summits. Less strenuously, you can take the cable car of Fuente Dé, which rises 900m (2 950ft) to a panoramic viewpoint. **Page 152**

7 Salamanca

Spain's prestigious university city, the equivalent of Oxford or Cambridge, has many outstanding **Renaissance and baroque buildings**, all made of the same warm-toned stone. Among them are two cathedrals, the old and the new, and the most magnificent Plaza Mayor ('main square') in Spain. **Pages 58–9**

8 Santiago de Compostela

This holy city was the third most important destination for pilgrims in the Middle Ages, after Jerusalem and Rome, and the Way of St James still attracts thousands of people a year to Santiago. The harmonious collection of monumental granite architecture grouped around the **Praza do Obradoiro** and other charming squares will not disappoint. **Pages 156–7**

9 Sevilla

New World gold was unloaded at Sevilla, the capital of Andalucia, making it Europe's richest port in the 16th century. Its fortunes show in the great architecture built before, during and after that time. The cathedral, with its **Giralda tower**, the **palace of the Reales Alcázares**, the **Maestranza bullring** and other sights will keep you busy for a few days. Unless you'd prefer to spend your time in some of Spain's best *tapas* bars. **Pages 188–95**

10 Toledo

This historic city is an incomparable assembly of **medieval architecture**. It is intimately associated with **El Greco** who, although a Greek, is considered one of the finest artists Spain has produced. Toledo is not far from Madrid, but warrants more than a day-trip. **Pages 74–7**

Madrid

MADRID

High up on the central plateau, far from any coast and in the dead centre of Spain, Madrid is one of western Europe's least-known capital cities. Undeservedly so. It may not have any memorable architecture but it more than makes up for this with museums crammed with an unparalleled collection of great art. If paintings are not your thing, you could spend weeks here just bar-hopping, without running out of new places to try.

MADRID

BEST OF Madrid

Getting around: walk around the twisting streets of the old centre if you can, but to cover any distance you will need to hop in a cab or arm yourself with a map and take advantage of the city's efficient **metro system** (0600–0130 daily). This has 12 numbered and colour-coded lines which extend to most places where you will want to go – even the airport. It is more economical to buy a ten-trip ticket called a **Metrobús** which, as its name suggests, can be used on buses as well.

MADRID

① *Puerta del Sol*

Start your sightseeing at the dead centre of Spain, in this bustling square, to get your bearings before launching into the sights (and innumerable bars) of old Madrid. **Page 24**

② *Plaza Mayor*

Madrid's spacious main square has been the site of executions and many other, less gruesome, public events. Now it is just a good place to sit at a café table and have a carefree drink in the sun or shade. **Page 26**

③ *El Rastro*

Hunt for bargains in this sprawling Sunday-morning flea market, or just enjoy the atmosphere in the packed streets of one of Madrid's most lively quarters. **Page 27**

④ *Palacio Real*

Spain's royal palace – now used for official functions rather than as a home – has a series of exquisite rooms to explore. **Page 28**

⑤ *Museo Thyssen-Bornemisza*

This extraordinary, privately assembled collection of paintings will take you on a complete tour of Western art as you move from floor to floor down the Villahermosa Palace. **Pages 32–3**

⑥ *Museo del Prado*

One of the greatest museums of art in the world, the Prado is worth a trip to Madrid in itself. In particular, it has outstanding collections by two very different Spanish artists: Velázquez and Goya. **Pages 34–7**

⑦ *Centro de Arte Reina Sofía*

Most people come to this collection of modern art to see just one painting, Picasso's gigantic canvas *Guernica*, a strident and timeless expression of the horrors of war, and one of the defining images of the 20th century. **Pages 38–9**

Tourist information

The main centres are: Aeropuerto de Barajas (*tel: 91 305 8556*); Duque de Medinaceli 2 (*tel: 91 429 4951*); Estación de Chamartín (*tel: 91 315 9976*); Mercado Puerto de Toledo (*tel: 91 364 1876*); and Plaza Mayor 3 (*tel: 91 588 1636*).

MADRID

Around Puerta del Sol

Puerta del Sol

Metro: Sol.

The natural place to start a tour of the city, indeed of Spain itself, is this semicircular square at the heart of old Madrid. A plaque set into the pavement on the south side of the square identifies the spot as 'Kilometre Zero', from where all road distances in the country are measured. Above the plaque is the clock Spaniards tune in to at midnight on New Year's Eve, gulping one grape for good luck each time it strikes. Across the square, on the corner of Calle del Carmen, is a **bronze statue** representing the symbol of Madrid, *El Oso y El Madroño* – a bear feeding from the foliage of a strawberry tree.

> " *This popular spirit has always existed in Spain; it is the bottomless well of Spanish vitality and exuberance, so that where there is deadness and corruption in the higher levels of society, there is always this creative energy underneath. It shows itself in the vitality of the popular arts.* "
>
> **V S Pritchett, *The Spanish Temper* (1954)**

The Puerta del Sol buzzes with life, but if you want to experience the leisurely side of old Madrid step into **Lhardy's**, a few steps up Calle de San Jerónimo from the square, on the right. This deli-cum-restaurant, a Madrid institution for over 160 years, still trades on good old-fashioned manners; well-heeled shoppers stand around chatting, sipping steaming cups of consommé and nibbling *croquetas* ('croquettes') and pastries.

MADRID

Real Academia de Bellas Artes de San Fernando

Calle de Alcalá 13. Tel: 91 522 1491. Metro: Sevilla or Puerta del Sol. Open: Tue–Fri 0930–1900; Sat–Mon 0930–1430. £.

Ranked as the third most important collection of art in the country (after the Prado and the Thyssen-Bornemisza), this academy for the promotion of art was founded in 1744 and is housed in a building by **Churriguera**. The highlight is the room devoted to **Goya's paintings** where you can see the carnival scene *The Burial of the Sardine* and two self-portraits, but there is much more Spanish art in the building, including works by **Velázquez** and the 17th-century masters **Ribera**, **Zurbarán** and **Murillo**. Another interesting item is *Spring* by **Arcimboldo** – a face made up of flowers, fruit and leaves. More mundanely, the Real Academia is one of the few galleries in the city that is open to the public on a Monday.

Convento de las Descalzas Reales

Plaza de las Descalzas, Arenal. Metro: Callao, Sol. Open: Tue–Thu, Sat 1030–1230, 1600–1730; Fri 1030–1245. £ (free on Wed afternoon).

King Felipe IV and his family look down at visitors from a balcony over the staircase of this royal convent, founded by Juana de Austria, sister of Felipe II and daughter of the emperor Charles V (Carlos I of Spain). It's only an illusion however, as the staircase is surrounded by **trompe-l'oeil frescos**. This staircase will take you to a cloister off which you will find several chapels filled with works of art. The convent with its treasures was only saved from the ravages of the dissolution of the monasteries in the 19th century because of its royal associations. The name of the convent refers to 'barefoot' (*descalzas*) nuns – shoeless, but not poor.

> " De Madrid al cielo – *'From Madrid to heaven'* "
>
> **Old Spanish saying, meaning that the only place better than Madrid is heaven**

MADRID

Old Madrid

Plaza Mayor

Metro: Sol.

The Spanish Inquisition once held its *autos-da-fé* in Madrid's largest and most monumental square, looked down upon by 237 balconies. The square has also been the scene of bullfights, pageants and public executions. Nowadays, a **stamp and coin market** is held in the arcades around the square on Sundays. On any sunny day there are tables to sit down at and have a drink or *tapas*.

> *On a sudden, the executioner, who stood behind, commenced turning the screw, which was of prodigious force, and the wretched man was almost instantly a corpse; but, as the screw went round, the priest began to shout, 'Pax et misericordia et tranquillitas,' and still as he shouted, his voice became louder and louder till the lofty walls of Madrid rang with it; then stooping down, he placed his mouth close to the culprit's ear, still shouting, just as if he would pursue the spirit through its course to eternity, cheering it on its way.*

George Borrow, witnessing an execution in Madrid, *The Bible in Spain* **(1842)**

The most prominent building on the square is the **Casa de la Panaderia**, which is covered with modern allegorical murals. In the middle of the square stands the 17th-century triumphant equestrian statue of King Felipe III. There are nine gateways leading into and out of the square. The one in the southwest corner has steps down to the Calle de Cuchilleros where stands **Casa Botín** (*see page 42*), the world's oldest restaurant, which specialises in roast suckling pig.

Plaza de la Villa

Metro: Opera, Sol.

This peaceful pedestrian square off the Calle Mayor has several handsome old buildings around it. The most interesting are the **Ayuntamiento** (town hall), the 15th-century **Torre de los Lujanes** and the **Casa del Cisneros**, connected to the town hall by an arch. In the square stands a statue of **Alvaro de Bazán**, hero of the battle of Lepanto (1571). The Calle Mayor, old Madrid's main street, still has several charming old-fashioned shops on it, notably the cheese specialists **El Palacio de los Quesos** (*No 53*) and the elegant cake shop **El Riojano** (*No 10*), which serves the royal household.

Catedral de San Isidro and Nuestra Señora de la Almudena

Madrid effectively has two cathedrals. For a long time the role was filled by the church of **Catedral de San Isidro** (*Calle de Toledo 37; tel: 91 369 2037; metro: La Latina; open: Mon–Sat 0800–1230, 1800–2045, Sun 0800–1430, 1745–2045*). It contains the remains of Madrid's patron saint, **St Isidore**, who is feted in May. Work began on **Nuestra Señora de la Almudena** (*Calle de Bailen; tel: 91 542 2200; metro: Opera; open: daily 1000–1330, 1800–1930*), next to the Palacio Real, in 1879 and continued, with an interruption caused by the Civil War, until the building was completed in 1993. It doesn't look much from the outside, but inside it has some pleasing decorative details.

El Rastro

Calle Ribera de Curtidores. Metro: La Latina, Embajadores. Open: Sun 0900–1400.

You name it and you are likely to find it on the stalls of Madrid's intense **flea market**, which snakes downhill from the irregular Plaza de Cascorro along Calle Ribera de Curtidores and its side streets every Sunday morning. Even if you are not shopping it can be an experience to squeeze through the packed crowds to see what is on sale: clothes, leather goods, books, CDs, plants, tools, household goods and plenty of junk. Most of the goods on sale are not, as would be expected, second-hand, but discounted new goods. At 0900, while the market is setting up, you can still move around freely, but by midday it will be almost impossible to move in any direction. And watch your bag – pickpockets thrive here.

Palacio Real

Calle Bailén. Tel. 91 542 0059. Metro: Opera, Plaza de España. Open: Oct–Mar, Mon–Sat 0930–1700, Sun 0900–1400; Apr–Sept, Mon–Sat 0900–1800, Sun 0900–1500. ££.

Construction of Spain's royal palace took 26 years and spanned the reigns of two monarchs. It was occupied from the late 18th century until 1931, when King Alfonso XIII was forced to abdicate by an angry republican crowd. During Franco's time the palace, known as the Palacio de Oriente, was used for state business. The present king, Juan Carlos I, lives elsewhere and the palace is now reserved for formal occasions.

The Palacio Real is entered via a massive square, the Plaza de la Armería. Off this is the **Botica Real**, a set of rooms used as a pharmacy, containing jars to store medicines and herbs. On the other side of the square is the **Armería Real** where suits of armour and weapons are on display.

> *… the breakwater of all the different Spains.*
>
> **Spanish poet Antonio Machado, on Madrid**

The interior of the palace proper shows off the high living of the Bourbon monarchs, especially Carlos II and Carlos IV. Highlights include the rococo **throne room**, which is used for royal receptions; the **Gasparini rooms** (named after their Neapolitan interior designer), in one of which hang royal portraits by Goya; the **Porcelain Room**, an overdose of green and white porcelain; and the huge **ceremonial dining room**, fitted out for lavish banquets of up to 160 guests, who dine opulently surrounded by frescos, chandeliers and tapestries.

Beside the palace, the Campo de Moro slopes majestically downhill towards the **Río Manzanares**. This spacious pleasure garden is entered from Paseo de la Virgen del Puerto.

Plaza de Oriente

Metro: Opera

This elegant square was laid out in 1844 as a means of separating the royal palace from the rest of the city. An equestrian statue of **Felipe IV** is the most prominent of the many sculptures that have been placed in it. A semicircle of buildings, some occupied by the elegant **Café de Oriente**

MADRID

and its offshoots (including a delicatessen), looks across at the palace from the east side of the square.

In the northwest corner of the square are the **Jardines de Sabatini**. This raised terrace garden is the closest green area to the sights of old Madrid. A much pleasanter place to sit, however, is the park a few minutes' walk to the northeast (skirting the Plaza de España), in which stands the **Templo de Debod**, a 4th-century BC Egyptian temple re-erected in the middle of an ornamental pond.

Teatro Real

Plaza de Oriente. Tel: 91 516 0600 (and check local press for details of performances). Metro: Opera. Open: Sat, Sun 1030–1330, guided tours only; closed Aug. £.

The eastern side of the Plaza de Oriente is dominated by the Teatro Real. Although inaugurated in 1859, Madrid's opera house has been closed for much of its history. After a costly restoration it finally reopened in 1997. It is bigger than it looks, with six floors below ground and nine above. The best part is the auditorium with its massive **crystal chandelier**, and there's an interesting collection of opera costumes on display in glass cases. Opera, ballet and classical music concerts are all staged here. The restaurant on the second floor is open to non-theatre-goers except when there are performances taking place. There is also a cafeteria on the sixth floor with views over the square below.

MADRID

Bourbon Madrid

Puerta de Alcalá and Plaza de Cibeles

Metro: Retiro for Puerta de Alcalá, Banco de España for Plaza de Cibeles.

These two open squares, both of them monumental traffic intersections, stand close to each other, separated by a short stretch of the Calle de Alcalá.

The Puerta de Alcalá is a five-arched 18th-century gateway which stands on a traffic island in the middle of the Plaza de la Independencia. The grid-pattern streets to the north of the Puerta de Alcalá comprise the fashionable residential, shopping and dining district of **Salamanca**.

In the middle of the square of the same name stands the Fuente de Cibeles, the goddess of nature in her chariot. There are four imposing buildings on or near to this square: the **Post Office**, jocularly called 'Our Lady of Communications', the **Palacio de Linares**, a 19th-century mansion, and the **Bank of Spain**. The fourth building, the **national air force headquarters**, is set back from the square.

A short way west from the Plaza de Cibeles, the Calle de Alcalá branches out and sprouts one of Madrid's most important streets, the busy **Gran Vía**. Near the junction of the two streets is the **Círculo de Bellas Artes**, an arts centre where you pay a small admission charge and can sit in a relaxing old café beneath painted ceilings and crystal chandeliers.

Café Gijón

Paseo de Recoletos 21. Metro: Colón or Banco de España. Open: daily.

One of the few legendary cafés of Madrid to survive into the 21st century, the interior of the Café Gijón is still redolent of

MADRID

> *Art lovers in the chattering classes sometimes play the 'what you would rescue' game. It consists of saying which treasure he or she would save, and why, were the Louvre, the Metropolitan, the Vatican Library, the National Gallery, the Prado or another major collection to be engulfed by an infernal blaze. If the game was amended to a discussion on 'which small neighbourhood you would spare from a global earthquake', Madrid's Paseo del Prado would top most art lovers' lists.*

Tom Burns, 'Madrid's Golden Triangle of Art', in *Spain Gourmetour* (July 1993)

the great literary and intellectual discussions that took place there before the Civil War. Today it is still a haven for those in search of quiet conversation, or a place to sit and read, and there is also a restaurant downstairs. The Gijón now has a pavement café on the Paseo de Recoletos, but it is not a patch on the **Pabellón del Espejo** further up the street.

Paseo del Prado

The Paseo de Recoletos and Paseo del Prado comprise the handsome, monumental artery of Bourbon Madrid. The two grandest hotels of Spain, the **Ritz** (*Plaza de la Lealtad 5; tel: 91 521 2857*) and the **Palace** (*Plaza de las Cortes 7; tel: 91 360 8000*), face each other across the Plaza Canovas del Castillo (better known as 'Neptune' after the fountain in the middle). If you want to escape the hoi polloi, take tea in either of these two great hotels and you may find yourself rubbing shoulders with visiting rock stars, footballers, bullfighters, screen actors and other celebrities.

Also on the Plaza Canovas del Castillo is the **Palacio Villahermosa**, which houses the Thyssen-Bornemisza Collection (*see pages 32–3*). A little further down the Paseo del Prado is the **Museo del Prado** itself (*see pages 34–7*), and not far from there is another of Madrid's great art museums, the **Reina Sofía** (*see pages 38–9*).

Beside the Reina Sofia is the 18th-century **Real Jardín Botánico** (*Plaza de Murillo; metro: Atocha; open: daily Oct and Mar, 1000–1900, Nov–Feb, 1000–1800, Apr and Sept, 1000–2030, May–Aug, 1000–2100; £*), where some 30,000 species are planted out on three terraces – Romantic, Isabelline and neo-classical in style – and in a greenhouse divided into climatic zones.

At the end of the *paseo* is Atocha station. When a new, functional station was built at Atocha it was decided to turn the great wrought-iron-and-glass original into a gigantic greenhouse. The temperature inside is a comfortable 24°C all year round, and the stone benches beneath the palm trees provide some peaceful places to sit.

Museo Thyssen-Bornemisza

The industrialist Baron Heinrich Thyssen-Bornemisza began assembling this extraordinary personal art collection in the 1920s, with the help of art experts. His son, Hans Heinrich, inherited the collection and continued to add to it. His Spanish wife, Carmen Cervera, proposed that it should be installed in a permanent home in Spain, and in 1993 care of the collection, some 775 paintings in all, passed to the Spanish state. Part of this important collection is on display in the Monestir de Pedralbes in Barcelona (see page 106), but the bulk is housed here in the 18th-century Palacio Villahermosa, often known in Madrid simply as 'La Thyssen'.

It is often said that the Thyssen-Bornemisza collection complements the contents of the pre-existing and far more extensive Museo del Prado. In crude terms, it is strong where the Prado is weak – for instance, it compensates for the Prado's lack of 17th-century Dutch paintings. And whereas the Prado can overwhelm by the sheer mass of paintings by the same artist, the Thyssen-Bornemisza collection is more selective and thus shows more clearly the progression from one artist to the next. Indeed, the idea of the collection is just that: to allow the visitor to learn about the development of European art. The paintings are arranged so that you travel anticlockwise around the patio descending floor by floor, following the history of Western art towards modern times.

The second or top floor (rooms 1–21) begins with early Italian art and takes the story up to the end of the 17th

MADRID

century. In these rooms you will see the great masters of the Renaissance. Side rooms boast Flemish, German, Spanish and French paintings. In room 3 are ***The Annunciation*** by **Jan Van Eyck** and ***Our Lady of the Dry Tree*** by **Petrus Christus**; the portrait of Henry VIII by **Hans Holbein the Younger** hangs in room 5; ***Jesus Among the Doctors*** by **Dürer** can be seen in room 8; ***St Jerome in the Wilderness*** by **Titian** is in room 11; and Rubens' popular painting ***The Toilet of Venus*** (*c* 1629) is in room 19.

The first floor (rooms 22–40) spans the period between Dutch 17th-century painting and German Expressionism, of which the gallery has a particularly valuable collection. There are three paintings by **Goya** in room 31; **Manet**, **Degas** (*Swaying Dancer*, 1877–9), **Renoir**, **Sisley** and other Impressionists feature in the next rooms, 32 and 33.

The ground floor (rooms 41–8) displays works of art typical of 20th-century movements such as Cubism, the Avant Garde and Pop Art. Highlights here include **Pablo Picasso**'s ***Harlequin with a Mirror*** (1923, from the artist's 'Classical' period), the ***Portrait of the Baron Thyssen-Bornemisza*** (1982) by **Lucien Freud**, **Edward Hopper**'s bleak ***Hotel Room*** (1931) and works by **Kandinsky**, **Grosz**, **Mondrian** and **Rothko**.

Getting there: Paseo del Prado 8. Tel: 91 420 3944; www.museothyssen.org. Metro: Banco de España. Open: Tue–Sun 1000–1700. £.

MADRID

Museo del Prado

*Reason enough alone for visiting Madrid, the Prado is one of the world's greatest art galleries, certainly the greatest collection of Spanish painting to be gathered in any one place. There are so many famous canvases in this building that you can't concentrate on more than a handful of them in one morning or afternoon. The best policy is to blinker yourself and head for one section, even one favourite painting if you can. If you are short of time, the Prado's real treasures are the paintings by the two Spanish artists **Goya** and **Velázquez**.*

The main building of the Prado, standing on the Paseo de Prado, is the neo-classical **Edificio Villanueva** by Juan de Villanueva, built in 1785 for Carlos III. This building houses paintings and sculptures from the 12th century up to the time of Goya, whose statue stands outside it. The core of the collection was built up by Spain's royal family prior to the opening of the museum, and the Prado now has a total of 8 600 paintings, as well as over 5 000 drawings, 2 000 etchings, almost 1 000 coins and medals and 700 sculptures. There is only room to show about a seventh of the whole collection at any one time.

The ground floor principally displays Flemish and Dutch paintings. One of the most striking pictures here is **Hieronymus**

MADRID

Bosch's *The Garden of Earthly Delights* (*c* 1516), the artist's stricture against what he considered the most deadly of the deadly sins: lust. Both compelling and disquieting, it comprises three panels that show, respectively, Paradise, man engaging in lust and the consequences of his actions, damnation. Other noteworthy paintings on the ground floor include works by **Rubens** and **Fra Angelico**'s *The Annunciation* (*c* 1430).

The first floor is mainly dedicated to Spanish works of art, outstanding among which is the collection of 17th-century Golden Age artists. **José de Ribera**, **Francisco Ribalta** and **Zurbarán** are among their number, but the greatest of all is **Velázquez** (*see next page*). Also represented here is a foreign artist inseparable from his adopted country, **El Greco**, but his work is better admired in Toledo (*see pages 74–7*).

The other building of the Prado is the **Casón del Buen Retiro**, an annexe round the corner on Calle Felipe IV, which contains 19th- and 20th-century art. The building is one of the few remains of the Palacio del Buen Retiro; the adjacent Parque del Retiro (*see page 39*) was the palace garden.

Getting there: Paseo del Prado. Tel: 91 330 2800; www.museoprado.mcu.es. Metro: Banco de España. Open: Tue–Sat 0900–1900; Sun 0900–1400. £.

> ... essentially it [the Prado] remains a period collection created by art-loving monarchs. Private collections ... reflect a series of variables such as the taste of the individual collector, the extent of his buying power and the availability of great works of art on the market. Fortunately the taste of Spain's kings ... was superlative. They could, moreover, buy most of what took their fancy. This was in part because Spain, then at the height of its imperial powers, controlled a good portion of creative Europe, from Brussels to Naples by way of Venice, and in part because the silver- and gold-laden fleets returning from the New World could finance patronage and acquisitions. By a happy coincidence there were great artists to whom the Habsburgs could turn.

Tom Burns, 'Madrid's Golden Triangle of Art', in *Spain Gourmetour* (July 1993)

Museo del Prado (continued)

Velázquez collection

The Prado has almost all of the significant works painted by the great Spanish artist **Diego de Velázquez**, who was for much of his life court painter to **King Felipe IV**. Velázquez was born in Sevilla in 1599 to a family of the lesser nobility. For six years he worked as an apprentice to the Sevillian painter **Francisco Pacheco**, who was also his father-in-law. In 1623 he executed a portrait of Felipe IV, which was favourably received, and he was appointed court painter. After two years spent travelling in Italy he resumed his work at court, painting *The Surrender of Breda* among other canvases, and in the 1630s he painted portraits of the royal family hunting, but also a series of portraits of court dwarfs which are remarkable in that the artist treats his subject with sympathy and respect.

Las Meninas (1656) is considered his greatest work. The name of this picture, which shows the Infanta Margarita and her court, refers to the maids of honour who looked after the royal children. Felipe IV, Velázquez's patron, is reflected in a mirror at the back of the painting, and Velázquez shows himself too, in the act of painting, his brush raised above his palette. Pablo Picasso produced no fewer than 44 paintings inspired by this one painting.

Velázquez continued to serve his king as court painter until his death in Madrid on 6 August 1660.

MADRID

Goya collection

The other great Spanish artist who dominates the Prado collection is **Francisco de Goya** (1746–1828). Like Velázquez, he served as a court painter, but not until he was 43 years old. Significantly, Goya was much influenced by the work of his predecessor, studying the latter's free brushstrokes and reproducing them. Two of his most famous works, *The Clothed Maja* and *The Naked Maja*, hang side by side for comparison. They are thought to have been painted for Godoy, the chief minister of King Carlos IV at the turn of the 18th century. Mystery has always surrounded the identity of the model.

Two qualities stand out in Goya's paintings: his expressiveness and his humanity. The latter is clearly seen in his other great painting which hangs in the Prado, *The 3rd of May*. This time the history of the subject is in no doubt. Painted in 1814, the picture shows French soldiers executing Spaniards during Napoleon Bonaparte's occupation of Spain in 1808. The man in front of the guns holds up his hands in the form of the cross, a gesture to which Picasso makes reference in his *Guernica* (*see page 38*). The painting makes a particular statement about Spanish independence, but also speaks volumes on war as a universal evil. Goya would later pursue this theme in a series of bitter etchings, the *Disasters of War*.

> ... this is less a picture that has been painted by a brilliant and deliberate expenditure of pigments than a vision that has been mysteriously evoked and that floats before us in its own atmosphere. If by a 'miracle' we mean an event in which the effect is beyond measure out of proportion with the seeming simplicity of the cause, then we may say that of all the great pictures of the world this may most precisely be called miraculous.

Havelock Ellis on Velázquez's *Las Meninas*,
***The Soul of Spain* (1926)**

Centro de Arte Reina Sofía

Most visitors to this museum of modern art come to see what is probably the single most famous painting of the 20th century, Pablo Picasso's Guernica, a wordless yet eloquent expression of the horrors of war. But a stroll around its four floors will give you a rounded picture of how Spanish art has developed over the last century.

The gallery is named in honour of the Queen of Spain, a great patron of the arts, and is housed in a rehabilitated late 18th-century hospital to which two highly modern glass lift shafts have been attached. The permanent collection, focusing on Spanish painters but including some foreign artists as well, is displayed on the second and fourth floors; the first (ground) and third floors are used for temporary exhibitions.

The second floor is dedicated to work from the early 20th century. A well-known painting in room 2, *La Tertulia del Café de Pombo* by José Gutiérrez Solana, gives the observer a good idea of what Madrid's thriving café society must have been like at the beginning of the 20th century. Such early works are followed by rooms on the versatile Joan Miró (*No 7*), the eccentric surrealist Salvador Dalí (*No 10*; compare his very different *The Great Masturbator* with *Girl at the Window*), cubist Juan Gris (*No 4*) and the sculptor Julio González (*No 8*). Room 12 lends further variety, as it is given over to the work of surrealist film-maker Luis Buñuel.

But it is the Picasso room (*No 6*) which draws the biggest crowds, and in particular the enormous canvas of *Guernica*. Critics agree that this is one of the few works of art successfully to combine artistic achievement with a propagandistic purpose. It was commissioned by the government in Spain in 1937 and was inspired by a bombing raid on a Basque town by German pilots in support of General Franco during the Civil War. Picasso ordained that the painting should not be returned to Spain until the dictatorship was at an end, and its arrival in 1981 was seen as confirmation of the stability of the new democracy.

The top floor of the gallery concentrates on Spanish art post-Civil War to the present day, and covers such movements as Abstract Art, Pop Art and Minimal Art. Look out here for the works of **Antonio Saura**, **Eduardo Chillida** and **Antoni Tapiès**.

Getting there: Calle Santa Isabel 52. Tel: 91 467 5062; www.museoreinasofia.mcu.es. Metro: Atocha. Open: Mon, Wed–Sat 1000–2100; Sun 1000–1430. £ (free on Sat afternoon and Sun morning).

Parque del Retiro

Metro: Retiro. Open: 24 hours all year round.

The grounds created for King Felipe IV's royal palace, the **Palacio del Buen Retiro**, now form a vast public park divided into areas connected by leafy avenues and planted with some 15,000 trees. The Retiro is generally quiet during the week, but heaving with people at the weekend. At the centre of the park is a boating lake partly framed by a monumental colonnade and overlooked by a statue of **Alfonso XII**. To the south of the lake are the **Palacio de Velázquez** and **Palacio de Cristal**. Beyond these is a sculpture of the devil, *El Angel Caído*, by Ricardo Bellver.

MADRID

Paseo de la Castellana

The Paseo de la Castellana is the monumental avenue of modern Madrid. Big business has its home here and the poshest restaurants and shops of the city are concentrated in the streets off it. Don't try to walk it; take a bus or a taxi along it or use the metro.

The first notable building north of its starting point in Plaza de Colón is, uncharacteristically, an old one: the 19th-century **Museo de Ciencias Naturales**. The *paseo* then executes a modest zig-zag and runs straight northwards, past a succession of towering examples of modern architecture. Azca, a vast commercial and shopping development intended as a new city centre, is identified by the skyward-pointing **Torre Picasso**, Madrid's tallest and most expensive office building. A complex of five branches, all together, of the department store **El Corte Inglés** stands on the junction of the Castellana with Raimundo Fernández Villaverde. Diagonally across the road from Azca is the **Estadio Bernabéu**, stamping-ground of Real Madrid, which can hold a crowd of 105,000 people. The climax of this parade of striking modern architecture is the **Puerta de Europa**, or Torres Kio, two tower blocks which lean towards each other over the Plaza de Castilla, near Madrid's principal station, Chamartín.

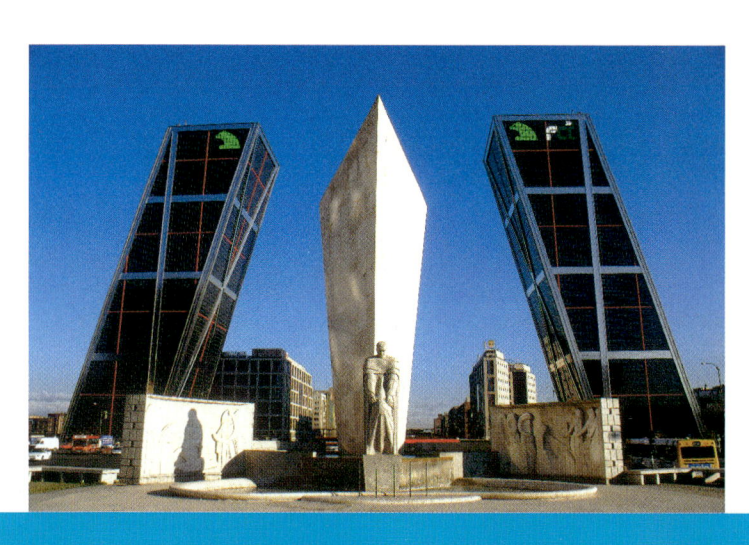

Tip

It has been said that the modern madrileño *no longer dreams of being a great bullfighter but a wealthy playboy banker. In reality, he'd probably like to be both at the same time.*

MADRID

Museo Arqueológico Nacional

Calle de Serrano 13. Tel: 91 577 7912; www.man.es. Metro: Serrano. Open: Mon–Sat 0930–2030; Sun 0930–1430. £.

Isabel II opened this splendid museum of antiquity in 1867. It houses exhibits from archaeological digs all over Spain, and artefacts deriving from Egypt and ancient Greece. Items of particular interest are a **Bronze Age sword** from Guadalajara and **Bronze Age gold bowls** unearthed in the Basque country; two ancient stone statues, the **Dama de Elche** and the **Dama de Baza**; a **Roman mosaic** with allegorical renderings of the months of the year; a 6th-century gold **Visigothic crown** set with precious stones; and a delicately carved 11th-century **ivory cross**. Outside the museum, underground, is a replica of the cave at Altamira with its prehistoric paintings (*see page 151*).

Estudio y Museo de Sorolla

Paseo General Martínez Campos 35. Tel: 91 310 1584. Metro: Rubén Darío. Open: Tue–Sun 1000–1500; closed Aug. £.

The searing sunlight of the Mediterranean infuses the works of **Joaquín Sorolla** (1863–1923), considered to be Spain's best Impressionist painter. His former home and studio, built in 1910, explain something of his life and work. It also has an interesting collection of ceramics, and stands in the garden Sorolla himself designed, inspired by those of Andalucía.

Museo Lázaro Galdiano

Calle de Serrano 122. Tel: 91 561 6084. Metro: República Argentina. Open: Tue–Sun 1000–1400; closed Aug. £ (free on Sun).

Almost 5 000 pieces are on display in this extraordinary collection assembled by a private collector, **José Lázaro Galdiano** (1862–1947), and given to the nation, along with the neo-Renaissance house, in 1948. Exhibits range widely across time and geography. Among the archaeological and other items on the ground floor are a 7th-century BC **Phoenician bronze jug** with its spout fashioned into a feline head (the *jarra púnica*) and the top of a bishop's crozier in **Limoges enamel**. There are furniture and paintings on the first floor and more paintings on the second floor, including works by **Hieronymus Bosch**, **El Greco** and **Goya**.

Eating and drinking

Restaurants

You can eat almost any kind of food in Spain, but Madrid's specialities are *patatas bravas*, a spicy potato *tapa*, and the hearty *cocido madrileño*, a kind of stew. The old town is full of good places to eat. For cheaper restaurants, look in the Malasaña district north of the Gran Via. The poshest restaurants are mostly in streets off the Paseo de la Castellana. They include **Príncipe de Viana**, **Cabo Mayor** and **Zalacaín**.

Artemisa
Ventura de la Vega 4. Tel: 91 429 5092. £. The best-known and most central vegetarian restaurant in Madrid.

La Bola
Bola 5. Tel: 91 547 6930. ££. Old *taberna* ('tavern', or 'bar') serving authentic *madrileña* cuisine. Its *cocido madrileño* is served in individual earthenware crocks straight from the stove.

Casa Botín
Calle de Cuchilleros 17. Tel: 91 366 4217. £££. A Madrid institution and the oldest restaurant in the world, according to the *Guinness Book of Records*. Its speciality is suckling pig cooked in a wood-fired oven.

Casa Lucio
Cava Baja 35. Tel: 91 365 3252. £££. It's essential to reserve a table here at least four or five days in advance – which tells you how good it is.

Cafés

The Civil War and its aftermath swept away most of the city's famous cafés. The few that are left include **Café Gijón** (*Paseo de Recoletos 21; see page 30*) and **Café Comercial** (*Glorieta de Bilbao*).

Bars and taverns

The main bar area of Madrid fans out from the Plaza Santa Ana. A good starting point for a night out is **Cervecería Alemana** (*Plaza Santa Ana 6*), a 1904 bar which was the sometime haunt of Ernest Hemingway. The nearby **Casa del Abuelo** (*Calle Victoria 12*) is a famous rough-and-ready bar serving only three *tapas*, all of them varieties of prawns.

Tabernas are a Madrid institution. It's estimated that some hundred of the old ones are still functioning. Their façades and interiors are often handsomely decorated with ceramic tiles. The oldest is **Taberna Antonio Sánchez** (*Mesón de Paredes 13*), which was founded in 1830. Two of the most attractive *tabernas* have been tarted up as nightspots for a youthful clientele: **Viva Madrid** (*Manuel Fernandez y Gonzalez 7*) and **Los Gabrieles** (*Calle Echegaray 17*).

Pastelerías

If you have a sweet tooth you are in for a treat as Madrid has a proud tradition when it comes to pastelerías *('cake shops'). The best include* **El Riojano** *(Calle Mayor 10) and* **Casa Mira** *(Carrera de San Jerónimo 30).* **Viena Capellanes** *is a chain with branches dotted around the centre.*

MADRID

Shopping

The best places for general shopping are branches of Spain's favourite department store, **El Corte Inglés**. Don't expect bargains there, but quality and service are usually reliable. The main branches are at Plaza del Callao and Calle Preciados, Calle Serrano 47 and Calle Raimundo Fernández Villaverde 79. For upmarket shopping, the **Salamanca district** is the place to go.

Nightlife

Café Central *(Plaza del Angel 10)* is a good venue for live jazz. To find the hippest dance places of the moment you will have to ask around, but good first ports of call are the massive seven-storey **Kapital** *(Calle Atocha 125)* and the 19th-century mansion of **Palacio de Gavira** *(Calle Arenal 9)*.

MADRID

PROFILE

Tapas

No Spaniard in his right mind would drink on an empty stomach, hence the existence of tapas *– little dishes of food ordered in a bar to accompany a glass of wine or beer.* Tapas *are casual, versatile and varied. Their main advantage is that you can order a small quantity of food to try without being landed with a plateful; conversely, you can ask for a larger quantity of something that you have just eaten which you particularly liked.*

At its simplest, a *tapa* can be no more than a few olives or nuts eaten as an appetiser before a meal. On the other hand, a selection of two or three *tapas* – ask for a *ración* to get a plateful instead of just a taster – can be enough for a light lunch or dinner. *Tapas*-eating can usually be regarded as an inexpensive way to eat out – in a few towns, a complimentary *tapa* is still served with each drink – although as you will rarely be given a menu with prices on it you can sometimes run up a larger bill than expected.

MADRID

Tapas (sometimes also called *pinchos*) are believed to have originated in Andalucia in the 19th century. A *tapa* is literally a 'lid' (*tapar* means 'to cover'), and the term first referred to a slice of cured ham or chorizo sausage which would be served on top of a glass of sherry to keep the flies out. Nowadays, *tapas* ingredients are legion, and they are served and devoured throughout Spain.

The main *tapas*-eating hours are roughly midday to 1430 and 2000 to 2200, but there are no fixed times and *tapas* are available all day – their *raison d'être* being to fill the protracted gaps between meals. You may choose to stay in one bar if it has sufficient variety or go on a '*tapas* crawl' between bars. But *tapas* shouldn't be thought of merely as fast food, to be gobbled in seconds on the hoof. They are a way of bringing people together, to be placed in the middle of a group of friends and shared over an animated conversation and a leisurely drink.

MADRID

Old Castile

Go north from Madrid, past Felipe II's great monastery-palace of El Escorial, and you reach the hills and plains of Old Castile, the modern region of Castilla y León. As its name suggests, this is a land of castles (the best of them at Segovia), but there are also monumental towns and cities to wander around, chief among them Salamanca, built of golden stone.

OLD CASTILE

OLD CASTILE

BEST OF
Old Castile

*Getting around: most visitors tackle this area from Madrid and its international airport, although it can be approached from the north coast via Burgos or León. Motorways (A6, NI, NII) radiate out from the capital, although they do not go directly to all the major cities; the major and minor connecting roads tend to be good, however, although expect to go more slowly in mountainous areas. Valladolid is the regional capital, where the main tourist office is located (*Dirección General de Turismo, Monasterio de Prado, Autovía Puente Colgante; tel: 98 341 1606, www.jcyl.es*), but the provincial capitals have their own tourist offices giving more details of local sights.*

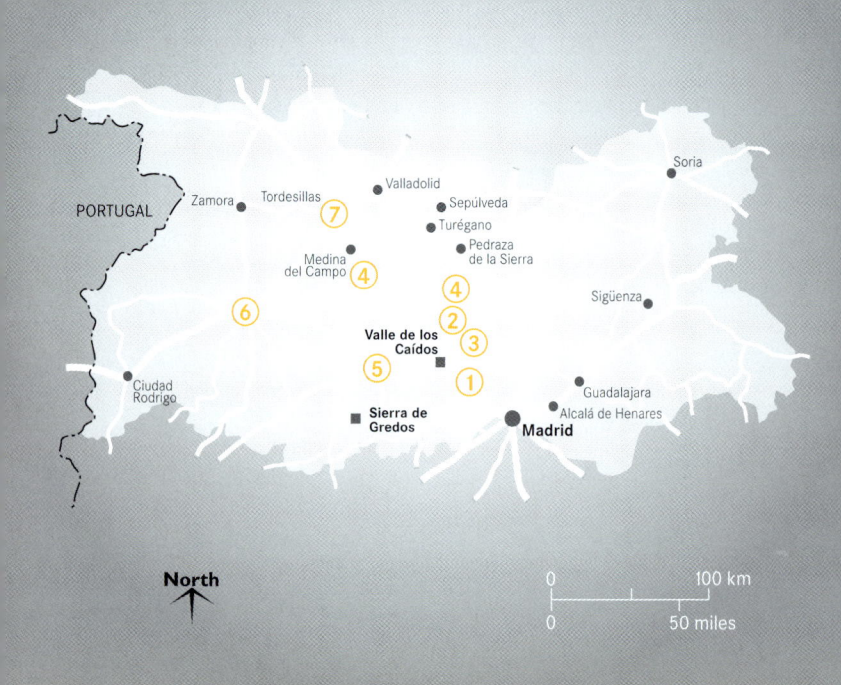

OLD CASTILE

① *El Escorial*

Felipe II's massive **monastery-cum-castle** was the centre of the Spanish empire at its height. With its royal apartments, pantheon of the kings of Spain, elegant library and works of art throughout it makes an ideal day-trip from Madrid. **Pages 50–1**

② *Segovia*

There are two exceptional sights to see here. The two-tiered **Roman aqueduct** – one of the best anywhere – strides defiantly across the city suburbs, and standing on a rocky outcrop is the **Alcázar**, a castle as they are meant to be, with battlements, patios, exquisite chambers and dreamy spires.
Pages 52-3

③ *La Granja de San Ildefonso*

A little bit of France in Spain: if this **regal country residence** is reminiscent of Versailles it is because Felipe V modelled his palace on that of his grandfather outside Paris. Take a guided tour of the interiors or explore the gardens of fountains and chestnut woods**. Page 53**

④ *Castillo de Coca and Castillo de la Mota*

These two castles still give you a good idea of different ways to build a castle in Spain. While the one is more ornamental than impregnable, the other has all the ingredients of a fortress prepared for a siege. **Page 55**

⑤ *Ávila*

The most complete set of **medieval city walls** in Europe encircles Ávila. Admire them from the outside or go through one of the nine gateways to see the cathedral and other fine buildings. **Pages 56-7**

⑥ *Salamanca*

Golden sandstone buildings are plentiful in Salamanca, a treasure chest of Spanish architecture and a delight to stroll around. This is an **ancient university city** and the façade of the university itself is an example *par excellence* of intricately carved Plateresque stonework.
Pages 58-9

⑦ *Convento de Santa Clara*

The historic town of Tordesillas hides a gem that deserves to be better known. Pedro the Cruel turned a former palace into this convent for the enjoyment of his mistress, embellishing it with Mudéjar (Moorish-Gothic) decoration. In the church is one of the finest **coffered ceilings** in Spain. **Page 61**

OLD CASTILE

El Escorial

*San Lorenzo el Real, better known as El Escorial, is both monastery and palace at the same time. It was commissioned by **Felipe II** and built by one of Spain's most influential architects, **Juan de Herrera**. The palace-monastery is dedicated to **St Lawrence** because it was on the saint's feast day, 10 August, in 1557 that Felipe's armies defeated the French at St Quentin in Flanders.*

The building took 1 500 workmen 21 years to complete and was finished in 1584; it is estimated to have 1 200 doors and 2 500 windows, and the grid-pattern layout is said to symbolise the martyrdom of St Lawrence, who was roasted alive on a gridiron. The building style and the stone – granite – create a sober, some would say austere, effect. To get an impression of the magnitude of the place, you need to drive up to the viewpoint known as the Silla de Felipe – 'Philip's Seat'.

That El Escorial once served as a palace is evidenced by the royal apartments. However, although ruler of a mighty empire stretching across the seas, Felipe II was famous for his restrained living and his rooms, at the east end of the church, are surprisingly modest. His bedroom looks directly on to the altar of the church. The Bourbon monarchs who came after Felipe preferred the other royal palaces to El Escorial, but none the less provided themselves with lavish quarters here too.

Beneath the chancel of the church is the **Royal Pantheon**, which contains the remains of all Spanish monarchs from the time of the emperor Charles V (Carlos I), except Felipe V, Ferdinand VI and the luckless Amadeo I of Savoy, who ruled for only two years before the First Republic was declared in 1873. They lie in bronze and marble sarcophagi in niches in the walls.

OLD CASTILE

Felipe's personal book collection has been incorporated into the library, a long gallery decorated with precious woods, which contains 40,000 volumes. **Priceless manuscripts** are on display here, including a poem by the 13th-century king Alfonso X, who is remembered in Spain as Alfonso 'the Wise' or 'the Learned'. There are also 16th-century frescos on the ceiling by **Tibaldi**.

Getting there: San Lorenzo del Escorial. Tel: 91 890 5902. Open: Apr–Sept, Tue–Sun 1000–1800; Oct–Mar, Tue–Sun 1000–1700. ££.

> The Spanish genius is for excess, for excesses of austerity as well as excesses of sensual decoration. The soldier architect of the Escorial and the King, half-monk, half-bureaucrat, who built it, disdained the sunlight of the Renaissance and built their tomb in the shadow of the wild mountains and in the hard military spirit of the Counter-Reform. The Escorial is the mausoleum of Spanish power.

V S Pritchett, *The Spanish Temper* (1954)

Valle de los Caídos

15km (9 miles) north of El Escorial by minor roads. Open: Apr–Sept, Tue–Sun 0930–1900; Oct–Mar, Tue–Sun 1000–1800. £.

It took 16 years, in the aftermath of the Civil War, for republican prisoners under Franco's direction to dig the immense basilica at the 'Valley of the Fallen' out of the rock face of the Guadarrama mountains. To some it is simply a massive war memorial but to others it is a lingering symbol of the dictatorship.

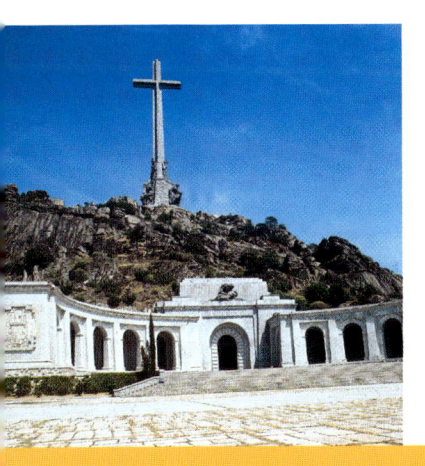

At 262m (860ft) the nave is longer than both St Peter's in Rome and St Paul's Cathedral in London. Next to the high altar are the tombs of **José Antonio Primo de Rivera**, founder of the fascist Falangist party, and **Franco** himself. Coffins of 40,000 soldiers and civilians from both sides who died in the fighting are also interred at Valle de los Caídos. Above the basilica rises a 150m (490ft) high cross by Diego Mendez.

OLD CASTILE

Segovia

This historic Castilian town is built around a spur of rock sticking out between two rivers, the Eresma and the Clamores. It has often been compared to a ship, with the cathedral and town centre as superstructure and the great fortress of the Alcázar as the prow.

That Segovia was an important Roman town can be seen by the presence of the long **aqueduct** that strides across the Plaza Azoguejo in a series of double arches, reaching 95m (312ft) above ground level at their highest point. It was built in the first century AD and was still in use in the 19th century.

The old town is grouped around the **Plaza Mayor**, where stands the **catedral** (*open: summer, daily 0900–1900, winter, Mon–Fri 0900–1300, 1500–1800, Sat–Sun 0900–1800*), Gothic in style but finished in the 18th century. Its tower was the highest in Spain until it was hit by lightning. The cloister is all that survives of an older cathedral which was built on a lower site.

The cathedral is a relative newcomer to Segovia which is better known for its **Romanesque churches**. The oldest of these, dating from the 11th century, is **San Juan de los Caballeros**. Outside the old town is an unusual church, the 13th-century **Vera Cruz** which was built by the Knights Templar and has 12 sides.

But all other buildings in Segovia are eclipsed in terms of importance by the royal castle of the **Alcázar** (*open: daily May–Sept, 1000–1900, Oct–Apr, 1000–1800; £*), a

> *Here is the real type of a 'dead city', still serenely sleeping, in a dream of which the spell has been broken neither by the desecrating hand of the tourist crowd, nor by the inrush of commercial activity, nor by any native anxiety for self-exploitation. How deeply Segovia sleeps the bats well know, and as evening falls they almost dare to enter one's window in the heart of the city.*

Havelock Ellis, *The Soul of Spain* (1926)

OLD CASTILE

magnificent building that is the epitome of everyone's idea of a castle. It was begun in the 12th century, but much of what can be seen today is the result of rebuilding after a fire in 1862. Inside are several ornate chambers including the **Throne Room** (with a Mudéjar ceiling), the **Galley Room** (so called because it looked like an inverted ship before the fire), the **King's Chamber** (where there is fine period furniture) and the **Monarchs' Room** (formerly the most important room in the castle). Before leaving the Alcázar, climb the **Torre de Juan II** for a view over Segovia.

If all that sightseeing has left you hungry, the culinary speciality of Segovia is *cochinillo asado,* roast suckling pig cooked in a wood-fired oven.

Tourist information: Plaza Mayor 10. Tel: 92 146 0334.

La Granja de San Ildefonso

11km (7 miles) southeast of Segovia on the CL601. Tel: 92 147 0019. Open: Tue–Sat 1000–1330, 1500–1700; Sun 1000–1400. £.

King Felipe V had fond memories of his grandfather Louis XIV's palace of Versailles in France, and in 1720 he ordered the construction of this magnificent palace in the foothills of the Sierra de Guadarrama, on the site of a 15th-century hunting lodge. Unfortunately, several rooms were damaged by fire in 1918 and had to be restored.

The guided tour takes you through chambers ornately decorated with marble, velvet and golden stucco. Notable among the fixtures and fittings are the great **chandeliers** made in the royal glass factory. The vast gardens are the work of French landscape gardeners and sculptors, and are particularly impressive as a result of their fountains and chestnut woods.

OLD CASTILE

Castles of Castille

> *The day was exceedingly hot, and we wended our way slowly along the plains of Old Castile. With all that pertains to Spain, vastness and sublimity are associated: grand are its mountains, and no less grand are its plains, which seem of boundless extent, but which are not tame unbroken flats, like the steppes of Russia. Rough and uneven ground is continually occurring ... There is little that is blithesome and cheerful, but much that is melancholy.*

George Borrow, *The Bible in Spain* (1842)

Pedraza de la Sierra

40km (25 miles) northeast of Segovia, off the N110.

The Plaza Mayor at the centre of Pedraza has all the ingredients of the typical square that is at the heart of almost every town of any size in Spain. It is overlooked by the twin powers-that-be: the town hall (*ayuntamiento*), with its public clock, and the church. On one side stands the residence of a noble family – distinguishable by the carved coat of arms – emphasising its social status at the centre of local life. The medieval porticos that run along the sides of the square provided a shady spot for shops and market stalls, among them at least one bar. The space in the middle was – and is – used for fiestas and other public events, and as a place simply for people to hang out when the sun has gone down. When arriving in any Spanish town, it is wise to head first for the Plaza Mayor to get your bearings.

At the end of town, on an outcrop of rock, is a somewhat austere **Gothic-style castle** which was once the home of the painter **Ignacio Zuloaga** (1870–1945).

Sepúlveda, 25km (15 miles) to the northeast, is another attractive town, spectacularly sited above the Río Duratón, while **Túregano**, 15km (9 miles) west, has a splendid castle.

OLD CASTILE

Castillo de Coca

50km (31 miles) northwest of Segovia, via the C605 to Santa Maria la Real de Nieva, and thereafter minor roads. Open: Mon–Sat 1030–1300, 1630–1900; Sun 1100–1300, 1600–1900; closed first Tue of the month.

Cruising across the rather drab plains of northern Segovia province, you would not expect to find one of Spain's finest castles ahead of you. The Castillo de Coca appears, as it were, out of nowhere, lying low on the horizon. The fact that it doesn't stand on a spot which lends any natural defence tells you that this is one of the later generation of Spanish castles, more a palace than a stronghold. Nevertheless, it is rooted in a **deep moat** and its **multiple battlements and turrets** make it look fearsome enough when you get close up to it.

Coca was built by the powerful 15th-century archbishop of Sevilla, **Fonseca**. The Mudéjar craftsmen responsible for its construction made skilful use of the rose-coloured bricks to produce different patterns and tones.

Castillo de la Mota

On the outskirts of the town of Medina del Campo, 25km (15 miles) south of Tordesillas, just off the NVI. Open: Mon–Sat 1100–1400, 1600–1900; Sun 1100–1400.

Like Coca, this is a brick castle standing in a deep moat. Gothic, with Mudéjar features, it is more austere than Coca and is dominated by a mighty **torre de homenaje** ('keep'). It dates from the 13th to the 15th centuries and once belonged to the 'Catholic Monarchs', Fernando and Isabel. Later it was used as a gaol to guard political and military prisoners.

It has been well restored, and its defensive features are clearly defined: windowless curtain walls, battlements, cross-and-orb loopholes to allow archers to shoot in all directions, twin bartizan turrets on the upper corners of the keep, and between them overhanging machicolations from which human excrement and searing hot oil could be poured over the heads of enemy soldiers.

The castle is entered over a drawbridge, and in the centre of it is a surprisingly gentle courtyard from which several rooms can be visited.

Western Castille

Ávlla

Tourist information: Plaza de la Catedral 4. Tel: 92 021 1387.

The most complete set of **medieval walls** in Europe encircles Spain's highest provincial capital, which stands at an altitude of 1 131m (3 710ft) above sea level. Altogether, the walls stretch for 2km (1 1/4 miles), with 88 towers and nine gateways spaced out along them. The road in from Salamanca is a good place from which to appreciate their dimensions.

> *God deliver us from sullen saints.*
>
> **St Teresa of Ávila**

The main intramural sight is the **catedral**, which actually forms part of the walls. It has a Gothic nave, 16th-century choir stalls and two pulpits of decorative wrought-iron. The **tomb of Cardinal Alonso de Madrigal**, a 15th-century bishop who was nicknamed 'El Tostado' ('the Swarthy') because of his dark complexion, is considered a masterpiece. On the square adjacent to the cathedral is the **Palacio de Valderrábanos**, which is now a hotel. The family crest of its former aristocratic owners can be seen over the doorway. Outside the walls, the large Romanesque church of **San Vicente** is worth seeing for its superbly carved west portal.

Ávila was the birthplace of the talented **St Teresa** (1515–82), but she spent most of her life travelling around building convents for her order, the Discalced (Barefoot) Carmelites, for which she was sometimes unkindly called by her critics 'the roving nun'. Not only did she found 15 convents herself directly and 17 more through intermediaries, but

> *The smell of Ávila is the aromatic smell of the wilderness which comes into every street, the reek of frying oil, or the cold sour smell of polish and charcoal in its stone doorways, of urine and excrement in the ruins, of the black pigs driven in at the great stone gates in the evening.*
>
> **V S Pritchett, *The Spanish Temper* (1954)**

OLD CASTILE

she is also remembered as one of the finest writers Spain has produced. More prosaically, she has lent her name to *yemas de santa Teresa*, a sweet delicacy of Ávila.

Sierra de Gredos

This mountain range west of Madrid is a popular weekend destination for hunting, hiking and fishing. It has long been a retreat from the capital; Spain's first parador, or state-run hotel, was built here in 1928 (*Parador de Gredos; tel: 92 034 8048*). The Reserva Nacional de Gredos now protects the wildlife in part of the area, which includes ibex and birds of prey.

The N502 crosses through the centre of the range, between Ávila and the NV Madrid to Extremadura motorway. It also crosses the Puerto del Pico, a pass at a height of 1 352m (4 435ft), and passes the 14th-century **Monbeltrán castle** to reach Arenas de San Pedro, the largest town. To the northwest of here is, at 2 592m (8 504ft), the highest summit in the Sierra de Gredos, **Pico Almanzor**. On the eastern fringe of the mountains, 6km (3 ¾ miles) northwest of San Martín de Valdeiglesias, four roughly carved granite figures of bulls stand in a field. The **Toros of Guisando** are known to be ancient but are of unknown origin and significance.

Ciudad Rodrigo

90km (56 miles) southwest of Salamanca on the N620.

You feel a long way off the beaten track in this small walled city near the Portuguese border. There are two **Renaissance mansions** to admire on the main square, one of them now the town hall. Adjacent to the walls stands a **14th-century castle** which has been converted into a parador (*Parador de Ciudad Rodrigo, Plaza Castillo; tel: 92 346 0150*). On the other side of the old town is the **catedral** which still shows marks of the cannon fire to which the town was subjected during an 11-day siege by the Duke of Wellington's troops in 1812, during the Peninsular War.

To the south of Ciudad Rodrigo is the attractive **Sierra de la Peña de Francia**. From the SA515 you can also reach the pretty village of **La Alberca**, and the 1 732m (5 682ft) Peña de Francia itself, on top of which is a monastery.

OLD CASTILE

Salamanca

This magnificent old university city has fine buildings almost everywhere you look, making it a joy to stroll around. The use of sandstone, which has mellowed over time into a golden hue, unites the Gothic, Renaissance, Plateresque and baroque architecture into a pleasing and memorable whole.

> " *Salamanca, that bewitches the will of anyone who has had the good fortune of enjoying a stay here, obliging him to return.* "
>
> **Cervantes,** *El Licenciado Vidriera* **(1613)**

The natural place to begin a tour of Salamanca is the **Plaza Mayor**, an 18th-century baroque square which is one of the largest and finest public spaces in Spain. Two buildings face each other across it: the **town hall** (*ayuntamiento*) on the northern side, with bells hanging above it, and the **Royal Pavilion** to the south. The rest of the square is flanked by uniform three-storey buildings with arcades filled with cafés below, but be warned: you'll pay for the privilege of sitting in one of the most beautiful squares of Spain. Look in the Plaza del Mercado or around the university for cheaper places to eat.

Leave the Plaza Mayor through one of the gateways on the southern side of the square and find your way on to the Rúa Mayor, which will lead you shortly to the **Casa de las Conchas** (*open: Mon–Fri 0900–2100, Sat 0900–1400, 1600–1900, Sun 1000–1400, 1600–1900*). This 16th-century mansion on a corner is named after the 400 scallop shells that are carved on its outer walls. They allude to the order of the Knights of Santiago, to which the owner belonged.

> " *About noon on the third day, on reaching the brow of a hillock, we saw a huge dome before us, upon which the fierce rays of the sun striking, produced the appearance of burnished gold.* "
>
> **George Borrow, on his first sight of Salamanca cathedral,** *The Bible in Spain* **(1842)**

The next most important stop in Salamanca is the **university** (*open: Mon–Sat 0930–1300, 1600–1900, Sun 1000–1300; £*) on Calle Libreros, which runs parallel to Rúa Mayor. Stand in the **Patio de las Escuelas** and

OLD CASTILE

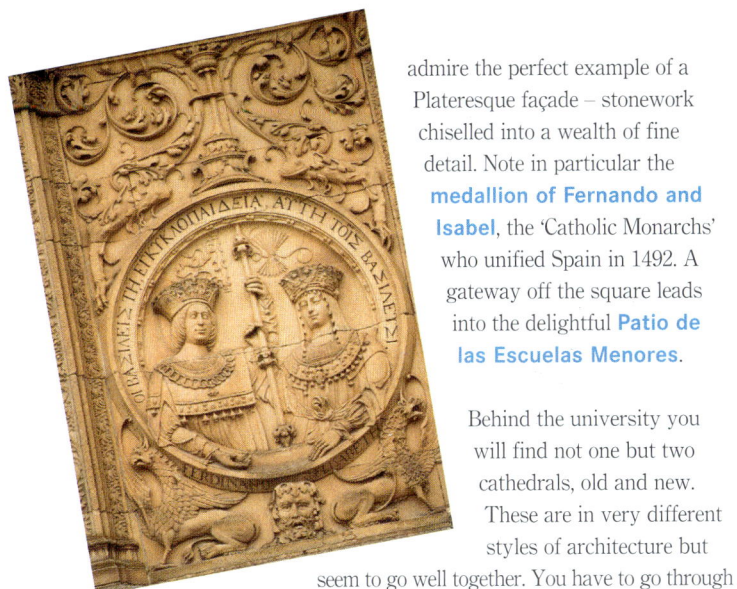

admire the perfect example of a Plateresque façade – stonework chiselled into a wealth of fine detail. Note in particular the **medallion of Fernando and Isabel**, the 'Catholic Monarchs' who unified Spain in 1492. A gateway off the square leads into the delightful **Patio de las Escuelas Menores**.

Behind the university you will find not one but two cathedrals, old and new. These are in very different styles of architecture but seem to go well together. You have to go through the **Catedral Nueva** (*open: daily 1000–1300, 1600–1800*) to get to the older, Romanesque **Catedral Vieja** (*open: daily 1000–1230, 1600–1730*), whose most interesting feature is the huge coloured altarpiece made of 53 painted panels by **Nicolás Florentino**. The new cathedral was built mainly in the 16th century but finished off in the 18th century, leaving it with Gothic, Renaissance and baroque elements. The best bit of it is outside: the west front is intricately carved into a mass of Gothic decoration. Don't forget to follow the old cathedral around to your right to have a look at its **Torre de Gallo**, a 12th-century dome in Byzantine style.

While you are down at this end of town, you may like to look at the **Puente Romano** ('Roman bridge') across the Rio Tormes, but it can be seen on your way out if you are going from here to Ávila or Ciudad Rodrigo.

There are plenty more fine buildings to see if you want to carry on walking. The **Convento de las Dueñas** (*open: daily 1030–1300, 1630–1800*) has a Renaissance patio on two levels. The so-called **Casa de las Muertes** ('House of the Dead') on Calle Bordadores has a skull carved into its façade. Two towers, the **Torre del Clavero** and the **Torre del Aire**, are all that are left of the mansions to which they belonged.

Tourist information: Plaza Mayor 14. Tel: 92 321 8342.

OLD CASTILE

From Zamora to Valladolid

Zamora

Tourist information: Calle de Santa Clara 20. Tel: 98 053 1845.

Zamora, on the banks of the Rio Duero, was once an important frontier settlement. Long stretches of its city walls still stand, and there are plans afoot to pull down the later buildings which obscure them. One narrow gateway through the walls is known as the **Portillo de la Traición** ('Traitor's Gate') because the assassin of Sancho II is said to have entered the city through it.

A number of Romanesque churches litter its streets, among them the **catedral** (*open: daily 1100–1400, 1600–2100; £ for museum*), built between 1151 and 1174 but with later Gothic additions. Stand back to look at the dome modelled on the Haghia Sophia in Istanbul, which is covered in grey, scale-like tiles. A friendly rivalry exists between Zamora and Salamanca as to which cathedral has the better Byzantine dome. Judge the contest for yourself.

The Renaissance **Palacio de los Condes de Alba y Aliste** is now a parador (*Parador de Zamora, Plaza de Viriato 5; tel: 98 051 4497*) and has a beautiful inner courtyard worth seeing. Next to it is a balcony from which you can watch storks building nests on nearby spires. Two other aristocratic mansions worth seeing for their façades are **Casa de los Momos** and **Casa del Cordón**.

Zamora holds a well-known Easter Week celebration and maintains the **Museo de Semana Santa** (*open: Mon–Sat 1000–1400, 1600–2100, Sun 1100–1400; £*) to display the processional floats during the year.

Some 20km (12 miles) northwest of Zamora is one of Spain's earliest churches, the 7th-century Visigothic **San Pedro de la Nave**.

OLD CASTILE

Convento de Santa Clara

Tordesillas, 30km (19 miles) southwest of Valladolid. Open: Oct–Mar, Tue–Sun 1030–1300, 1600–1730; Apr–Sept, Tue–Sun 1000–1300, 1530–1830. £.

It would be easy to drive past Tordesillas, which is clustered along the north bank of the River Duero, without noticing that it contains one of the most interesting buildings in Spain. The Convento de Santa Clara was built as a palace by King Alfonso XI in 1350 and transformed into a convent by his son, Pedro the Cruel, as a place to install his mistress, María de Padilla. The Mudéjar decoration of the convent was intended to remind María of her native Andalucía.

The guided tour begins with the patio and then moves into the chapel, in which stands an organ belonging to Juana the Mad, who retreated here for the remaining 46 years of her life after the death of her husband, Felipe, in 1506. The tour then passes through the nuns' refectory and along the side of the cloister to reach the oratory, choir and church, which has one of the most superb, multicoloured **coffered ceilings** in Spain, peopled by 43 figures of saints. In a chapel off the church is a richly decorated 15th-century portable altar.

The town of Tordesillas is remembered in Spanish history for the treaty signed here between Spain and Portugal in 1494, by means of which the two imperial powers divided up the New World between them. Unwisely, Spain ceded Brazil to Portugal.

Valladolid

Tourist information: Plaza de Zorrilla 3. Tel: 98 335 1801.

Valladolid, at the confluence of the Río Esgueva and Río Pisuerga, was the capital of the Catholic kings, and **Columbus** died here in 1506. Another name associated with the city is that of **José Zorrilla**, who promoted the legend of Don Juan through his 1844 play.

The most important sight is the **Museo Nacional de Escultura Religiosa** (*open: Tue–Sat 1000–1400, 1600–1800, Sun 1000–1400; £*), located in the Colegio de San Gregorio, with its superb façade, Plateresque staircase and patio with twisting columns. The exhibits are mainly multicoloured sculptures on religious themes, made between the 13th and 18th centuries.

OLD CASTILE

East of Madrid

Alcalá de Henares

30km (19 miles) east of Madrid on the NII. Tourist information: Callejón de Santa Maria 1. Tel: 91 889 2694.

The reputation of this industrial city in the shadow of Madrid is mainly founded on the university established here by Cardinal Cisneros in 1498. The university was moved to Madrid in the mid-19th century, but since then a new one has been founded. The colleges that made up the university have disappeared except for one, the **Colegio de San Ildefonso** (*guided tour only, normally every half hour 1100–1400 and 1600–1900, but check with tourist information office first; £*). This has a Plateresque façade and several patios. The carved tomb of Cisneros is in the 15th-century chapel.

Alcalá has other claims to recognition. In 1547, **Miguel de Cervantes**, the author of *Don Quixote*, was born in the house which is now run as a museum, the **Museo-Casa Natal de Cervantes** (*open: Mon–Sun 1015–1330, 1615–1830; £*). Alcalá was also the birthplace of **Catherine of Aragón** (1485–1536), the first wife of England's Henry VIII.

OLD CASTILE

Guadalajara

55km (34 miles) northeast of Madrid on the NII. Tourist information: Plaza de los Caidos 6. Tel: 94 921 1626.

The main attraction in this small provincial capital is the 15th-century **Palacio de los Duques del Infantado** (*tel: 94 921 3301; open: Tue–Sat 1000–1400, 1600–1900, Sun 1000–1400; £*), built in a Gothic-Mudéjar style with a florid façade and a two-storey patio. It was badly damaged by bombs in 1936 but has since been restored.

To the east of Guadalajara is the region of La Alcarria, described in a classic book by Nobel Prize-winner Camilo José Cela, **Journey to the Alcarria**. At its centre are three large reservoirs called, collectively, the Mar de Castilla ('Sea of Castile'). **Pastrana** is the most charming town of the Alcarria.

Sigüenza

80km (50 miles) northeast of Guadalajara on the CM1101.

Many tourists head for Sigüenza to stay in regal splendour in the magnificent parador (*Parador de Sigüenza, Plaza del Castillo; tel: 94 939 0100*) that is housed in the imposing castle at the top of the town. The lounge was formerly the throne room.

The old town below the castle has steep streets lined with numerous churches and elegant stone buildings. At its heart is the handsome 15th-century **Plaza Mayor** on which stands the Renaissance town hall.

The **catedral** (*open: daily 1100–1200, 1700–1900*) is full of treasures, most notably a sepulchral sculpture known as **El Doncel**. The young nobleman reading and dreaming his way through immortality is **Martín Vasquez de Arce**, who was killed during the fight for Granada in 1486.

Atienza, 30km (19 miles) northwest of Sigüenza, is a delightful medieval town of old stone houses on cobbled streets. It also has a handsome Plaza Mayor and a 12th-century castle. It is known for its annual fiesta, **La Caballada**, which takes place on Whit Sunday, a colourful costumed pilgrimage on horseback to a local shrine.

OLD CASTILE

Eating and drinking

Restaurants

La Casita
Zamora. Carretera de Carrascal. Tel: 98 053 9046. ££. This charming restaurant is in an old house in peaceful countryside 4km (2 1/2 miles) outside the city. It serves delicious traditional dishes.

Chez Víctor
Salamanca. Espoz y Mina 26. Tel: 92 321 3123. £££. An institution in Salamanca, serving French and Spanish food, and excellent chocolate desserts.

Duque Maestro Asador
Segovia. Cervantes 12. Tel: 92 146 2487. ££. One of the best places to try *cochinillo asado*. Can get crowded at the weekends.

El Mesón
Salamanca. Plaza del Poeta Iglesias 10. Tel: 92 321 7222. ££. Typical Castilian cuisine, with interesting specialities on the menu.

El Molino de la Losa
Ávila. Bajada de la Losa 12. Tel: 92 021 1102. ££. Restaurant in a pretty setting, which serves good *cordero*, *cochinillo asado* and *chuletón de Ávila*.

Nuevo Racimo de Oro
León. Plaza de San Martin 8. Tel: 98 721 4767. ££. One of the best restaurants to eat at in the area around Plaza de San Martin.

La Parrilla de San Lorenzo
Valladolid. Pedro Niño 1. Tel: 98 333 5088. ££. Located in the Real Monasterio de las Monjas Recoletas. Traditional Castilian dishes and delicious desserts.

El Yantar de Pedraza
Pedraza. Plaza Mayor. Tel: 92 150 9842. ££. Lamb is cooked in a wood-fired oven in this restaurant in the centre of town.

What to try

The cooking of Castilla y León makes wide use of red meats, in particular **cochinillo asado** (suckling pig), which should be so tender that it can be cut with a plate; **cordero** (lamb); and the T-bone steak from Ávila called **chuletón**. This area also has excellent cured meats: **jamón serrano** and **chorizo de camtimpalo** are favourites. In winter, try the delicious **sopa castellana** (made from bread and garlic) or **cocido maragato** (chick-pea stew). This region is also good for game and for its pulse vegetables from El Barco de Ávila. Castilla y León also has three excellent wine areas: **Toro**, **Rueda** and **Ribera del Duero**.

OLD CASTILE

Shopping

What to buy

Traditional crafts worth looking for are **pottery** in Alba de Tormes, Arrabal de Portillo, Moveros, Perelada and Jiménez de Jamuz; **wooden clogs** in Sajambre; **textiles** in Val de San Lorenzo; **lace** in La Alberca; and **silver** in Salamanca.

Fiestas

'Landscapes that are old and harsh, as good fortune would have Spain's, steep their fiestas in blood, fire, gunpowder and wine,' wrote the Spanish novelist Camilo José Cela, words that will chime with anyone who has ever experienced one of the bigger, more established fiestas in this country.

But not all are so fiery. The **Semana Santa** ('Holy Week') rites of Castilla y León are very different to those of the Mediterranean. Valladolid and Zamora have solemn but impressive processions. An unusual tradition is enacted on Corpus Christi (in May or June) in the town of **Castrillo de Murcia** (near Burgos) when a devil-like figure called El Colacho jumps over the town's babies to protect them from illnesses in the coming year. And at the beginning of February the women of **Zamarramala**, in the province of Segovia, rule the town for the day in an amusing festivity called Las Alcaldesas ('The Mayoresses').

Spanish in Salamanca

Salamanca, one of the old universities of Spain, specialises in teaching Spanish to foreigners and always has a lively student atmosphere. You can find all the information you need about Spanish language courses on the internet (*www.castillayleon.com/turismo/castellano/index.htm*).

OLD CASTILE

PROFILE
Castles

Spain's turbulent history, combined with its rugged terrain, has left it a land filled with castles. During the bellicose Middle Ages as many as 10,000 fortresses and fortifications may have been built; of these, about 2 500 remain. Many are in ruins, but others are preserved intact and some have been restored and put to new uses.

Although there are remains of prehistoric fortifications at **Los Millares** in Almeria dating back to 2700 BC, it was the Romans who built the first proper castles. Every civilisation since then has added to earlier fortifications or built its own; indeed, most of the surviving castles are not the product of a single age but of successive generations. Even during the Civil War ancient defensive positions were re-fortified to withstand bombs and artillery.

Many of the castles that can be seen today were built during the wars of the Reconquest between the Moors and the Christians. Almost as soon as they had arrived in the peninsula the Moors began to fortify their possessions. The most common type of Moorish defence is the *alcazaba*, built on high ground as an integral part of a town's defences. The *alcazaba* of **Almería** was once the most extensive in Spain, but that of **Málaga** (*see page 209*), with its gardens and courtyards, has survived the ages better.

> " *Castles in Spain: a visionary unattainable scheme; a daydream.* "
> **The New Oxford Dictionary of English (1998)**

OLD CASTILE

The Moors also created Spain's most famous castle, the **Alhambra** in Granada (*see page 214*). The best examples of Christian fortified buildings are the handsome palaces, or *alcázares*, of **Segovia** and **Toledo**.

Most medieval castles were built to police the shifting frontier between the two sides. The last, triumphant wave of Christian 'reconquerors' came from Castile, a name that derives from the Latin for 'castle', and where castles are most densely concentrated. Some of these castles doubled as monasteries or the headquarters of quasi-religious orders of knights. A fine example of the Spanish castle-monastery is that of the **Knights of Calatrava**, near Almagro in La Mancha.

Castles continued to be built even after the defeat of the Moors. Some of these served a military purpose, but many were little more than the product of aristocratic caprice. **Coca** (*see page 55*), near Segovia, belongs to this period, but perhaps the fairy-tale spires and turrets of the **Castillo de Olite** in Navarra (*see page 145*) mark best this transition between fortification and pleasure palace.

OLD CASTILE

Castilla-La Mancha and Extremadura

CASTILLA-LA MANCHA AND EXTREMADURA

Wonderful sights are spread out on the plains of Castilla-La Mancha, south of Madrid, the stamping-ground of the fictional Don Quixote. *To the east and west are two cities not to be missed: Cuenca and Toledo. Beyond Toledo is the region of Extremadura, one of Spain's best-kept secrets, with many historic towns to visit and some great countryside in between.*

CASTILLA-LA MANCHA AND EXTREMADURA

BEST OF Castilla-La Mancha and Extremadura

Getting around: Madrid is the natural departure point for these two regions, although southern Extremadura is within reach of another international airport, that of Sevilla. The NV goes to Extremadura, the NIV through the heart of La Mancha towards Extremadura, and the NIII takes you at least part of the way towards Cuenca. Toledo has its own motorway spur (N401). The main tourist information offices are in the regional capitals of Toledo (Plaza Santiago de los Caballeros 5; tel: 92 521 0900, www.jccm.es) and Merida (Calle Cárdenas 11; tel: 92 438 1300, www.junatex.es).

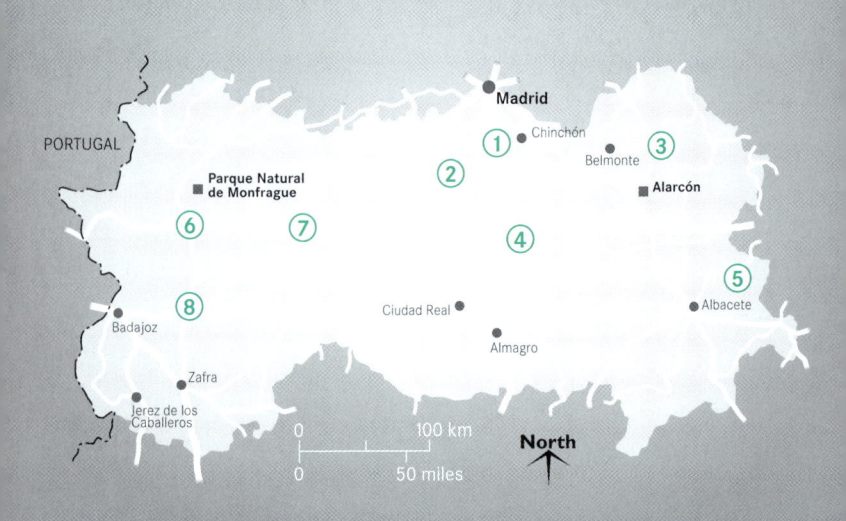

CASTILLA-LA MANCHA AND EXTREMADURA

① Aranjuez

The royal palace and gardens beside the Rio Tajo at Aranjuez make a good day out from Madrid. During the summer months you can get there on the old-fashioned 'Strawberry Train' from Atocha station. **Pages 72-3**

② Toledo

One of the truly special cities of Spain, Toledo needs time dedicated to it. A mixed medieval community of Christians, Jews and Moors left behind it a **rich collection of architecture**, especially in Mudéjar (Moorish-Gothic) style. Later, Toledo was home to the singular painter **El Greco**, and his greatest masterpiece hangs here in the Iglesia de Santo Tomé. **Pages 74-7**

③ Cuenca

The famous **'Hanging Houses'** – now a museum of abstract art – are permanently poised over the gorge on which the old town of Cuenca is spectacularly sited. The Serranía de Cuenca to the north has many beauty spots, including the 'Enchanted City' where rocks have been eroded into bizarre formations. **Pages 78-9**

④ La Mancha

It may seem like a big empty space in the middle of Spain, but La Mancha has its charms. Follow Spain's answer to literary tourism, in the steps of *Don Quixote,* to the inn where he got himself knighted, the village where he chose his beloved and the windmills he mistook for giants. **Pages 80-1**

⑤ Alcalá del Júcar

This brilliant-white village is built on the wall of a river meander with a castle on top, and many of its houses are carved into the soft rock. **Page 80**

⑥ Cáceres

There are stone mansions with carved façades at every turn in the perfectly preserved nucleus of this old seigneurial town in Extremadura. **Page 82**

⑦ Monasterio de Guadalupe

One of the most important shrines in Spain, this enormous monastery was built to venerate a statue of the black Virgin of Guadalupe. It is richly decorated with works of art. **Page 83**

⑧ Mérida

The Roman theatre and National Museum of Roman Art are what draw most people to ancient *Augusta Emerita,* which was one of the largest cities in the Roman world. There is also an amphitheatre, a Roman bridge and the remains of two villas with mosaic floors. **Pages 84-5**

CASTILLA-LA MANCHA AND EXTREMADURA

Aranjuez

The royal town of Aranjuez, renowned for its palace and gardens, stands in fertile farmland on the banks of the Río Tajo (Tagus), near its confluence with the Jarama, and can easily be visited on a day-trip from Madrid. Throughout the summer an old-fashioned steam train runs from Atocha station along the second railway line to be built in Spain (in 1850); its evocative name, the 'Strawberry Train', recalls the days when fruit was sent up the line to the capital from Aranjuez.

The **Palacio Real** (*open: Apr–Sept, Tue–Sun 1000–1830, Oct–May, Tue–Sun 1000–1715; £, guided tours only*) and its accompanying gardens were laid out in the 18th century on the south bank of the river. They have inspired a number of works of art and literature, as well as perhaps the most famous classical music to come out of Spain. **Joaquín Rodrigo**, blind from the age of three, was Spain's greatest composer of the Civil War period, and his best-known composition is a 1940 piece for guitar and small orchestra entitled *Concierto de Aranjuez*.

The palace's great staircase was designed by the Italian **Giacomo Bonavia** during the reign of Felipe V. One of the finest rooms is the rococo **Porcelain Room**, which was used as an audience chamber. Also on the itinerary are the **Throne Room** and the king's **Smoking Room**. The palace's walls are adorned with Brussels tapestries and the floors spread with fine carpets.

Behind the palace is the **Parterre**, a formal French garden. Two larger gardens snake along the riverside, west and east: the **Jardín de la Isla**, an artificial island between the river and a mill stream, and the **Jardín del Príncipe** ('Prince's Garden'), in which stands the **Casa de Marinos** (a museum displaying some of the launches used to take the royal family on their trips along the river) and the **Casa del Labrador** ('Labourer's House'), a pavilion built by Carlos IV.

CASTILLA-LA MANCHA AND EXTREMADURA

> *A lovely spot is Aranjuez, though in desolation: here the Tagus flows through a delicious valley, perhaps the most fertile in Spain; and here upsprang, in Spain's better days, a little city, with a small but beautiful palace shaded by enormous trees, where royalty delighted to forget its cares. Here Ferdinand the Seventh spent his latter days, surrounded by lovely señoras and Andalusian bull-fighters …*
>
> **George Borrow, *The Bible in Spain* (1842)**

Neighbouring **Ocaña**, 15km (9 miles) southeast of Aranjuez, has an impressive Plaza Mayor, built of brick in the 18th century and almost big enough to rival the squares of Madrid and Salamanca. The Hospital de la Caridad in **Illescas**, 25km (15 miles) to the northwest on the Madrid–Toledo road, houses five paintings by **El Greco**.

Getting there: 55km (34 miles) south of Madrid on the NIV.

Chinchón

45km (28 miles) southeast of Madrid on the M311.

Chinchón is a picturesque town grouped around an irregular, 16th-century wooden galleried plaza, the setting for an **Easter Week passion play** and **August bullfight**. Shops and bars here sell the renowned local spirit Anis de Chinchón. The parish church, hovering over the square, has a painting of the Assumption of the Virgin, by **Goya**, and near the square is an 18th-century **Augustinian monastery**, now a parador, arranged around a verdant courtyard. For a view of the town, head for the old castle which stands above it.

The Rio Jarama, between Chinchón and Madrid, was, in 1937, the site of one of the fiercest battles of the Spanish Civil War.

CASTILLA-LA MANCHA AND EXTREMADURA

Toledo

Toledo is one of Spain's most beautiful and interesting cities, and should be on every visitor's list of must-sees. It has been called a complete history of Spain in architecture. Romans, Visigoths, Arabs, Mozarabs, Jews, Mudéjars, Christians, Moriscos – they all lived here, built monuments and left behind them strong traditions.

Until the ascendancy of Madrid in the 16th century, Toledo was for a short time the country's capital. Although it is now no more than a provincial capital, it is still something of a spiritual centre for the nation – the Archbishop of Toledo is the Primate of Spain.

The city centre is a complex tangle of steep, narrow streets spilling over a mound which is edged on three sides by the Rio Tajo (Tagus) and protected on the fourth by a wall. There are good viewpoints on the ring road across the river, but for a better view climb up to the parador (*Parador de Toledo, Cerro del Emperador; tel: 92 522 1850*) for a coffee on the terrace.

Toledo's skyline is dominated by the **Alcázar** (*Cuesta del Alcázar; tel: 92 522 3038; open: Tue–Sat 0930–1330, 1600–1730, to 1830 in summer, Sun 1000–1330, 1600–1730; £*), a huge 16th-century palace-fortress built on the site of Roman, Visigothic and Muslim castles. It was set fire to three times, and in 1936 came close to destruction yet again when it was the scene of a famous siege during the Civil War.

A story, well known in Spain, is attached to this siege, but no one can be sure how authentic it is; perhaps it was embellished as propaganda. Leading the defenders inside the castle was one Colonel Moscardó. One of the republican soldiers besieging the Alcázar telephoned to say that he was holding Moscardó's son hostage and that he would kill the young man if the garrison did not surrender. 'Shout "Viva España!" and die like a hero,' the colonel supposedly instructed his son over the phone. It is said that the son was shot later for other reasons. The Alcázar, meanwhile, held out until it was

CASTILLA-LA MANCHA AND EXTREMADURA

> *… canons, prebendaries, curates, and twenty different orders of friars are seen standing in groups, strolling under the piazzas or seated upon benches, refreshing themselves with melons or grapes. There cannot be a more perfect realization of 'fat, contented ignorance' than the Plaza presents every day after dinner.*

Henry Inglis on Toledo's Plaza Real, quoted in David Mitchell, *Travellers in Spain* **(1990)**

relieved by Franco's rebel forces, a psychological blow to republicans.

Toledo's splendid **Gothic cathedral** (*open: Mon–Sat 1030–1200, 1600–1800, Sun 1400–1800*) stands on the site of a 7th-century church. It took over 250 years to build and combines several styles: outside it is conspicuously Gothic but inside it makes use of Mudéjar, Plateresque and other Spanish styles. Particularly interesting features of the cathedral are the **carvings in the choir** showing the fall of Granada to Christian forces, the colourful **reredos** behind the high altar and the **Transparente**, a baroque altarpiece lit up by a special skylight. In addition, the chapterhouse has a **superb Mudéjar ceiling**, and the cathedral treasury contains a 3m (10ft) tall **silver monstrance**, made in the 16th century and carried through the streets during Toledo's Corpus Christi processions. In the sacristy are paintings by **El Greco**, **Titian**, **Van Dyck** and **Goya**.

Another of the city's splendid buildings is the **Monasterio de San Juan de los Reyes** (*open: daily Apr–Sept, 1000–1345, 1530–1845, Oct–Mar, 1000–1345, 1530–1745; £*), built at the behest of the 'Catholic Monarchs' Fernando and Isabel in celebration of the defeat of the Portuguese at the battle of Toro in 1476. The church, finished in the year 1492, is largely in the style known as Isabelline, although the upper galleries of the cloisters have Mudéjar vaulting.

Tourist information: Puerta de Bisagra. Tel: 92 522 0843.

CASTILLA-LA MANCHA AND EXTREMADURA

Toledo (continued)

The city of El Greco

The career of the painter Domenikos Theotokopoulos, better known as El Greco ('The Greek', because he was born in Crete), is inextricably linked to Toledo. El Greco (1541–1614) lived and worked here for 30 years and his paintings can be seen in many buildings.

The **Casa-Museo El Greco** (*Calle Samuel Levi; tel: 92 522 4046; open: Tue–Sat 1000–1400, 1600–1800, Sun 1000–1400; £*) may or may not be the house he actually lived in, but it is now a museum dedicated to his memory, displaying several of his works, including *View of Toledo*. The **Museo de Santa Cruz** (*Calle Cervantes 3; open: Mon–Sat 1000–1830, Sun 1000–1400; £*), a handsome Plateresque building in its own right, has 18 paintings by El Greco (displayed on the first floor) among its outstanding collection of 16th- and 17th-century art – some of the works from monasteries and convents dissolved in the 19th century. Another item of interest here is **Don Juan of Austria's pennant** from the battle of Lepanto (1571), one of the greatest victories in Spanish history.

CASTILLA-LA MANCHA AND EXTREMADURA

> *Highly esteemed in his own lifetime, El Greco was subsequently dismissed as technically inept and mentally unstable until 'rediscovered' in the 20th century by avant-garde artists such as Picasso.*

Robert Cumming, *Annotated Art* (1995)

El Greco's best-known painting, **The Burial of the Count of Orgaz**, hangs in a church, the **Iglesia de Santo Tomé** (*Plaza del Conde; open: daily 1000–1345, 1530–1745; £*). Only two figures are looking out of the painting towards the spectator: one is El Greco's son Jorge, in the bottom left; the other, among the bystanders across the middle of the painting, is thought to be the artist himself.

Mudéjar Toledo

In medieval times Jewish, Moorish and Christian cultures co-existed in an atmosphere of mutual respect and Toledo became a city of churches, mosques and synagogues. This intermingling of cultures is nowhere better evidenced than in the architecture, particularly in the proliferation of the Mudéjar style.

Toledo had a particularly large and prosperous Jewish community until a persecution began in 1355, culminating in the expulsion of Jews from Spain in the year 1492. Having no architectural style of their own to draw on, the Jews had turned to Mudéjar craftsmen for their synagogues, of which only two remain. **Santa María la Blanca** (*open: daily Apr–Sept, 1000–1200, 1530–1900, Oct–Mar, 1000–1400, 1530–1800; £*) was converted into a church but has been restored to its former appearance, with plain white horseshoe arches and carved stone capitals; **El Tránsito** (*open: Tue–Sat 1000–1400, 1600–1800, Sun 1000–1400; £*) looks deceptively uninteresting from the outside, but inside has the most **magnificent Mudéjar decoration** in the city.

Tip

Damascene – a technique of inlaying black steel with gold, silver and copper wire – is the craft most associated with Toledo, and swords and other souvenirs can be bought in many shops.

CASTILLA-LA MANCHA AND EXTREMADURA

Cuenca

Cuenca is a small provincial city, superbly sited above a deep gorge of the Río Huécar. Part of the old city actually overhangs the gorge, and the Casas Colgadas ('Hanging Houses') have become the city's trademark. No one knows who built them but it appears they were there in some form in the 15th century. They now house the atmospheric Museo del Arte Abstracto (open: Tue–Fri 1100–1400, 1600–1800, Sat 1100–1400, 1600–2000, Sun 1100–1400; £). For a good view of the Casas Colgadas cross the nearby Puente San Pablo.

The 12th to 13th-century **catedral** has a magnificent façade, and the nearby **Museo Diocesano** (*open: Tue–Fri 1100–1400, 1600–1800, Sat 1100–1400, 1600–2000, Sun 1100–1400; £*) houses the cathedral treasury and paintings and has a display of early carpets.

Beyond the urban area to the north is the **Serranía de Cuenca**, a beautiful area of forests, crags and rivers which is well worth exploring. Wildlife – roe deer, wild boar, mouflon (mountain sheep), vultures, birds of prey, otters – abounds here; in certain parts you can truly get off the beaten track

CASTILLA-LA MANCHA AND EXTREMADURA

and deep into rural Spain. Most people, however, make for the **Ciudad Encantada** (*open: daily, sunrise to sunset; £*), which is signposted from the city. The so-called 'Enchanted City' can be overrun with coach parties in season, but there's still something awesome about this remarkable collection of naturally sculpted rocks.

Not far from the Ciudad Encantada, just outside Villalba de la Sierra, is the **Ventano del Diablo** – a cave-balcony framed by two natural arches from which there are great views over the gorge of the Rio Júcar below. And if you don't mind driving 40km (25 miles) further into the sierra you will reach another, very different, beauty spot, the **Nacimiento del Río Cuervo** ('Source of the River Cuervo'). There's a marked walk to the source from the car park which takes about an hour. The moss-hung waterfalls could have come straight out of a fairy-tale, and are particularly impressive in winter.

Tourist information: Plaza Mayor 1. Tel. 96 923 2119.

Alarcón

60km (37 miles) south of Cuenca off the N111.

The stunning castle of Alarcón hangs over a deep valley of the Júcar. The Moors considered the castle to be impregnable, but in 1184 the Christians managed to wrest it from them. According to legend, it was one Fernán Martín de Ceballos who scaled its walls at night, inching his way up to the battlements using two daggers dug into the cement between the stones. Alarcón castle is now a parador (*Parador de Alarcón; tel: 96 933 0315*).

Belmonte

100km (62 miles) southwest of Cuenca on the N420.

Belmonte is a village of white houses beneath a late-Gothic castle (*open: daily 1000–1400, 1700–1900; £*) built by the Marquis of Villena in the 15th century. The castle was constructed to a star-shaped plan, with double walls and its six corners marked by round towers. Inside it has decorated galleries and coffered ceilings. It was used as one of the sets for the 1961 film *El Cid* starring Charlton Heston and Sophia Loren.

CASTILLA-LA MANCHA AND EXTREMADURA

La Mancha

Alcalá del Júcar

60km (37 miles) northeast of Albacete on the AB862/863.

Brilliant white to match the rock it is built on, Alcalá del Júcar looks as if it has been glued precariously to the inner curve of a tight river meander. It spills down the steep slope from the walls of its castle – perched on a rocky pinnacle – to an old stone bridge that bounds across the olive-green waters of the Río Júcar below. Park either at the top or the bottom of the village and plunge yourself into the complex of steps and narrow streets.

Many householders in Alcalá del Júcar have tunnelled extra rooms into the soft chalk. Some have even dug tunnels that pierce the meander and emerge up to 90m (300ft) away, high above the river. Two of the largest caves, **Cuevas de Masagó** and **Cuevas del Diablo**, are open to the public as bars.

For a spectacular view of the whole village in its natural setting, go up to the hamlet of **Casas del Cerro**, across the river on the lip of the gorge.

Don Quixote's La Mancha

The route taken by Don Quixote in Cervantes's novel of the same name is now touted as a tourist trail; you can pick up leaflets on this at tourist information offices, but you have to have a car to drive between the sights and not everything on the trail is worth seeing – and what there is should be approached with a sense of humour.

Don Quixote is knighted by an inn-keeper at **Puerto Lápice**, which he sees as 'a fortress with its four towers and pinnacles of shining silver, complete with a drawbridge and a deep moat'. Painted bright blue and surrounding a rustic courtyard,

CASTILLA-LA MANCHA AND EXTREMADURA

Unknown village

Cervantes deliberately leaves the location of Don Quixote *vague; the book begins with words famous in Spain: 'In a certain village in La Mancha, which I do not wish to name …'. Some towns in La Mancha seem to think this is a compliment, and they use the phrase as a promotional slogan.*

the inn still serves meals to the weary traveller (*see page 86*).

The confused knight then chooses his lady love, Dulcinea, almost at random in the pretty village of **El Toboso**. His sidekick, Sancho Panza, laments his choice, noting that she is 'a brawny girl … the one who pitches rocks as well as the strongest lad in the whole village'. The supposed 'Dulcinea's House', decorated in a local style, can be visited.

The **Lagunas de Ruidera** is another Don Quixote location, but the reason to stop by here is to see the scenery. The 16 lakes comprise a veritable oasis in the parched plains of La Mancha, feeding a population of waterfowl and marsh harriers (there's a nature reserve information centre in the village of Ruidera).

But of course it is windmills with which Don Quixote is most associated (he attacked them, mistaking them for menacing giants – hence our phrase 'tilting at windmills', meaning to try to overcome imaginary obstacles). The ones Cervantes had in mind are thought to be those at **Mota del Cuervo**, but the best windmills in the area are at **Consuegra** and **Campo de Criptana**. Nowadays they may look part of the landscape, but in Cervantes's day they represented new technology imported from the Low Countries.

Almagro

25km (15 miles) southeast of Ciudad Real.

Almagro's cobbled streets lined with 16th- and 17th-century houses lead to a picture-postcard central square, the **Plaza Mayor**, flanked by two tiers of green bay-windows. Just off the square is the **Corral de las Comedias** (*tel: 92 688 2244; better still, ask about visits and/or performances at the tourist information office: Calle Mayor Carnicerías 5; tel. 92 686 0717*), a theatre which has survived from Spanish literature's Golden Age. Lace-making is the traditional craft of Almagro, if you want a souvenir.

About 35km (22 miles) to the north is Spain's smallest national park, the **Tablas de Daimiel,** a chain of wetlands supporting a large population of waterfowl.

CASTILLA-LA MANCHA AND EXTREMADURA

Cáceres

You may not guess it from the modern outskirts, but the core of Cáceres is a perfectly preserved old town of palacios *(stone mansions).*

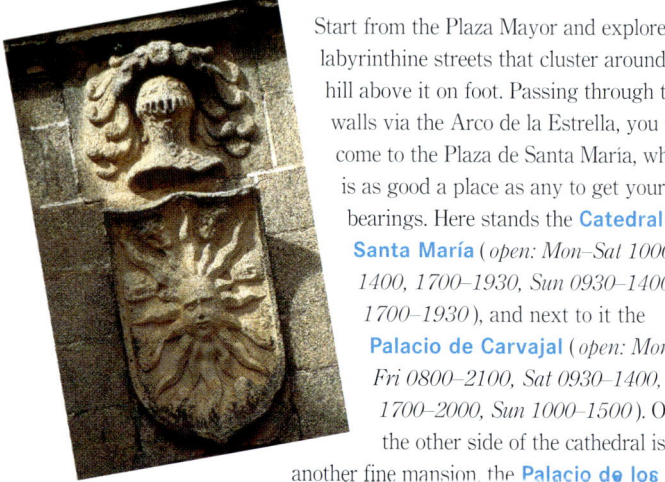

Start from the Plaza Mayor and explore the labyrinthine streets that cluster around the hill above it on foot. Passing through the walls via the Arco de la Estrella, you will come to the Plaza de Santa María, which is as good a place as any to get your bearings. Here stands the **Catedral de Santa María** (*open: Mon–Sat 1000–1400, 1700–1930, Sun 0930–1400, 1700–1930*), and next to it the **Palacio de Carvajal** (*open: Mon–Fri 0800–2100, Sat 0930–1400, 1700–2000, Sun 1000–1500*). On the other side of the cathedral is another fine mansion, the **Palacio de los Golfines de Abajo**, which has an ornate façade.

From here, head up the hill to the Plaza de las Veletas. The Casa de las Veletas contains the **Museo Provincial** (*Plaza de las Veletas; tel: 92 724 7234; open: Tue–Sat 0900–1400, Sun 1015–1430; £, but free for EU citizens*), which includes an Arab cistern. Also on this square stands the **Palacio de la Cigüeñas** (*open: Mon–Fri 1100–1300, 1700–2000*). This house is distinguished by a tower which, as the name suggests, is topped by a stork's nest (*cigüeña* is Spanish for 'stork') – not that this is unusual as most rooftops in Cáceres are inhabited by storks. Going downhill again, look out for the **Casa del Sol**, which has a handsome carved shield showing the sun.

Trujillo, 50km (31 miles) east of Cáceres, is a pretty, unspoilt hilltop town of narrow old streets. A statue of **Francisco Pizarro**, conqueror of Peru, stands in the main square.

Tourist information: Plaza Mayor 33. Tel: 92 724 6347.

CASTILLA-LA MANCHA AND EXTREMADURA

Parque Natural de Monfrague

25km (15 miles) south of Plasencia on the C524. Tourist information: Villarreal de San Carlos.

In the countryside around this nature reserve you often see black pigs grazing – they are the source of Spain's finest cured ham. If you are just driving through, the best place to stop and watch birds is the car park in front of the **Salto del Gitano**, a craggy peak with vultures wheeling round it.

Monasterio de Guadalupe

80km (50 miles) east of Trujillo on the C40. Open: summer, Mon–Sun 0930–1245, 1530–1845; winter, Mon–Sun 0930–1245, 1530–1830. £.

The spires and turrets of this **great royal monastery**, one of the major centres of pilgrimage in the Hispanic world, dominate the hill town of the same name in eastern Extremadura. A shrine to the Virgin of Guadalupe was probably first built here in around 1300. In the 14th century Alfonso XI had a Hieronymite monastery constructed on the spot in thanks for the Virgin's help in a victory against the Moors.

The guided tour of the monastery first visits the **Mudéjar cloisters** and the three museums off them: the **Embroidery Museum**, the **chapterhouse** containing illustrated plainsong manuscripts, and a **museum of religious works of art**. Next comes the **choir**, with its beautiful painted ceiling. The **sacristy** is a triumph of the baroque style, with a series of paintings by **Zurbarán**. From here you move into the **octagonal reliquary** where the jewels and crowns used to dress the figure of the Virgin for processions are stored. The climax of the tour is the **camarín**, the chamber behind the image of the Virgin who sits above the altar of the church. A priest will turn the Virgin's enamelwork throne around to reveal the black statue with the child Jesus on her knee.

> *Kings, conquistadores, saints – every kind of person has passed through here.*
>
> **Tour guide, Monasterio de Guadalupe**

CASTILLA-LA MANCHA AND EXTREMADURA

Mérida

The Romans founded Augusta Emerita *(ancient Mérida) in 25* BC*, and it became the capital of their western province of* Lusitania.

As a result, Mérida has one of the most exceptional collections of **Roman monuments** in Europe. Foremost among them is the **Teatro Romano** (*tel: 92 433 0312; open: daily summer, 0930–1345, 1700–1915, winter, 0930–1345, 1600–1815 – for performances, check at the local tourist information centre; ££ – a single combined ticket gets you into most of the monuments of Mérida*), which could seat 6 000 people. The magnificent **colonnaded stage wall** cannot fail to impress, and the theatre is still used for a summer drama festival. Next to it is the **Anfiteatro** ('amphitheatre'), which doesn't seem so impressive after seeing the theatre, but it once entertained crowds 14,000 strong with chariot races and gladiatorial contests.

> *Hispania's greatest city was Emerita Augusta (Mérida) … During the Pax romana, Mérida ranked ninth in size in the entire empire, ahead of cities such as Athens …*
>
> Mark Williams, *The Story of Spain* (1990)

Across the road from the theatre and amphitheatre is the excellent **Museo Nacional de Arte Romano** (*open: Tue–Sat 1000–1400, 1600–1800, Sun 1000–1400; £, but free on Sun*). The strikingly designed, purpose-built museum is made of brick and is light, cool and airy inside, where you will find displays of sculptures and other Roman finds. You can also see mosaics *in situ*, and imagine how the Romans must have lived in the remains of two houses carefully prepared for visitors. In the **Casa del Anfiteatro** (*open: daily summer, 0930–1345, 1700–1915, winter, 0930–1345, 1600–1815; £*), close to the museum, you can actually walk over the mosaics. In the

Casa de Mithra (*same opening times; £*), a short walk away from the other Roman sights, walkways keep you off the ground but enable you to look down on a depiction of Roman cosmology. Reproduction mosaics, skilfully made by local craftsmen and women, are on sale in the museum shop.

On the way out of town towards Cáceres are the extensive ruins of the **Los Milagros aqueduct**, a glorious perch for the storks nesting on it. Other sights in Mérida include a very early Moorish fortress, the **Alcazaba**, and a **Roman bridge** across the Río Guadiana.

Tourist information: Calle José Alvarez Sáez de Buruaga. Tel: 92 431 5353.

Zafra

60km (37 miles) south of Mérida on the N432.

This attractive old town is affectionately nicknamed 'Sevilla La Chica' ('Little Sevilla') because of its unmistakably Andalucian character (the real Sevilla is, in fact, only 140km, or 87 miles, away). It has two arcaded main squares: **Plaza Grande** and **Plaza Chica** (the older of the two). The **Iglesia de la Candelaria** has an altarpiece by **Zurbarán**, who was born nearby at Fuente de Cantos in 1598. The castle, **Alcázar de los Duques de Feria**, is now a parador (*Parador de Zafra, Plaza Corazón de María 7; tel: 92 455 4540*), with a handsome marble courtyard by **Juan de Herrera**.

Jerez de los Caballeros

40km (25 miles) southwest of Zafra on the C4311. Tourist information: Plaza de San Agustín 1. Tel: 92 473 0384.

The name, 'Jerez of the Knights', refers to the Knights Templar to whom King Alfonso IX of León gave the town when it was captured from the Moors in 1230. It is not to be confused with the more famous Jerez de la Frontera to the south, where the sherry comes from. When the Templars were disgraced, the local members of the order were supposedly beheaded in the Torre Sangrienta ('Bloody Tower') of Jerez's castle. The town was the birthplace of explorer **Vasco Núñez de Balboa**, who discovered the Pacific Ocean.

CASTILLA-LA MANCHA AND EXTREMADURA

Eating and drinking

Restaurants

Asador Adolfo
Toledo. Granada 6. Tel: 92 522 7321. ££. Eat in an old house with a splendid Mudéjar coffered ceiling. The Asador Adolfo's specialities include stuffed partridge and marinated venison.

Figón de Eustaquio
Cáceres. Plaza San Juan 12. Tel: 92 724 8194. ££. Rustic *mesón* ('inn') offering game and other regional dishes of Extremadura.

Figón de Pedro
Cuenca. Cervantes 13. Tel: 96 922 6821. ££. In the new part of the city, this restaurant specialises in *ajo arriero* (garlic-and-pepper vegetables), *morteruelo* (a pâté of mixed meats) and roasts.

Hostal del Cardenal
Toledo. Paseo de Recaredo 24. Tel: 92 522 0862. ££. A hotel in a fine 18th-century mansion with a restaurant recommendable in its own right. On the menu are roast lamb and roast suckling pig cooked in a wood-fired oven.

Parador de Toledo
Toledo. Cerro del Emperador. Tel: 92 522 1850. £££. Although principally a working hotel (one of the state-run parador chain), you can still come here to eat, or to have a snack in the bar. Either way, the reason to come here is to enjoy from its terrace the magnificent view of the city of Toledo.

Rufino
Mérida. Plaza Santa Clara 2. Tel: 92 431 2001. ££. Big selection of *tapas* on the bar and good homemade dishes on the menu.

Venta del Quijote
Puerto Lápice. El Molino 4. Tel: 92 657 6110. ££. Presumed to be the inn Miguel de Cervantes had in mind while writing about the adventures of his fictional character Don Quixote. It will still serve you meat and ale.

What to try

La Mancha has lent its name to two dishes well known throughout Spain: *gazpacho manchego*, a hearty dish of chicken and rabbit cooked with a kind of wafer (not to be confused with the cold soup, *gazpacho andaluz*), and the much-imitated *pisto manchego*, a concoction of mixed vegetables. Other regional favourites are *migas* (a simple savoury delicacy based on fried breadcrumbs), roast lamb and *caldereta* (lamb stew). The tangy sheep's cheese *queso manchego*, which is made in La Mancha, is exported all over the country and abroad. Extremadura makes great use of pork in its cooking and also produces some of the best *jamón serrano* in Spain.

CASTILLA-LA MANCHA AND EXTREMADURA

Shopping

What to buy

Lace is made in Almagro, and Largartera has a long tradition of **embroidery**. Distinctive **blue and yellow ceramics** come out of the kilns at Talavera de la Reina, a town famed for its tiles since the 15th century (*some workshops in Talavera are open to visitors*). Toledo is, of course, known for its damascene work and its **swords**. High-class reproductions of pieces of Roman art, particularly **mosaics**, are made in Mérida. They can be bought in the shop of the Museo Nacional de Arte Romano, but a much better selection can be found in **Mithra** (*José Ramón Mélida 35*), a shop down the road.

Wines of La Mancha

La Mancha is Spain's largest area of vineyards, producing almost half the wine consumed by Spaniards. The climate of cold winters and hot summers with low rainfall is perfect for the ripening of the native *airén* grape, source of the region's principal output: low-alcohol, low-acidity white table wines. More sophisticated vintages are made in **Valdepeñas**, which has had a wine industry since Roman times.

PROFILE
Don Quixote

The Golden Age writer Miguel de Cervantes captured the essence of the Spanish character in his comic masterpiece The Adventures of Don Quixote, *about a country squire who decides to become a knight long after the age of chivalry has passed.*

Dressed in hand-me-down armour and wearing a barber's bowl for a helmet, the well-intentioned but befuddled Knight of the Rueful Countenance roams the dreary plains of his native La Mancha looking for heroic deeds to perform. He is accompanied by his earthy sidekick Sancho Panza, who is mainly concerned with knowing where his next meal is coming from. Together, they are taken to represent the two extremes battling within the soul of all Spaniards: a desire to search for the unattainable forever at odds with the practical needs of life. There is also something of a universal appeal about the story. We may laugh at the man, but we also admire his courage in acting out his fantasies in a world which does its best to deflate every one of his dreams.

Miguel de Cervantes was a contemporary of Shakespeare and is regarded as Spain's greatest literary genius. Born in 1547 in Alcalá de Henares, near Madrid, he was to live an eventful life before achieving fame. He lost an arm in the battle of Lepanto in 1571 and was held as a prisoner of war by the Turks for the next five years. Success came to him

CASTILLA-LA MANCHA AND EXTREMADURA

late, at the age of 60. It is said that he began writing his masterpiece while in prison in Argamasilla de Alba, and that the personality of Don Quixote was modelled on a local *hidalgo* (minor noble). He died on 23 April 1616 – curiously, the same day on which Shakespeare died.

In recent years, the tourist authorities in La Mancha have created a Don Quixote trail, and there is soon to be a Don Quixote museum in Ciudad Real, but apart from windmills and a pretty inn there isn't much worth seeing. It was not for nothing that Cervantes chose the sparse La Mancha as the setting for his book. It is easy to see how endless dry plains can turn the mind of a man to dreaming of more glorious times.

CASTILLA-LA MANCHA AND EXTREMADURA

BARCELONA

Barcelona

Stylish Barcelona, the capital of Catalonia, has always looked outwards to Europe as much as to the Iberian peninsula. In the Middle Ages it became a great port; now it is a dynamic business centre, as close in spirit to Paris and Milan as it is to Madrid. The city has an endless capacity for reinventing itself: creative and chic, Barcelona is bursting with energy and fizzing with life.

BEST OF Barcelona

*Getting around: the old town from Las Ramblas to the Parc de la Ciutadella and from Plaça de Catalunya to the waterfront is compact enough to walk around; indeed, it can sometimes be faster to negotiate its narrow streets on foot than by taxi. To get around the rest of the city, Barcelona has an excellent **metro system** (0630–2300 daily). It interconnects with the **FGC urban rail system**, useful for taking a day-trip to Montserrat monastery.*

BARCELONA

① Barri Gòtic

The oldest part of Barcelona is known as the Barri Gòtic ('Gothic Quarter'), though it also incorporates Renaissance elements and traces of the old Roman city. This is a rich and delightful area in which to take a leisurely stroll.
Pages 94–5

② Catedral

Barcelona's Gothic cathedral is dedicated to **Santa Eulàlia**, a 4th-century martyr and patron of the city who is believed to be buried in the crypt. A flock of white geese is kept in the cloister, possibly in order to reflect the purity of the virgin saint. Pages 94–5

③ Las Ramblas

The most famous promenade in Spain is **street theatre** at its best, with a non-stop cast of florists, newspaper vendors, artists, musicians, low-life characters, bemused tourists and locals out for a stroll beneath the plane trees. A walk along Las Ramblas is the essential Barcelona experience, without which no day in the city is complete.
Pages 98–9

④ La Sagrada Família

This remarkable unfinished cathedral is the culmination of **Antoni Gaudí**'s creative genius. Long after his death, it continues to arouse controversy, as the architects and builders work on in an attempt to realise Gaudí's dream.
Page 103

⑤ Poble Espanyol

A legacy of the 1929 Exhibition is the 'Spanish Village', with reproductions of traditional architecture from the various Spanish regions. Among the highlights are Andalucian patios, a main square modelled on Segovia and a complete Catalan Romanesque monastery. Pages 104–5

⑥ Museu Nacional d'Art de Catalunya

The glory of Catalonia's art museum is an outstanding collection of **Romanesque murals**, recovered from remote Pyrenean churches. The museum is housed in the Palau Nacional, the main building of the 1929 International Exhibition.
Page 105

⑦ Monestir de Pedralbes

The last surviving monastic complex in Barcelona is still home to a community of nuns, as well as a superb collection of **medieval art**. A chapel off the cloister contains 14th-century frescos by the Catalan painter **Ferrer Bassa**.
Page 106

Travel tip

It is worth buying a one-, two- or three-day Barcelona Card from the tourist information office in Plaça de Catalunya (open: daily 0900–2100, closed 1 Jan and 25 Dec; www.barcelonaturisme.com). This allows you to use public transport as you please and gives you discounts on admission to some tourist attractions.

BARCELONA

Barri Gòtic

The oldest part of Barcelona is known as the Barri Gòtic ('Gothic Quarter'), though you can also find Renaissance-style architecture and evidence of the old Roman city. It is wonderful just to walk around the area and take it all in; you will come across shady squares, Gothic churches and palaces, and narrow streets containing some of Barcelona's most appealing and eccentric shops. The prettiest squares are Plaça de Sant Felip Neri and Plaça del Pi. In the large Plaça Sant Jaume the rival power bases of the city and Catalan governments – the Casa de la Ciutat and Palau de la Generalitat respectively – face each other.

Getting there: Metro: Jaume I and Liceu.

Catedral

Plaça de la Seu. Tel: 93 315 1554. Metro: Jaume I. Open: daily 0900–1300, 1600–1900; museum daily 1030–1300. £ (for museum only).

Barcelona's cathedral has been at the centre of the city's life for over 1 500 years. It is built on the remains of an early Christian basilica destroyed by the Moors in the 10th century, at which time a Romanesque cathedral was put up in its place. The present building dates from 1298 and is a **fine example of Catalan Gothic art**, though the neo-Gothic façade was only added in the early 20th century.

With three naves of roughly equal width and an intricately carved wooden choir at the centre, the

BARCELONA

cathedral is typical of the Catalan Gothic style. In contrast to the simplicity of Barcelona's other great Gothic church, **Santa María del Mar**, it is filled with richly decorated side chapels, Gothic altarpieces and an abundance of gold leaf. Together with the choir, these lend it a dark, rather cluttered appearance and make it harder to appreciate the whole.

The cathedral is dedicated to **Santa Eulàlia**, a 4th-century Christian convert of legendary beauty and purity who was tortured and eventually put to death by the Roman rulers of Barcelona. Of the many torments she is said to have suffered, one was to be rolled down the nearby Baixada de Santa Eulàlia in a barrel perforated with knives. Her **alabaster tomb**, carved in Pisa in the 13th century, is kept in the crypt, situated directly beneath the main altar and reached by a staircase from the centre of the nave. A flock of 13 white geese is kept here, some say as a reminder of the 13 torments suffered by Santa Eulàlia, or that they reflect her age when she died. Nearby, hanging on the wall to the right of the altar, are the painted wooden tombs of Count Ramón Berenguer I and his wife, who founded the second Romanesque cathedral on this site.

The 14th-century **cloisters**, with their magnolia, palm and orange trees, are particularly attractive. Look out, too, for the fountain with a 15th-century **statue of St George**, as well as side chapels that once belonged to the medieval guilds. On the floor you will see the symbols of the guilds, such as scissors for tailors and a boot for shoemakers, carved into the stone. The cloisters also give access to the cathedral museum, which contains silver treasures and altarpieces by the Gothic painters **Jaume Huguet** and **Bernat Martorell**.

> *I began to haunt the old city. I could hardly wait for darkness to fall, when the lamps would be lit high up on the walls, and the streets would become shadowy, ghostly. This was the late medieval world of master craftsmen, stonecutters, masons and architects surviving intact in the middle of a city.*

Colm Tóibín, *Homage to Barcelona* **(1990)**

Museums in old Barcelona

Museu d'Història de la Ciutat

Plaça del Rei. Tel: 93 315 1111. Metro: Jaume I. Open: June–Sept, Tue–Sat 1000–2000, Sun 1000–1400; Oct–May, Tue–Sat 1000–1400, 1600–2000, Sun 1000–1400; closed Mon. ££.

This museum has underground remains of the Roman city on display and gives access to the complex of buildings called the **Palau Reial Major**. Here you can visit the **Saló del Tinell** ('throne room') where Fernando and Isabel are said to have received Columbus on his return from America in 1492. The 14th-century **chapel of Santa Agata** is built directly on to the Roman wall; from it you can go into the **Torre del Rei Martí**, a 16th-century watchtower offering splendid views of the city.

Museo Picasso

Carrer de Montcada 15–19. Tel: 93 319 6310. Metro: Jaume I. Open: Tue–Sat 1000–2000; Sun 1000–1500; closed Mon. ££ (free on first Sun of each month).

The most visited museum in Barcelona was founded in 1963 in the 15th-century Palau Berenguer d'Aguilar but has gradually expanded to take over an entire row of Gothic palaces on Carrer de Montcada. It is devoted to **Pablo Picasso** (1881–1973), the Málaga-born painter who spent his formative years in Barcelona. His masterpieces may be elsewhere, in Paris, Madrid and New York, but the appeal of this museum lies mostly in the light it sheds on his early development, including his so-called Blue Period, which he spent in Barcelona.

BARCELONA

Tip

When Picasso moved from Málaga to Barcelona, apart from a brief spell in Paris he remained in the city for nine years, and Catalans like to claim him as their own, as part of the 'holy trinity' of 20th-century Catalan artists with Joan Miró and Salvador Dalí.

Picasso moved to Barcelona at the age of 13 when his father was appointed professor of fine arts at an academy in El Born. It was here that he came into contact with the ideas of Catalan Modernism, meeting painters like Ramón Casas and Santiago Rusiñol in Els Quatre Gats café (*see page 108*) and establishing a lifelong friendship with his secretary Jaume Sabartés, who was later to found this museum. It contains over 3 000 paintings, sketches and lithographs, together with ceramics donated by Picasso's widow, though only a small selection is on display at any one time. The collection is arranged chronologically, making it easy to follow Picasso's development from schoolboy drawings and landscapes of Barceloneta beach through experiments with Impressionism and then his Blue Period (1902–4).

Palau de la Música Catalana

Carrer de Sant Francesc de Paula 2. Tel: 93 295 7200. Metro: Urquinaona. Open: daily 1000–1500, except when performances are taking place. ££. Box office open Mon–Sat 1000–2100 and one hour before performances on Sun.

This lavish concert hall was designed in 1905 by Lluís Domènech i Montaner as the home of the Catalan choral society Orfeo Català. In 1997 Unesco declared it a World Heritage Site.

From the extravagant façade, rich in mosaics and floral columns, to the sumptuous main hall with its skylight dome, this building is a classic example of the Catalan Modernist style. The only way to visit the interior is on one of the excellent guided tours, which take place every half-hour in Catalan, Spanish and English. The remarkable sculptural group on the façade, *La Canço Popular Catalana*, refers to Catalan folk traditions.

The entire building was restored during the 1980s by the architect Oscar Tusquets, who is now working on an extension to the building on the site of a demolished church.

BARCELONA

Las Ramblas

*Las Ramblas (or La Rambla) is a boulevard which seems to sum up the entire city. For the poet **Federico García Lorca**, it was 'the only street in the world which I wish would never end'. Traffic is now allowed to pass along either side, but this is one street in Barcelona where the pedestrian reigns supreme, most of the action taking place on the wide central pavement.*

Las Ramblas is just over a kilometre (two-thirds of a mile) long; although it is split into five distinct sections, most people refer to the entire street as Las Ramblas. At the seaward end stands the **Mirador a Colom** (Columbus monument; *see page 101*). Heading inland is **Rambla de Santa Mònica**, which takes its name from a former convent on this site, converted into an arts centre during the 1980s as part of a plan to clean up what had become a sordid stretch used for highly visible drug-dealing and prostitution. Further up the street are the portrait painters, who are joined, at weekends, by an assortment of charlatans, including fortune-tellers and tarot-readers.

> " *The women, beautiful, graceful and coquettish, preoccupied by the fold of their mantillas and the play of their fans; the men by their cigars, as they strolled along, laughing, chatting, ogling the ladies, discussing the opera, and seeming not to care in the least what might be happening beyond the city walls.* "
>
> **George Sand on Las Ramblas, *Winter in Majorca* (1855)**

Passing the **Teatre Principal** (*Rambla 27; tel: 93 301 4750*), built in 1847 on the site of Barcelona's first theatre, lies the **Rambla dels Caputxins**, the start of the long, straight section which runs all the way to Plaça de Catalunya. On the left, the **mosaic façade** of the Ramblas Hotel is worth seeing.

On the most animated stretch of Las Ramblas, buskers and magicians compete for attention with Barcelona's famous 'living statues'. The action reaches a peak at **Pla Boqueria**, the halfway point of Las Ramblas, marked by a mosaic pavement designed by **Joan Miró** in 1976.

BARCELONA

A short way up on the left is Barcelona's main market, **La Boqueria** (*open: Mon–Sat 0800–2100*), also known as Mercat Sant Josep because it stands near the start of Rambla de Sant Josep, which in turn is usually known as **Rambla de les Flors** because of the picturesque flower stalls lining the promenade well into the evening. Almost as well known are the newspaper vendors, some open 24 hours a day, selling newspapers from all over Europe.

On the left, the **Palau de la Virreina** is a splendid neo-classical palace, built for the Viceroy of Peru and now used as an exhibition centre. It is followed by the baroque façade of the **Betlem church**. Across the street is another 18th-century palace, **Palau Moja**, now the Catalan government bookshop. In the stretch known as **Rambla dels Ocells** ('birds'), flowers give way to songbirds and stalls selling pets from goldfish to tortoises and guinea pigs.

Finally, **Rambla de Canaletes** is a wide open space with metal chairs for hire. The small fountain here is where supporters of FC Barcelona gather before and after important matches. According to legend, whoever drinks from the Canaletes fountain is sure to return to Barcelona.

Getting there: Metro: Plaça de Catalunya, at the top end of La Rambla; Liceu, midway along La Rambla; and Drassanes, at the seaward end.

BARCELONA

Ciutadella and the Waterfront

Parc de la Ciutadella

Metro: Arc de Triomf, Barceloneta or Jaume I. Open: daily 0800–2100.

The oldest, largest and greenest of all central Barcelona's parks is known by many people simply as 'the park'. Families come here in summer to row boats on the lake or to visit the **Zoo de Barcelona** (*open: daily May–Aug, 0930–1930, Sept–Apr, 1000–dusk; £££*), which contains the world's only albino gorilla in captivity.

> *Gardens are to a city what lungs are to the human body.*
>
> **Josep Fontseré (1829–97), chief architect of Parc de la Ciutadella**

The park was laid out in the 1870s on the site of the former citadel built by Felipe V in 1715, and it became the central setting for the 1888 World Fair. To the north of the park is another World Fair structure, the **Arc de Triomf**, an early example of Modernist art built of Moorish-style red brick with ceramic domes.

The arsenal of the military citadel is now the Catalan parliament. It first met here in 1932, before being suppressed under Franco, to be restored to life only in 1980. A wing of the parliament building houses the **Museu d'Art Modern** (*open: Tue–Sat 1000–1900, Sun 1000–1430; ££*), which features a selection of Catalan art from the 19th century to the 1940s.

BARCELONA

Mirador a Colom

Plaça Portal de la Pau. Tel: 93 302 5224. Metro: Drassanes. Open: Oct–May, Mon–Fri 1000–1330, 1530–1830, Sat–Sun 1000–1830; daily June–Sept, 0900–2030. £.

The monument to Christopher Columbus at the foot of Las Ramblas is a favourite image of Barcelona. Erected in 1888 at the start of the World Fair, this was a defining symbol of the new Barcelona that was showing itself off to the world.

At 60m (197ft) tall, this is the largest monument of its type anywhere in the world. Around the base are **stone sculptures** representing the medieval kingdoms of Spain, while the cast-iron column has **capitals** symbolising the four major continents of the world. You can take the lift up to the viewing gallery to have a look at **Port Vell**, the city's premier entertainment district, where there is a large shopping centre, an IMAX cinema and what is claimed to be the largest aquarium in Europe.

Museu Marítim

Avinguda de les Drassanes. Tel: 93 318 3245. Metro: Drassanes. Open: daily 1000–1900. ££.

Barcelona's maritime museum is located in the former royal shipyards, built in the 13th century at the time of Catalonia's Mediterranean expansion. This unique example of civil Gothic architecture, with its **cathedral-like arches and columns**, is worth a visit for the building alone. The exhibits cover the full range of Barcelona's seafaring history and include maps, navigational instruments, fishing boats and a collection of carved figureheads, as well as the story of Catalonia's Mediterranean conquests, which included the Balearics, Sicily and Sardinia. Pride of place goes to a full-scale reproduction of the **royal galley**, built here in 1568.

> " *Barcelona had always been and continued to be a maritime city; it had lived off and for the sea; it was nourished by the sea, and gave back the fruit of its endeavours to the sea; the streets of Barcelona guided the wanderer's steps down to the sea, and that sea linked the city with the outside world.* "
>
> **Eduardo Mendoza,** *City of Marvels* **(1986)**

L'Eixample

The rigid grid plan of L'Eixample ('the extension') was devised in the 19th century, when Barcelona needed to expand beyond its medieval limits. It was here that the Modernist architects were given free rein to develop their fantasies, especially along the elegant main thoroughfare, Passeig de Gràcia.

The Antoni Gaudí-designed Casa Milà (*Passeig de Gràcia 92; tel: 93 484 5995; metro: Diagonal; open: daily 1000–2000; £££*) was nicknamed La Pedrera ('the stone quarry') because of its wavy architecture and lack of straight lines. This building is considered a masterpiece, one of the most emblematic sights of Barcelona, and it contains an exhibition on Gaudí's life and work. The nearby Casa Batlló (*No 43; not open to the public*) was designed by Gaudí in 1905 and features all his familiar trademarks.

Casa Casas (*No 96*) was built in 1899 by Antoni Rovira for the Modernist painter Ramón Casas; this is now the home of Vinçon, Barcelona's leading furniture and household goods design store. An art gallery, Sala Vinçon (*open: Tue–Sat 1000–1400, 1630–2030, closed Mon*), in Casas' original studio, hosts regular exhibitions of avant-garde furniture and design.

Casa Lleó Morera (*No 35; not open to the public*) was designed by Domènech i Montaner in 1902 for the Lleó Morera family. Lions and mulberry trees on the façade are a reference to the family name, while sculpted figures of women holding a light bulb and a camera are symbols of technological progress. Casa Amatller (*No 41; tel: 93 488 0139; open: Mon–Sat 1000–1900, Sun 1000–1400; tours on the hour; ££*) was designed by Josep Puig i Cadafalch in 1898 for the chocolate manufacturer Antoni Amatller. The façade is a strange mix of neo-Gothic and Dutch gabled styles, with patriotic symbols including the rose and the legend of St George.

BARCELONA

A tourist route, **La Ruta del Modernisme**, involving a walk of some 3½ km (2¼ miles) followed by a few metro and bus journeys, has been devised. It begins in Casa Amatller, and the price of a ticket, valid for a month, includes entry discounts and a guidebook with a detailed description of the route.

Getting there: Metro: Catalunya, Diagonal or Passeig de Gràcia.

La Sagrada Família

Carrer de Mallorca 401. Tel: 93 207 3031. Metro: Sagrada Família. Open: daily Nov–Feb, 0900–1800; Mar, Sept–Oct, 0900–1900; Apr–Aug, 0900–2000. ££.

This building was begun in 1882 as a neo-Gothic church by another architect, but in 1883 Antoni Gaudí was appointed chief architect to the project with a brief to build a new cathedral, and he devoted the last 40 years of his life to it – many of them spent living frugally on site. Tragically, he was knocked down by a tram in 1926 before he could complete it. He died three days later and is buried beneath the nave.

Gaudí's designs were incredibly ambitious, with 18 crenellated towers and an enormous central nave, but only the crypt, apse and part of the **Nativity façade** – its exquisite stone carvings undoubtedly making it the high point of the building – were completed during his lifetime.

Many of Gaudí's plans for the cathedral were destroyed during the Civil War, but building work resumed in the 1950s. The **Passion façade**, with sculptures by Josep Subirachs, was finished in 1990 and has been the focus of considerable comment. Although the inside of the cathedral resembles a building site it is intended that the entire building should be roofed by 2010.

> " I think the Anarchists showed bad taste in not blowing it up when they had the chance. "
>
> **George Orwell on the Sagrada Família,** *Homage to Catalonia* **(1938)**

BARCELONA

Montjuïc

The green hill overlooking Barcelona has long been a place of recreation, where people could come to escape the stifling heat and spend a day in the country. Landscaped in 1929 for the International Exhibition and spruced up for the 1992 Olympics, Montjuïc has twice been at the centre of Barcelona's attempts to show itself off to the world.

To get there, take **bus 50** in Plaça d'Espanya which continues up to Montjuïc. A more enjoyable way is to take the **metro** to Espanya and walk down Avinguda María Cristina before ascending to Montjuïc on the outdoor escalators. In summer there is also a '**tourist train**' with regular departures from Plaça d'Espanya. Another alternative is to take the metro to Paral.lel and then the **funicular** to Montjuïc, which connects with the **Telefèric cable-car** to the castle.

Poble Espanyol

Avinguda del Marquès de Comillas. Tel: 93 325 7866; www.poble-espanyol.com. Metro: Espanya. Bus: 50. Open: Mon 0900–2000; Tue–Sat 0900–0200; Sun 0900–0000. ££.

This 'Spanish Village' was designed for the 1929 International Exhibition by Catalan architect **Josep Puig i Cadafalch** as a way of emphasising the diversity of the Spanish nation and celebrating its different cultures. Undeniably touristy, it nonetheless serves as a useful introduction to the various styles of Spanish architecture.

The basic idea was to include **vernacular architecture** and copies of **historic buildings** from the various Spanish regions, grouped together in streets with a distinctive regional flavour; so, it has a Romanesque gateway from Ávila, a

Gothic portico from Navarra, a main square from Segovia, an Aragonese town hall, Basque farmhouses, whitewashed Andalusian patios, a Mudéjar bell-tower and a Catalan Romanesque monastery complete with cloister.

Museu Nacional d'Art de Catalunya

Palau Nacional. Tel: 93 622 0360; www.mnac.es. Metro: Espanya. Open: Tue–Sat 1000–1900; Sun 1000–1430; closed Mon. ££.

Barcelona's only world-class museum collection is housed in a mock-baroque palace built for the 1929 International Exhibition by the Modernist architect **Puig i Cadafalch**.

The main attraction of the museum is its collection of **Romanesque frescos**, unrivalled anywhere in Europe; especially notable are those from the church of Sant Climent de Taüll, consecrated in 1123. The museum's second major collection is of **Catalan Gothic art**, spanning the period of Catalonia's Mediterranean expansion and showing the Flemish and Italian influences that came to the fore as a result. The museum concludes with the Cambó bequest, a collection of **Renaissance and baroque art** donated by the financier Francesc Cambó.

Fundació Joan Miró

Plaça Neptú. Tel: 93 329 1908; www.bcn.fjmiro.es. Bus: 50. Open: Tue, Wed, Fri, Sat 1000–1900; Thu 1000–2130; Sun 1030–1430; closed Mon. ££.

One of the greatest artists of the 20th century was born in Barcelona and has become indelibly linked to the city. The son of a Catalan watchmaker, **Joan Miró** (1893–1983) has sometimes been described as 'more surrealist than the surrealists', but what most people remember are his childlike spontaneity, playful sense of humour and use of bright primary colours.

> *When I pick up a rock, it's a rock; when Miró picks it up, it's a Miró.*
>
> **Joan Prats, hatmaker, friend and patron of Joan Miró**

The foundation was established by Miró himself in 1971, in a building designed by his friend **Josep Lluís Sert**. The collection includes paintings and sculptures donated by Miró and others given by his wife Pilar Juncosa and dealer Joan Prats.

BARCELONA

On the outskirts

Monestir de Pedralbes

Baixada del Monestir 9. Tel: 93 280 1434. FGC: Reina Elisenda. Bus: 22, 63, 64, 75. Open: Tue–Sun 1000–1400; closed Mon. £.

Barcelona's only surviving medieval monastery was founded in 1326 by Queen Elisenda, the fourth and last wife of Jaume II of Aragón, who is buried in the church. The highlight is the **Capella de Sant Miquel**, a tiny chapel decorated with frescos by the court painter **Ferrer Bassa**, creator of the Italian-Gothic style in Catalonia.

Since 1993 the monastery has housed, in the nuns' old dormitory, part of the **Colección Thyssen-Bornemisza** (*open: same hours as monastery; £; see page 32*), mostly religious art from the medieval to baroque periods. The collection is small and manageable but contains several minor masterpieces, making it very appealing to visit. Its strength is an assemblage of European old masters, including works by **Fra Angelico**, **Cranach**, **Titian**, **Tintoretto**, **Rubens**, **Velázquez** and **Canaletto**. The oldest pieces on display are an anonymous 13th-century sculpture of the *Virgin and Child* from northern France and a 13th-century Umbrian polychrome figure of the dead Christ.

Parc Güell

Carrer d'Olot. Metro: Vallcarca. Bus: 24, 25. Open: daily 1000 to dusk.

Of all **Antoni Gaudí**'s contributions to Barcelona, none is more enjoyable than this park overlooking the city. It was commissioned in 1900 by his patron Count Eusebi Güell, whose idea was to create a fashionable residential district along the lines of English garden cities.

BARCELONA

> *His brain is at the tips of his fingers and tongue.*
>
> **Salvador Dalí (1904–89) on Gaudí**

It was here that Gaudí's sense of playfulness and fantasy was given full rein. The main entrance on Carrer d'Olot is flanked by a **pair of gatehouses** based on Gaudí's drawings for the fairy-tale 'Hansel and Gretel'. On the left is the children's house; on the right, the house of the witch, topped by a fly agaric mushroom. Inside the gates, a double stairway divided by a waterfall is watched over by a **colourful mosaic dragon**, the symbol of the park. The park's high point is the **central esplanade**, surrounded by an undulating bench created with pieces of broken ceramic rearranged to form abstract patterns and shapes.

The **Casa-Museu Gaudí** (*open: daily Oct–May, 1000–1800, June–Sept, 1000–2000; £*) is the house where Gaudí lived for the last 20 years of his life.

Tibidabo

FGC to Avinguda del Tibidabo, followed by tram and funicular.

The mountain at the summit of the Serra de Collserola range has been a playground for the people of Barcelona for more than a hundred years.

To get there, take the **Tramvia Blau** (in Plaça John Kennedy), a charming relic of the early 20th century, which trundles up Avinguda del Tibidabo, passing Modernist mansions. One of the tram's stops is close to the **Museu de la Ciència** (*Carrer Teodor Roviralta 55; open: Tue–Sun 1000–2000, closed Mon; ££*), an interactive science museum with hands-on exhibits, a planetarium and a scientific playground for younger kids. The tram also stops in **Plaça Dr Andreu**, a square lined with café terraces overlooking the city, from where a funicular takes you to the summit (it operates whenever the funfair is open and also on winter weekends). The journey ends close to the **Parc d'Atraccions** (*open: Easter–Oct, Sat–Sun 1200–2000, extended hours throughout summer period, daily Jul–Aug, 1200–0100; £££*), still as popular as ever with its ferris wheel, haunted castle and ancient fairground rides.

Eating and drinking

Restaurants

Barcelona's restaurants naturally specialise in Catalan cuisine (*see page 130*), but there is plenty of choice of non-Catalan, even non-Spanish, food. For outdoor dining beside the sea, head for the fashionable seafood restaurants in the Palau de Mar or the more down-to-earth establishments along Passeig Joan de Borbó.

Can Culleretes
Carrer Quintana 5. Tel: 93 317 3022. ££. Barcelona's oldest restaurant was founded in 1786. The speciality here is seafood, but the menu also features Catalan meat dishes such as chicken with *samfaina* (a Catalan version of ratatouille) and *botifarra* (cured pork) sausage with beans.

Can Ramonet
Carrer Maquinista 17. Tel: 93 319 3064. ££. The oldest restaurant in Barceloneta was opened in 1763. You can eat outside on a charming market square, sit at the bar or splash out on black rice and grilled lobster in the restaurant at the back.

Los Caracoles
Carrer dels Escudellers 14. Tel: 93 302 3185. ££. This busy, traditional restaurant is best known for its snails and the spit-roast chicken, which you can watch being cooked out on the street. It is more popular with tourists than locals but is still worth a visit for its lively atmosphere.

Les Quinze Nits
Plaça Reial 6. Tel: 93 317 3075. £. No bookings. The queues across the square at weekends testify to the popularity of this restaurant, which offers solid Catalan cuisine at excellent prices. Arrive early for one of the outdoor tables on the square.

Bars and cafés

Café de l'Opera
Rambla 74. This Modernist coffee house, all dark wood and panelled mirrors, has long been popular with intellectuals who while away their time over coffee and newspapers, or hold *tertulias* (literary debates) in the salon upstairs.

Café Moka
Rambla 128. In *Homage to Catalonia*, George Orwell described a Civil War shoot-out here from the relative safety of a rooftop across the street. The café is still there, with plenty of historical atmosphere and a simple menu of pizzas, *tapas* and grills.

Els Quatre Gats
Carrer Montsió 3. A Modernist landmark where Picasso used to meet his bohemian friends.

BARCELONA

Shopping

Barcelona is the capital of design and even small souvenirs are tasteful and easy to find. On Passeig de Gràcia, look out for the **Centre Català d'Artesania** (*No 55*), a large, bright gallery highlighting the best in contemporary Catalan design, including jewellery, ceramics and glassware. Barcelona's design temple, however, is still **Vinçon** (*No 96; see page 102*), further up the street. For a taste of old Barcelona, head for **Els Encants** (*Plaça de les Glòries Catalanes; metro: Glòries; open: Mon, Wed, Fri, Sat 0900–1900*), a flea market where you might pick up a bargain among the heaps of walking-sticks, wind-up gramophones, porn videos and second-hand furniture.

Nightlife

Since the opening up of the waterfront, the focus of after-dark activity has shifted increasingly down to the port. There are numerous bars, clubs and discos in and around the Port Olímpic area offering everything from techno and house music to designer *tapas* and *nuevo flamenco*. The fashions here change so quickly that the only thing to do is to arrive after midnight, wander around and find something that appeals. The young crowd gathers every night, and especially on summer weekends, at the discos on the top floor of the Maremagnum complex, of which **Nayandei** is the biggest and best known.

BARCELONA

PROFILE

Gaudí and *Modernisme*

At the end of the 19th century a new artistic and architectural style appeared in Europe, known simply as 'art nouveau'. Spain quickly developed its own variation of it, called Modernismo – *or* Modernisme *in Catalonia, where it reached its peak. Many artists – especially* **Lluís Domènech i Montaner** *and* **Josep Puig i Cadafalch** *– built houses and furnished them in the new style. But one creative genius stands out from the rest as the greatest exponent of Catalan* Modernisme: **Antoni Gaudí** *(1852–1926), who left behind him a great catalogue of work, most of it in his native Barcelona.*

Gaudi graduated as an architect in 1878, and in 1889 finished his first major building in the centre of Barcelona, the **Palau Güell** near Las Ramblas, in which his originality of thought can already be seen. This was followed by the **Casa Batlló** (1904–6) on Passeig de Gràcia in what was then Barcelona's expanding suburbs, L'Eixample. Another house on the same street, **Casa Milà** (or La Pedrera) (*see page 102*), was completed in 1910 and has become one of his best-known works, despite being criticised at the time by intellectuals. Gaudi also completed the major part of

BARCELONA

another of his much-loved works, **Parc Güell** (*see page 106*), a garden city that formed part of the estate of the financier Eusebi Güell.

Elsewhere in Spain, Gaudí's work can be seen at Astorga, near León (the **Palacio Arzobispal**), and at Comillas in Cantabria (the folly of **El Capricho**, now a restaurant; *see page 151*). But his most astonishing work, and the building with which he will forever be associated, is **La Sagrada Família** (*see page 103*), the extravagant church in Barcelona which became his life's project. Work on it recommenced in the 1950s, as far as possible to Gaudí's original plans, which have always generated controversy, although, as Evelyn Waugh commented in his *Mediterranean* Journal, 'In one's first brush with Gaudí's genius, it is not so much propriety that is outraged as one's sense of probability.'

BARCELONA

Catalonia and the Pyrenees

CATALONIA AND THE PYRENEES

Catalonia considers itself a country within a country and it has a rich history and culture of its own. It's a relatively small corner of Spain, but with a lot crammed into it: beaches, Romanesque churches, old towns and, of course, that majestic mountain range, the Pyrenees, which also stretches across the neighbouring region of Aragón.

CATALONIA AND THE PYRENEES

BEST OF
Catalonia and the Pyrenees

Getting around: prosperous and independent-minded, Catalonia has an excellent road network with a tangle of motorways around Barcelona, the regional capital and site of the tourist information HQ (*Passeig de Gràcia 107; tel: 93 238 4000, www.gencat.es*). From Barcelona, the A7 motorway is the best access road to the coast and its hinterland; main roads reach almost everywhere else. Expect hairpin bends and high-altitude passes as you approach the Pyrenees. Barcelona has the main airport, but charter flights also land at Girona and Reus.

CATALONIA AND THE PYRENEES

① Tarragona

From its amphitheatre near the sea shore to its necropolis, Tarragona is a **Roman city** with a thin layer of modernity on top. It's well organised for tourism with a single ticket admitting you to several monuments.
Pages 116–17

② Monestir de Santa María de Poblet

This carefully restored **Cistercian monastery** standing among vineyards contains the tombs of the kings of Catalonia. **Page 117**

③ Montserrat

It would be hard to imagine a more spectacular setting for a monastery than the mountain of Montserrat, the **sacred mountain of Catalonia**. The place can be heaving with tourists and pilgrims but there are walking routes to get away from them and see the monastic buildings from afar.
Page 119

④ Costa Brava

The so-called 'Wild Coast' was one of the first in Spain to open up to tourism. Much of it consists of attractive wooded cliffs, but here and there are coves, bays and beaches. It has both brash resorts, led by **Lloret de Mar** and **Platja d'Aro**, as well as more sophisticated ones, such as **Begur**. **Pages 120–1**

⑤ Teatre-Museu Dalí

Figueres is a pleasant town, but the only reason most people visit it is to see the last great creation of the most eccentric artist of the lot. Even if you loathe **Salvador Dalí** you'll probably have a secret admiration for the over-the-top approach he took to his memorial-cum-museum. **Pages 122–3**

⑥ Parque Nacional de Ordesa

The third highest peak in the Pyrenees is the focal point for this national park which backs on to one over the border in France. The best of Pyrenean flora and fauna can be seen, when weather conditions permit. **Page 126**

⑦ Monasterio de San Juan de la Peña

The monastery church of San Juan de la Peña is extraordinarily sited underneath a rock overhang. Most impressive of all are the galleries of the **12th-century cloisters**.
Pages 126–7

Tourist information

Tourist information for **Aragón** can be found at Torreón de la Zuda, Zaragoza (*tel: 97 639 3537; www.aragon.es*).

CATALONIA AND THE PYRENEES

Tarragona

What is now a modern city of boulevards and ring roads was once imperial Tarraco, *the capital of Rome's western Mediterranean empire. A single entrance ticket (£) admits you to several monuments.*

The **Amfiteatre Romà** (*open: Oct–June, Tue–Sat 1000–1330, 1530–1730, Sun 1000–1400, closed Mon; July–Sept, Tue–Sat 0900–2100, Sun 0900–1500, closed Mon; £*), built into the hillside beside the sea in the 2nd century AD, was once the venue for gladiatorial contests and the martyrdom of Christians. Above the amphitheatre, the oldest part of Tarragona is still enclosed within its Roman walls, now the base for a pleasant walk along the **Passeig Arqueològic** (*access from Via de l'Imperi Romà; same hours as amphitheatre; £*).

The streets of the old town lead up towards the **catedral** (*Plaça de la Seu; open: mid-Mar–mid-Nov, Mon–Sat 1000–1300, 1600–1900, closed Sun, mid-Nov–mid-Mar, 1000–1400, closed Sun; £*), built between the 12th and 14th centuries on the site of a Roman temple in a mix of Romanesque and Gothic styles. The **Museu Nacional Arqueològic de Tarragona** (*Plaça del Rei; open: Oct–May, Tue–Sat 1000–1330,*

CATALONIA AND THE PYRENEES

> *There is never any doubt ... that one has arrived in Spain ... There is a faint sound of drums, a smell of crude olive-oil, and current of strong, leaking electricity.*
>
> **Anthony Carson,**
> *A Train to Tarragona*
> **(1957)**

1600–1900, Sun 1000–1400, closed Mon, June–Sept, Tue–Sat 1000–2000, Sun 1000–1400, closed Mon; £) features Roman pottery and coins, and an outstanding collection of Roman mosaics.

The **Forum Romà** (*Carrer de Lleida; same hours as amphitheatre; £*) is the old forum outside the city walls, the centre of political and commercial Roman life. The **Museu i Necròpolis Paleocristiana** (*Avinguda Ramón i Cajal; same hours as Museu Nacional Arqueològic and entered on same ticket*) is a late-Roman burial ground on the banks of the Rio Francoli, and the **Pont de les Ferreres** is a magnificent Roman aqueduct 4km (2½ miles) north of Tarragona, visible from the A7 motorway but best reached by taking the N240 towards Valls.

Tourist information: Carrer Major 39. Tel: 97 724 5203.

> *Spain – a country that has sold its soul for cement and petrol and can only be saved by a series of earthquakes.*
>
> **Cyril Connolly**

Costa Daurada

The coast of Tarragona province is not as developed for tourism as other parts of Spain. The leading resort is the rather brash **Salou**, which runs into the much more authentically Catalan fishing port of Cambrils. Outside Salou, behind the new resort of La Pineda, is the massive theme park of **Port Aventura**. The southern extreme of the Costa Daurada is marked by the wetlands of the delta of the Rio Ebro.

Monestir de Santa María de Poblet

5km (3 miles) southwest of L'Espluga de Francoli on the N240 from Tarragona to Lleida. Tel: 97 787 0089. Open: daily 1000–1230, 1500–1730 (to 1800 Mar–Oct). Guided tour only. £.

A 50-km (31-mile) drive inland from Tarragona and the Costa Daurada brings you to the peaceful 12th-century royal Cistercian monastery of Poblet, which stands amid vineyards. It was all but destroyed in the 19th century but has since been carefully restored, and presently has a small community of monks in residence. The church contains the **tombs of the kings of Catalonia**.

CATALONIA AND THE PYRENEES

Around Barcelona

Sitges

Tourist information: Carrer Sinia Morera 1. Tel: 93 894 4251.

This cosmopolitan, low-rise beach resort has long attracted a different kind of tourist, ever since it became the meeting-place for a group of Modernist painters in the late 19th century. Artists still come, day-trippers flock here from Barcelona at weekends and gay tourists are drawn by its tolerant lifestyle – especially in February, when Rio comes to Catalonia with extravagant **carnival parades** and outrageous costumes.

The setting is perfect: a succession of beaches joined by a long promenade, beneath a rocky bluff overlooking the harbour. On the cliffs are the **Museu Cau Ferrat** (*Carrer Fonollar; open: summer, Tue–Sun 1000–1400, 1700–2100, winter, Tue–Fri 1000–1330, 1500–1830, Sat 1000–1900, Sun 1000–1500; £*), with a remarkable collection of wrought-iron and paintings by **El Greco**, **Picasso** and **Rusiñol**, and the **Museu Maricel** (*same hours; £*), with Romanesque frescos, Gothic paintings and Catalan Modernist art.

Sant Sadurni d'Anoia

12km (7½ miles) northeast of Vilafranca del Penedès on a minor road.

Tip

Codorniu alone has more than 200,000 square metres of underground cellars, producing 30 million bottles of Cava each year, 75 per cent of which is consumed within Spain. One of their biggest customers is the Spanish royal family.

This small town is the home of Cava, Catalonia's sparkling wine. Some 90 per cent of all Cava is produced here at more than a hundred cellars, ranging from huge international companies to small family-run firms and local farmers' co-operatives. The best bodegas to visit are **Codorniu** (*signposted from the road to Igualada; tel: 93 818 3232; open: Mon–Fri 0900–1700, Sat–Sun 0900–1300*), the biggest name in Cava and one of the leading producers of sparkling wine in the world, and **Freixenet** (*Carrer Joan Sala 2; tel: 93 891 7000; free tours: Mon–Thu 0900, 1000, 1130, 1530, 1700, Fri 0900, 1000, 1130*).

CATALONIA AND THE PYRENEES

The capital of this wine region is **Vilafranca del Penedès**, to the southwest, an industrious town with a lovely old Gothic centre and modernist buildings. There is a wine museum, the **Museu de Vilafranca** (*Plaça Jaume I; open: Tue–Sat 1000–1400, 1600–1900, Sun 1000–1400; £*), in the 12th-century palace of the kings of Aragón.

Montserrat

40km (25 miles) northwest of Barcelona, off the A18 or C1411. Tourist information: Plaça de la Creu, across from the cable-car station. Tel: 93 877 7701.

The 'serrated mountain', one of the symbols of Catalonia, climbs steeply out of the Llobregat plain. The monastery on the mountainside owes its fame to a legend: St Peter placed a statue of the Virgin, carved by St Luke, here after Christ's death. For many years the statue was hidden from the Moors, then in 880 it was rediscovered by shepherds who were led to a cave by angelic voices and heavenly light. The local bishop tried to move the statue but it refused to budge, a sure sign from God that the Virgin was to be worshipped at Montserrat (*access to the Virgin: daily 0800–1030, 1200–1830, and 1930–2030 at weekends*). A chapel was built to house the statue and a Benedictine monastery was established. The nearby museum, **Museu de Montserrat** (*open: summer, daily 0930–1900, winter, Mon–Fri 1000–1800, Sat–Sun 0930–1830; £*) has a superb art collection, and the **Santa Cova** (*open: daily summer, 0915–1730, winter, 1015–1630*) is the cave where the statue was found.

CATALONIA AND THE PYRENEES

Costa Brava

Catalonia's 'Wild Coast' has, perhaps, more variety than any other coast of Spain. It begins, in the south, with **Lloret de Mar**, the biggest resort on the Costa Brava and a classic example of mass tourism gone berserk. The main attraction is the beach, stretching all the way along the promenade to the mock castle at its northern end, where the rocky cove of **Sa Caleta** offers sheltered swimming. The most notable sight is the 16th-century parish church, with its striking **Modernist roof** of brightly coloured tiles.

Although it is one of the Costa Brava's busiest summer resorts, **Tossa de Mar** retains a good deal of its charm – largely because of the survival of its fortified old town, Vila Vella, founded on a headland by the Abbot of Ripoll in 1186. The sight of Tossa's medieval walls rising above the beach is one of the most enduring images of the Catalan coast. Within the walls is a warren of narrow streets, reached by a fairly easy climb. At the heart of the old town, the **Museu Municipal** (*Plaça Roig i Soler; open: Oct–May, Tue–Sun 1000–1300, 1500–1800, June–Sept, Tue–Sun 1000–1900; £*), in the former abbot's palace, displays archaeological finds and modern art. The main beaches are **Platja Gran**, and **Platja Mar Menuda** at the northern end of the promenade.

Palafrugell's Calella resort consists of a series of pretty coves strung out like pearls. Development here has been low-rise and low-key, with everything on a human scale. Calella de Palafrugell is particularly agreeable. A cliff path leads from here to Llafranc (about 30 minutes' walk), making a delightful pre-dinner stroll. A path going in the opposite direction from Calella takes you to the **Jardí Botànic de Cap Roig** (*Castell Cap Roig; open: daily winter, 0900–1900, summer, 0900–2000; £*), a botanical garden designed by Russian emigré Nicolai Woevodsky and his English wife Dorothy in the 1920s.

CATALONIA AND THE PYRENEES

Begur, a hilltop town with a ruined castle at its summit, is the access point for Aiguablava as well as the nearby coves at Aiguafreda, Sa Riera and Sa Tuna. It is worth climbing up to the defensive towers for views of the coastline, stretching north from the Medes islands to the Gulf of Roses.

The walled village of **Pals** was abandoned after the Civil War, but then slowly and lovingly restored by a local doctor. The restoration has won many architectural awards, with the result that Pals has become something of a showpiece and, consequently, a tourist trap. The village has narrow lanes and Gothic houses, medieval walls and a **Romanesque clock tower**.

The charming **Castelló d'Ampurias**, set back just a short distance from the coast, is a town of Gothic palaces and cobbled streets. The main attraction is the **basilica of Santa María**, sometimes referred to as the cathedral of the Costa Brava. This Gothic church, built in the 14th century, has retained some Romanesque elements.

With its whitewashed houses and boats moored in a peaceful bay, the fishing village of **Cadaqués** was one of Dalí's favourite spots. His house and studio there is now a museum, the **Casa-Museu Dalí** (*Port Lligat; tel: 97 225 8063 – tickets must be booked in advance; open: daily 15 June–15 Sept, 1030–2100, 15 Mar–14 June, 16 Sept–1 Nov, Tue–Sun 1030–1800; £*).

CATALONIA AND THE PYRENEES

Figueres and Girona

Teatre-Museu Dalí (Dalí Theatre-Museum)

Figueres. Plaça Gala-Salvador Dalí. Tel: 97 251 1800. Open: daily June, 1030–1800; July–Sept, 0900–2000; Oct–May, Tue–Sun 1030–1800. £.

Figueres, the county town of the Upper Empordà region, has a fair sprinkling of attractions, but most visitors come here for just one thing: to see the museum **Salvador Dalí** created as his own memorial, built in the gutted ruins of the town's theatre, where Dalí had his first exhibition.

Dalí did not want a conventional museum; he wanted his 'audience' to create their own surrealist experience, without the distractions of catalogues and guided tours. And from the moment you set foot inside the building, its façade adorned with trademark Dalí symbols, you enter a fantasy world created by one man's fertile imagination.

The best way to explore it is to do as Dalí wished, allowing your senses to guide you. In this museum, nothing is quite what it seems: a bright pink sofa turns into the lips of Mae West, and a portrait of Gala (the artist's muse) becomes Abraham Lincoln when seen from a different angle. In the courtyard, visitors feed coins into a meter to spray water over the inhabitants of a Cadillac, the centrepiece of a sculpture, *Rainy Taxi*, which also features a bronze statue of Queen Esther, a column of tractor tyres and Gala's fishing boat.

Among all the tricks and illusions are some remarkable paintings. Look out for *Self-Portrait with L'Humanité*, a statement of Dalí's communist sympathies produced in 1923; *Soft Self-Portrait with Grilled Bacon*, in which

CATALONIA AND THE PYRENEES

> *Figueres on Thursdays [market day] bulges at the seams, the cafés buzz with excited chatter ... when Dalí was in New York or Paris, he would think of Figueres on Thursdays and recall the animation in the streets and squares.*

Ian Gibson, Dalí's biographer, Condé Nast Traveller (1997)

his familiar obsessions are starting to emerge; **Galarina**, an enigmatic portrait of Gala; and **The Happy Horse**, a grim premonition of death painted in 1980.

Girona

Tourist information: Rambla de la Llibertat 1. Tel: 97 222 6575.

Founded by the Romans, sacked by the Moors, captured by Charlemagne and besieged by Napoleon, Girona is sometimes known as 'the city of a thousand sieges'. Girona is proud of its history, and the restoration of the old town has given many of its ancient buildings a new lease of life. The medieval ramparts have been painstakingly restored, and it is possible to walk along certain sections of them.

The **Banys Arabs**, or Arab baths (*Carrer Ferran el Catòlic; open: Apr–Sept, Tue–Sat 1000–1900, Sun 1000–1400, Oct–Mar, Tue–Sun 1000–1400; £*), were built in the 13th century to resemble a Roman bath-house, and remain one of the best preserved examples in Spain.

The **Museu Arqueòlogic** (*Carrer Santa Llúcia 1; open: Tue–Sat 1000–1400, 1600–1800, Sun 1000–1400; £*), in the Romanesque monastery of **Sant Pere de Galligants**, contains artefacts from prehistoric to medieval times, and the **Museu d'Art** (*Pujada de la Catedral 12; open: Oct–Feb, Tue–Sat 1000–1800, Sun 1000–1400, Mar–Sept, Tue–Sat 1000–1900, Sun 1000–1400; £, free on Sun*), located in the former episcopal palace, houses a representative collection of Catalan art from the Romanesque period to the present day.

CATALONIA AND THE PYRENEES

The Catalan Pyrenees

Parc Nacional d'Aigues Tortes

Tourist information: Centro de Información de Espot. Tel: 97 362 4036.

Spectacular Pyrenean mountain scenery is contained within Catalonia's only national park. There is water everywhere here; pretty streams rush down steep wooded slopes and flow through meadows to feed into the many lakes within the borders of the park, the most scenic of which is the **Estany de Sant Maurici**. The area is rich in wildlife, too: beaver and otter can be spotted in the waterways; birds include golden eagles, grouse and capercaillie. The main point of access into the park is the village of **Espot** (*85km, or 53 miles, northwest of La Seu d'Urgell, by mountain roads*).

La Seu d'Urgell

Tourist information: Avda de les Valls d'Andorra 33. Tel: 97 335 1511.

The chief town of the Catalan Pyrenees was ruled for many years by a prince who also shared joint sovereignty over Andorra. This is a small town with a big history, and a delightful base from which to explore Andorra and the Cerdanya region. The main sight is the 12th-century **catedral** (*open: Mon–Sat 1000–1300, 1600–1800, Sun 1000–1300*), the only remaining Romanesque cathedral in Catalonia. The **Museu Diocesà** (*open: June–Sept, Mon–Sat 1000–1300, 1600–1900, Sun 1000–1300, Oct–May, Mon–Fri 1200–1300, Sat–Sun 1100–1300; £*), reached off the cloister, contains an **illustrated 10th-century *Beatus***.

CATALONIA AND THE PYRENEES

Andorra

Tourist information: Plaça de la Rotonda, on the main road through Andorra la Vella. Tel: 82 7117.

According to legend, Andorra was founded by the emperor Charlemagne in 784 as a reward to the people of the valleys for their support in driving out the Moors. For several centuries from 1278 it was ruled as a feudal possession, then it was transferred to the French crown, and in 1993 became an independent state and took its seat at the UN. Andorra's tiny parliament chamber is housed inside a 16th-century mansion, **Casa de la Vall** (*Carrer de la Vall; tel: 82 9129; free guided tours daily, 1000–1300, 1500–1800*), in the old quarter of the capital, **Andorra la Vella**. The building also contains the courts of justice and a working prison in the basement.

A single main road runs across the country: it leaves Spain as N145, transforms into CG1 and CG2 through Andorra and emerges in France as N22. During the skiing season and in summer, this road can get clogged with traffic as day-trippers visit Andorra for its duty-free shopping or pop across the border to fill up on cheap petrol.

The **Museu Nacional de l'Automòbil** (*on the main road through Encamp; open: Tue–Sat 0930–1330, 1500–1800, Sun 1000–1400; £*) is a great place for little boys of all ages, with vintage cars, bicycles, motorbikes and toys.

Vall d'Arán

Tourist information: Carrer Sarriulera 10, Vielha. Tel: 97 364 0110.

The only north-facing valley in the Catalan Pyrenees is located on the French side of the Pyrenean watershed, which accounts for both its Atlantic climate and its legendary greenness. This is a bucolic landscape of lush, flower-filled meadows watered by the Río Garona and shady slopes hemmed in by towering mountain peaks. In the Nautaran ('Upper Valley') are several pretty villages with slate and granite cottages and fine Romanesque churches. It is certainly worth stopping at **Salardú** to see the 13th-century **church of Sant Andreu** with its original carved wooden crucifix. **Bossòst**, the capital of Baixaran ('Lower Valley'), has a 12th-century **Romanesque church** and a number of French-style restaurants.

CATALONIA AND THE PYRENEES

The mountains of Aragón

Parque Nacional de Ordesa

Tourist information: Avda de Ordesa, Torla. Tel: 97 448 6472.

The Ordesa valley was declared a national park in 1918. The park includes **Monte Perdido**, the third highest peak in the Pyrenees, and forms a continuous link with the Parc National des Pyrénées in France, creating a sizeable area where Pyrenean flora and fauna are protected. Within the park the most dramatic elements of Aragón's mountain scenery are to be found, from pine and beech woods to limestone cliffs, canyons and crystal streams. Bearded vultures and golden eagles can be seen flying above the cliffs, and it is possible to see chamois, red deer and the **rare Pyrenean ibex**. The park is open all year, but conditions are best for walking between April and October. From October to June it is possible to take your car into the park; between July and September, and in Holy Week, a bus service operates from Torla.

Tip

The lammergeier, or bearded vulture, a resident of the Ordesa National Park, is known in Spanish as quebrantahuesos *('bone breaker') because of its habit of dropping bones from a height in order to break them open and get at the marrow inside.*

Monasterio de San Juan de la Peña

30km (18 1/2 miles) southwest of Jaca. Open: Tue–Sun 1000–1300, 1600–1900; mid-Oct–mid-Mar, Wed–Sun 1100–1400. £.

A twisting mountain road leads to this monastery church, spectacularly situated beneath an overhanging rock. Since Muslim times it has had special significance as the spiritual home of the Aragonese Reconquest. Medieval pilgrims would stop off here hoping for a glimpse of the **Holy Grail**, a Roman chalice hidden in the monastery and now on display in Valencia cathedral (*see page 166*).

There are three distinct parts to the monastery. The **lower church** was built in the 10th century in Mozarabic style, with the horseshoe arches typical of the period and a pair of aisles with apses hollowed out of the rock. The **upper church**, built in the 11th century, has a single aisle with the rock face acting as a roof. In it is the **royal pantheon**, which contains the tombs of the early Aragonese kings. But most impressive of all are the two remaining galleries of the **12th-century cloisters**, with richly carved capitals by the Maestro of San Juan de la Peña.

Sos del Rey Católico

45km (28 miles) southeast of Pamplona, on the A127.

The Catholic king after whom this atmospheric medieval town is named is Fernando II of Aragón, who, with his wife Isabel, unified Spain in the 15th century. He was born in the Palacio de Sada, one of several grand stone mansions that stand on the cobbled streets. The town centres upon the **Plaza Mayor**, with its 16th-century town hall and Gothic-style *lonja*, or commercial exchange. Other monuments worth seeing are the **ruined castle** and the **Iglesia de San Esteban** (*open for services*), a church containing 13th-century frescos. Sos is the most handsome of the so-called 'Five Towns' which were loyal to Felipe V during the War of the Spanish Succession.

CATALONIA AND THE PYRENEES

Huesca and Zaragoza

Castillo de Loarre

30km (19 miles) northwest of Huesca, off the A132. Open: Tue–Sun 1000–1330, 1600–1900.

> " To the foreigner who comes as a friend no country is more hospitable than Spain. The armed invader, however, has always fared badly. "
>
> **Delano Ames,**
> *introduction to Spain*

This magnificent 11th-century fortress, built high upon a rock by **Sancho Ramírez**, king of Navarra and Aragón, is everyone's fantasy of what a medieval castle should be like. You can clamber over the ruins, get lost among a labyrinth of stairways and ancient dungeons, or admire the views across the Ebro plain from the round towers that flank the walls. Inside the castle is a **Romanesque chapel and crypt**, a reminder that this was once home to a religious community.

Zaragoza

Tourist information: Plaza del Pilar. Tel: 97 620 1200.

The Roman town of *Caesaraugusta* was founded in the 1st century BC on the banks of the Río Ebro. For 400 years a thriving Islamic city, it was captured by Alfonso I in 1118 and became the capital of the young kingdom of Aragón. It is a bustling, modern city, the fifth largest in Spain, with some fine examples of Mudéjar (Moorish-Gothic) architecture.

The most impressive sight, the **Aljafería** (*Calle Diputados; open: 15 Apr–15 Oct, Sat–Wed 1000–1400, 1630–2000, Fri 1630–1800, closed Thu, 16 Oct–14 Apr, Mon–Wed, Sat 1000–1400, 1600–1830, Fri 1600–1830, Sun 1000–1400, closed Thu; £*), a short distance west of the city centre, is an Islamic fortress-palace, begun in the 11th century. It has been used by Aragonese kings and Spanish monarchs, and now houses the regional assembly of Aragón. The oratory inside the northern portico has a *mihrab* (a prayer niche pointing towards Mecca) and finely decorated **stuccowork**. You can also see the Gothic quarters added by Fernando and Isabel, with a stone stairway leading to a gallery and a throne room with an **ornate, polychrome coffered ceiling**.

CATALONIA AND THE PYRENEES

In the huge Plaza del Pilar stands the **Basílica del Pilar** (*open: daily 0600–2130, museum daily 0900–1400, 1600–1800; free guided tours daily at 1000, 1100, 1200, Mon–Sat, also at 1700, 1800 and 1900, departing from the tourist office on Plaza del Pilar*), whose domes and minaret-like towers dominate the city from the north bank of the river. This site, the leading Marian shrine in Spain, owes its existence to the legend of the pillar, on which the Virgin is said to have appeared to St James in AD 40, commanding him to use it as the foundation stone of a church. It is worth going in to see the cupola frescos by **Goya** and the fine Renaissance altarpiece by **Damián Forment**.

La Lonja (*Plaza del Pilar; open for exhibitions only: Tue–Sat 1000–1400, 1700–2100, Sun 1000–1400*), the former commodities exchange, is the best piece of civil Renaissance architecture in Zaragoza. Outside in the square, a modern entrance leads down to the **Foro Romano** (*Plaza del Pilar; open: Tue–Sat 1000–1400, 1700–2000, Sun 1000–1400; £*), the underground remains of the Roman city. Near here, too, is the cathedral, **La Seo** (*open: daily 1000–1400, 1700–2000*), built between the 12th and 18th centuries in a number of architectural styles.

Monasterio de Piedra

Near Nuévalos, 120km (75 miles) southwest of Zaragoza, on the A202.

In the 12th century Cistercian monks discovered this verdant spot in an otherwise dry, drab landscape and they built a monastery (since converted into a hotel; *tel: 97 684 9011*). Beside it is a wooded park littered with waterfalls and grottoes, all of them connected by paths, tunnels and steps built in the 19th century. Sights to look out for are the **Lago del Espejo** ('Mirror Lake'), framed by high cliffs, and the **Cola de Caballo** ('Horse's Tail') waterfall.

CATALONIA AND THE PYRENEES

Eating and drinking

Restaurants

Catalan food is rich, varied and sometimes surprising. It is described as *mar i muntanya* ('sea and mountain') because of its unlikely combinations, such as chicken with lobster. The neighbouring, landlocked region of Aragón serves much more orthodox meat dishes.

Albereda
Girona. Carrer Albereda 7. Tel: 97 222 6002. £££. Widely considered to be Girona's top restaurant, this serves modern Catalan cuisine in a quiet back street just off the Plaça de Catalunya. (For bar-hopping, head for the area around **Plaça del Vi**, or join local students and expatriates at the **Excalibur** ale house on Plaça de l'Oli. There are also several outdoor cafés on the Rambla.)

Bahía
Tossa de Mar. Passeig del Mar 19. Tel: 97 234 0322. ££. Fresh fish dishes on a seafront terrace, with specialities including squid and *cim i tomba*, a fish, potato and garlic stew.

Can Pep
Calella de Palafrugell. Carrer Lladó 20. Tel: 97 261 5000. ££. This popular restaurant is situated in a typical village house, with whitewashed walls and flower-filled courtyards. The emphasis is on local seafood, cooked in rice dishes and fish stews.

Casa Anita
Cadaqués. Carrer Miquel Rosset 16. Tel: 97 225 8471. ££. This back-street restaurant was one of Dali's favourite haunts. The cooking is rustic, the portions huge, and you eat at crowded wooden tables. The whitewashed walls are covered with photos of former clients and signed prints by Dali.

Casa Irene
Vall d'Arán. Carrer Major 3, Arties. Tel: 97 364 4364. £££. When King Juan Carlos comes here to ski, he eats in this restaurant, famed for its elegant informality and Michelin-starred cuisine. The menu is heavy on treats like *foie gras* and truffles, and the specialities include stuffed rabbit and an unusual green tea sorbet.

Durán
Figueres. Carrer Lasauca 5. Tel: 97 250 1250. ££. The walls of this central hotel are adorned with Dali memorabilia, a reminder of the days when this was one of his favourite haunts. The restaurant continues to serve up classic regional cuisine.

El Prior
Zaragoza. Calle Santa Cruz 7. Tel: 97 620 1148. ££. This fashionable art-deco restaurant, set around the Renaissance patio of a former priory, serves an eclectic range of *tapas* plus roast meat, game and seafood specialities. (For *tapas* bars, look in the alleys of the old town between Plaza España and Plaza del Pilar.)

CATALONIA AND THE PYRENEES

Nightlife on the Costa Brava

If you want to sample the nightlife, Lloret de Mar's **Tropics** (*Avinguda Just Marles I Vilarrodona; open: 2200–0600; ££*) is the best-known disco on the Costa Brava, although every major resort has its own popular dance spot, usually just out of earshot of the town and its inhabitants.

Shopping in Andorra

The entire country of Andorra (not that there's much of it) has been likened to a cut-price supermarket. The main shopping areas are **Andorra la Vella**, the neighbouring town of **Escaldes** and the ski resort of **Pas de la Casa** on the French border. In Andorra la Vella, most of the duty-free shops are strung out along a single road, which changes its name from Avda Princep Benlloch to Avda Meritxell as it cuts across the old town. The largest department store is **Pyrénées** (*Avda Meritxell 21*). Most shops are open seven days a week, though many close on Sunday afternoons, and alcohol, tobacco, perfume, jewellery, clothing and electronic goods are all likely to be cheaper here than in Spain or France. Prices are usually quoted in Spanish pesetas, though French francs are also accepted.

CATALONIA AND THE PYRENEES

PROFILE

Wildlife of Spain

*Spain is said to have 'half the wildlife' of the EU, in both quantity and quality. It harbours, for instance, 1 300 species of plant found nowhere else – more than any other Western European country – and is also home to rare and elusive creatures, such as the ethereal pale-green Spanish Moon Moth (*Graellsia isabellae*), one of the most beautiful moths in the world.*

In 1916 Spain became the first country in the world to pass a law to create a national park. This was Covadonga, in the mountains of Asturias and Cantabria, since enlarged and renamed Picos de Europa; today there are 11 national parks, the largest of them Doñana, in Andalucia. Altogether, there are now over a hundred protected areas of countryside, including the national parks and *parques naturales* ('natural parks') administered by regional governments. And the popularity of 'green tourism' has given an impetus to conservation as people in rural areas realise that Spain's wildlife can be an attraction, bringing money into impoverished village economies.

But it is not all good news. Nineteen animal species in Spain are considered in 'immediate danger of extinction', and a further 350 are on the critical list. The most

CATALONIA AND THE PYRENEES

endangered animals include the lynx, brown bear, golden eagle, lammergeier, osprey and white-headed duck.

The brown bear, in particular, has been hunted almost to the point of no return; its numbers in the Pyrenees and the mountains of Cantabria went down from the thousand mark to under a hundred during the 20th century. Wolves have fared only slightly better. Spain is one of the few Western European countries still to have wolves, but the population wavers between 1 500 in spring, before the mating season, and 2 000 in the autumn, before winter sets in, most of them confined to Galicia and Castilla y León. Griffon vultures are a common sight around high crags in Spain, but there are now only about 52 pairs of lammergeier, or bearded vulture (*Gypaetus barbatus*).

However, one large species of bird which is happy nesting near people, and which you'll see in relative abundance if you travel anywhere in central Spain in spring or summer, is the white stork.

CATALONIA AND THE PYRENEES

The North

THE NORTH

From the western end of the Pyrenees to Galicia's 'Land's End' is the so-called 'Green Spain', where high rainfalls produce lush landscapes and the Atlantic carves out attractive coastal scenery. The Basque country and the regions of Navarra, Cantabria, Asturias and Galicia don't look anything like 'typical Spain', but they're perfect if you like countryside, quiet beaches and unspoilt historic towns.

THE NORTH

Best of The North

Getting around: ferries from Britain dock at Santander and Bilbao. Bilbao airport has the best range of flights serving the region, but given the distances here you may be better flying into Santiago de Compostela, or Asturias airport near Gijón. The mountainous geography impedes travel, but the main route you will need is the road along the coast, which is mainly called the N634 but has some motorway stretches by other names. Burgos is best reached from Bilbao by the A68 and A1, and León from Oviedo via the A66, a spectacular road in its own right.

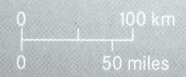

THE NORTH

① Bilbao

Not long ago hardly anyone visited Bilbao as a tourist, but the heavy industry has gone and the extraordinary Guggenheim Museum has arrived in its place. You'll probably only want to visit the city for this, but what a reason! See the collection or just marvel at the hi-tech building itself. **Pages 138–9**

② San Sebastián

This handsome *belle-époque* holiday resort, historically patronised by Spanish royalty, curves around the near-perfect crescent of a bay. A great place to laze on a beach or take an aperitif on a pavement café. **Pages 140–1**

③ Burgos

Three great religious buildings can be seen in this city at the heart of Castile: the cathedral, a monastery and a convent. You'll probably want to make an excursion to the monastery of Santo Domingo de Silos to the southeast, to see its famous cloister and hear the monks chanting mass. **Page 148**

④ Santillana del Mar and Las Cuevas de Altamira

Santillana, one of Spain's prettiest towns, looks as if it has been frozen in time. Next door are the caves of Altamira, famous throughout the world for their prehistoric paintings. You're unlikely to see the actual caves, but you can always visit the on-site museum. **Page 151**

⑤ Picos de Europa

This massive mountain block close to the north coast rises to 2 600m (8 500ft). Take a cable-car to a viewpoint, drive through spectacular gorges or climb slopes covered with wildflowers. **Page 152**

⑥ León

Explore the cathedral filled with stained-glass windows and the ancient royal pantheon of the kings of León with its ceilings covered in Romanesque frescos. **Page 154**

⑦ Santiago de Compostela

After Jerusalem and Rome, this venerable city was the most important shrine in medieval Christendom. The town centre is a harmonious collection of great stone buildings with a magnificent cathedral as centrepiece. **Pages 156–7**

⑧ Rías Baixas

Deep inlets of the Atlantic create one of Spain's most attractive coastlines. There are beaches, islands and historic towns to visit here. This corner of Galicia produces excellent seafood, and vineyards provide highly regarded wines to go with it. **Page 157**

Tourist information

Navarra (*Blas de la Serna 1, Pamplona; tel: 94 810 7730, cmn.navarra.net*);
Basque country (*Gran Via 44–1, Bilbao; tel: 94 424 2277, www.euskadi.net*);
La Rioja (*Portales 46, Logroño; tel: 94 129 1230, www.calarioja.es*); **Cantabria**
(*Plaza Velarde 1, Santander; tel: 94 231 0708, www.turismo.cantabria.org*);
Asturias (*Plaza de España 5, Oviedo; tel: 98 525 0184, www.asturnet.es/turismo*);
and **Galicia** (*Salvador de Madariaga, A Coruña; tel: 98 118 4681, www.xacobeo.es*).

THE NORTH

Bilbao (Bilbo)

For years a byword for heavy industry, Bilbao was facing a lingering decline until it decided to give itself a new, post-industrial image.

At the heart of its renaissance is the **Museo Guggenheim** (*Avda Abandoibarra 2; tel: 94 435 9000; metro: Moyua; open: Tue–Sun 1000–2000; £; free guided tours take place twice daily in Basque, Spanish and English – book in advance at the information desk*), which opened in 1997 and is already one of the most visited museums in Spain.

In the early 1990s, the New York-based Solomon R Guggenheim Foundation chose Bilbao as a European home in which to display its expanding collection of modern art. **Frank Gehry**'s masterpiece, a triumph of titanium, glass and limestone in organic, free-flowing forms, is one of the most influential buildings of the 20th century. A surrealistic touch is added by Jeff Koons's playful **floral sculpture** of a giant puppy standing guard outside. Inside, the soaring central atrium is filled with natural light, the huge windows forming a symbolic link between the city, the river and the university on the far bank. The exhibits are constantly changing, and much space is given over to temporary exhibitions, but the focus of the permanent collection is firmly on the second half of the 20th century.

Most visitors would not dream of coming to Bilbao were it not for the Guggenheim, but the city has always had its other attractions. The heart of Bilbao remains the medieval enclave, the **Casco Viejo**, on the right bank of the river. From Plaza Nueva, an arcaded square lined with *tapas* bars, the pedestrian shopping streets converge on the **Catedral de Santiago** (*contact tourist information for opening times*).

South of the cathedral, the atmospheric **Siete Calles** ('Seven Streets'), the original centre of Bilbao, leads to **Mercado de la Ribera**, an art-deco market-hall.

The **Museo de Bellas Artes** (*Plaza del Museo 2; open: Tue–Sat 1000–1330, 1600–1930, Sun 1000–1400; £, free on Wed*) was the fine arts museum of Bilbao before the arrival of the Guggenheim. It contains Spanish painting from the 12th to the 20th centuries, including works by **El Greco**, **Morales** and **Zurbarán** and a series of portraits by **Goya**. The museum also incorporates the collection of the former Modern Art Museum, with works by foreign artists including **Gauguin** and **Bacon** as well as the Basque sculptor **Eduardo Chillida**.

Tourist information: Paseo del Arenal. Tel: 94 479 5760.

Gernika-Lumo (Guernica)

20km (12 miles) northeast of Bilbao, on the BI635.

This small town is of symbolic significance for the Basque people. For centuries the representatives of the various communities met there under an oak tree, continuing a form of democracy practised since ancient times. But on a market day in April 1937, warplanes of Hitler's Condor Legion, allied to Franco, attacked Gernika, killing at least 200 people and reducing the town to rubble. Although 99 per cent of the buildings were destroyed, the **Arbol de Gernika** ('Tree of Gernika') was left unscathed. Gernika was made famous by Picasso's painting (now in the **Reina Sofía arts centre** in Madrid; *see page 38*) depicting the bombing of the town. The neo-classical **Casa de Juntas** (*Allende Salazar Etorbidea; open: daily 1000–1400, 1600–1800, to 1900 in summer*) has a large hall containing a museum of Basque history and a stained-glass ceiling depicting the sacred oak. The tree itself stands in the garden and is still used for oath-taking by newly elected presidents of the Basque government.

" *The Spaniards have a genius for adapting everything to their own life; their indolence, the obstinate, individual refusal to break easily with custom, has given them enormous, natural power of resistance.* "

V S Pritchett, *The Spanish Temper* (1954)

THE NORTH

San Sebastián (Donostia)

San Sebastián is the pearl of the Basque coast. Beautifully situated on a crescent bay at the mouth of the Río Urumea, it was first popularised by the Spanish royals, who came to take the waters in the 19th century. The resort reached its heyday in the belle-époque *era immediately before the First World War, when the Spanish aristocracy would stay at its lavish hotels. Such decadence, however, belies a violent history: this border town has been destroyed by fire at least a dozen times.*

Its shell-shaped beach, **Playa de la Concha**, set between two green hills, is protected from the harsh Atlantic winds by the calming presence of the Isla de Santa Clara just offshore. In summer, it is packed with people and deckchairs; in winter, the locals come out to play football on the sand and couples take romantic moonlit walks beside the sea. The beach promenade, **Paseo de La Concha**, with its white railings, Edwardian lamp-posts and tamarind trees, is the focal point of San Sebastián. During the early evening the entire population of the city puts on its best casuals for a stroll here and an apéritif at one of the beachfront cafés.

> *" A Basque joint, all roasted red and green peppers, fat olives, fresh salmon, lobster and prawn. I could not believe it the first time I went there. You stand there and help yourself to the range of delights on display … "*
>
> **John Carlin, *Daily Telegraph* (2000)**

The promenade runs out at the **Palacio Miramar**, a summer palace built in Queen Anne-style by the English architect Selden Wornum in 1893. Beneath the palace gardens (*open: daily summer, 0900–2100, winter, 1000–1700*), a tunnel leads to **Ondarreta beach**, a continuation

THE NORTH

of La Concha. At the far end is an extraordinary sculpture, **El Peine de los Vientos** ('Comb of the Winds'), by sculptor Eduardo Chillida. Nearby, a rickety 1912 funicular (*open: daily summer, 1000–2200; winter, Thu–Tue 1100–1800*) leads up to Monte Igueldo for **panoramic views** over the bay.

Tourist information: Calle Reina Regente. Tel: 94 348 1166.

Hondarribia (Fuenterrabia)

15km (9 miles) northeast of San Sebastián, off the N634 or A8.

A fishing port and holiday resort, this historic town stands at a strategic location close to the French border at the mouth of the Rio Bidasoa. The older, higher part of the town is ringed by 15th-century ramparts which are entered through the gateway of Puerta de Santa Maria. Hondarribia's **castle** dates from the 10th century but was restored by the emperor Charles V in the 16th century and is now a parador (*Parador de Hondarribia, Plaza de Armas 14; tel: 94 364 5500*).

Vitoria (Gasteiz)

Tourist information: Parque de la Florida. Tel: 94 513 1321.

The old centre of the capital of the Basque country focuses upon the **Plaza de la Virgen Blanca**, a square which has numerous *miradores* (glass-enclosed balconies) overlooking it. Above the square is the **Iglesia de San Miguel** (*open during services; check with tourist information*), with a carving over its door depicting the life of St Michael, after whom the church is named. In the city's curious annual fiesta in August a dummy is lowered on a rope from this church to the square below. Worth seeing, too, is the **Catedral de Santa María** (*open during services; check with tourist information*), also 14th century. The most interesting of Vitoria's several museums, the **Museo del Naipe 'Fournier'** (*Palacio de Vendaña, Calle Cuchilleria 54; open: Tue–Sat 1100–1400, 1700–2100, Sun 1100–1400; £*) in the modern part of the city, testifies to an unusual local industry: the manufacture of playing cards.

THE NORTH

Eastern Navarra

Roncesvalles (Orreaga)

45km (28 miles) northeast of Pamplona on the N135. Tourist information: Antiguo Molino de Roncesvalles. Tel: 94 876 0301.

The pass above the diminutive village of Roncesvalles is one of the traditional gateways to Spain for pilgrims on the **Way of St James**. It is also the setting for the *Chanson de Roland*, a medieval epic recounting the defeat of Charlemagne's rearguard at the hands of the Navarrese. All other buildings in Roncesvalles are dwarfed by the zinc-roofed monastery **Real Colegiata de Santa María** (*open: daily 0800–2000*), founded in the 13th century to give spiritual and physical succour to pilgrims. It has a peaceful cloister off which is a chapterhouse containing the tomb of Sancho the Strong (1154–1234), who lies beneath his life-size statue.

Leyre

40km (25 miles) southeast of Pamplona, off the N240.

The old **Cistercian Monasterio de San Salvador de Leyre** (*tel: 94 888 4150; open: Mon–Fri 1000–1400, 1530–1830, Sat–Sun 1600–1800*), picturesquely situated above the Yesa reservoir beneath white rock pinnacles and cliffs inhabited by vultures, was the spiritual centre of old Navarra and the pantheon of its monarchs. Since it was restored in the 1950s the monastery has been inhabited by Benedictines. You can visit the singular **Romanesque crypt** (with its primitively carved capitals supported on stocky columns) and the church, which has a **Gothic nave** and **Romanesque sanctuary**. Time your visit to include Vespers (*1900 in winter, 2000 in summer*) to hear the monks' Gregorian evensong.

Sangüesa

10km (6 miles) southwest of Leyre on the C127.

The bridge across the Río Aragón is part of the Aragonese branch of the pilgrim route to Santiago de Compostela. Beside it stands the 13th-century church of **Santa María la Real**, which has an extraordinarily detailed **carved southern doorway**. Immediately above the door, on the tympanum, is a representation of the Last Judgement. Above this are two rows of figures or saints in blind arcades, but it is the details on the arches of the doorway and on the flat space outside the arch that make this doorway most interesting: they show a range of mythical beasts, geometric motifs and medieval characters.

North of Sangüesa are two gorges. The nearest, but least spectacular, of the two is the **Hoz de Lumbier**, visible from the N240 back towards Pamplona. Take the NA211 beyond Lumbier to see the far more impressive **Hoz de Arbayún** – 6 kilometres (3¾ miles) of vertical cliffs which are home to vultures. There is a car park and viewing platform along this road, between the Iso Pass and Aspurz.

Javier

11km (6½ miles) northeast of Sangüesa on a minor road.

The **Castillo de Javier** (*open: daily 1000–1300, 1600–1900, guided tours only; £*), the oldest parts of which date from the 10th or 11th century, would probably have fallen into decay had it not been the birthplace of **St Francis Xavier** (or Javier), patron saint of Navarra and of missionaries everywhere. Because of this, the castle has been carefully restored and is immaculately maintained by the Jesuits, the order St Francis jointly founded with Ignatius Loyola.

> *Spain is the very native land of carnage and of the saints. Of those who martyrise and those who are martyred.*
>
> **Hilaire Belloc (1870–1953)**

The museum devoted to the life of the saint is of interest; St Francis (1506–52) travelled extensively and is considered by the Catholic Church to have been the greatest missionary after St Paul. Thousands of people congregate in Javier to honour the saint on two Sundays every March. But the building is of interest in itself. The guided tour (*times as advertised on the day*) takes in the guardroom and chapel, in which there is a bizarre mural, **The Dance of Death**, peopled by grinning skeletons.

THE NORTH

Pamplona and the rest of Navarra

Pamplona (Iruña)

Tourist information: Calle Duque de Ahumada 3. Tel: 94 822 0741.

Founded by the Romans, occupied by the Moors and sacked by Charlemagne, Pamplona has played a central role in Navarrese history. It is a prosperous and modern university city of wide boulevards and spacious parks, best known for the **Sanfermines**, the July bull-running festival made famous by the writer Ernest Hemingway, whose statue stands outside the bullring. From there, a stroll along the ramparts, looking down over the river, leads to the **catedral** (*Plaza San José; open: 16 Sept–14 July, Mon–Fri 1030–1330, 1600–1800, Sat 1030–1330, 15 July–15 Sept, Mon–Fri 1000–1900, Sat 1000–1330; ££*), its fine Gothic nave and cloister hidden behind a stern 18th-century neo-classical façade.

West of the cathedral, the narrow streets of the **Navarrería** (the old Basque artisan quarter) merge with the **Judería** (Jewish quarter) to form an atmospheric pedestrian shopping district. Behind Santo Domingo market, the **Museo de Navarra** (*Calle Santo Domingo; open: Tue–Sat 1000–1400, 1700–1900, Sun 1100–1400; £*), housed in a 16th-century hospital, contains **Roman mosaics** and Gothic and Romanesque art.

The nerve centre of Pamplona is **Plaza del Castillo**, a porticoed square ringed with cafés and Hemingway's favourite hotel. From here a wide promenade, **Paseo Sarasate**, connects the old town to the 19th-century extension, squeezed between two of the city's finest parks: **La Ciudadela**, based around the remains of a 16th-century fortress, and **La Taconera**, a romantic park with a botanic garden.

> *The Spanish have a genius for popular display: the bullfight, the religious procession, and the fiesta. They have a genius for dancing and popular song. In the past thirty years there has been a slight decline in the typical regional character of this popular culture, but it remains easily the strongest and most lively in Europe.*
>
> **V S Pritchett**, *The Spanish Temper* (1954)

THE NORTH

Puente la Reina

25km (15 1/2 miles) southwest of Pamplona, on the N111. Tourist information: Plaza de la Mena 1. Tel: 94 834 0845.

This small town stands on the banks of the Rio Arga at the junction of the two main routes to Santiago. The entry to the oldest part of the town is the medieval gate **Portal de Suso**, which leads into Calle Mayor where shops sell scallop-shells and rosaries for pilgrims, local sausages and wine. The street leads to the graceful humpbacked 11th-century bridge from which the town takes its name.

Estella (Lizarra)

20km (12 1/2 miles) west of Puente la Reina, on the N111. Tourist information: Calle San Nicolás 1. Tel: 94 855 6301.

To pilgrims in the Middle Ages, Estella was a popular resting-place astride the Rio Ega with a wealth of beautiful Romanesque buildings. The Palacio de los Reyes de Navarra, a fine example of 12th-century civil Romanesque architecture, houses the **Museo Gustavo de Maeztu** (*open: Tue–Sat 1100–1300, 1700–1900, Sun 1100–1300*), dedicated to the works of the Basque painter.

Olite

30km (19 miles) south of Pamplona on the N121 or A15.

All other buildings in Olite are dwarfed by the **Castillo** (*open: daily winter, 1000–1400, 1600–1800, spring, 1000–1400, 1600–1900, summer, 1000–1400, 1600–2000; £*) which was the residence of the kings of Navarra until their realm was swallowed up by the kingdom of Castile. It was one of the most luxurious palaces of its time in Europe, a **Gothic labyrinth** of towers, patios, staircases, galleries and turrets. For the amusement of the royal family there were hanging gardens within the complex and a pen to keep lions. The oldest part of the fortress is now a parador (*Parador de Olite, Plaza Teobaldos 2; tel: 94 874 0000*).

THE NORTH

La Rioja

Haro

40km (25 miles) northwest of Logroño, via the A68 or the N232. Tourist information: Plaza Monseñor Rodriguez. Tel: 94 130 3366.

Haro is the main wine town of Rioja Alta. Although winemaking in Haro dates back to Roman times, the town really took off at the end of the 19th century when French viticulturalists, devastated by the phylloxera plague in Bordeaux, moved to Haro to experiment with the local grapes.

Most of the wineries are situated in the area around the station; they can usually be visited, though it is best to book by telephone at least a week in advance. Of the 17 bodegas in Haro, **López de Heredia** (*tel: 94 131 0244*) is the most old-fashioned and **Muga** (*tel: 94 131 0498*) the most geared up to receiving visitors. Other interesting bodegas are **Bilbaínas** (*tel: 94 131 0147*), **La Rioja Alta** (*tel: 94 131 0346*), **CVNE** (*tel: 94 130 4800*) and **Paternina** (*tel: 94 131 0550*). And you can get a good overview of the wine production process at the **Museo del Vino** (*Calle Bretón de los Herreros 4; open: Mon–Sat 1000–1400, 1600–2000, Sun 1000–1400; £, free on Wed*).

Santo Domingo de la Calzada

50km (31 miles) west of Logroño, on the N120. Tourist information: Calle Mayor 70. Tel: 94 134 1230.

This charming town on the Rio Oja is named after an 11th-century hermit who built a causeway (*calzada*) and a hospital for the many pilgrims who passed through the town on the road to Santiago de Compostela. King Alfonso VI of Castile built a church here, it was consecrated in 1106, and it is now the **catedral**. Although parts of it can be visited free of charge, the cloisters, museum and crypt are reached by a separate entrance on Calle del Cristo (*open: Mon–Sat 1000–1830; £*).

The **tomb of Santo Domingo** lies in the crypt. A live cock and hen, permanently kept inside a henhouse in the south transept, are a reminder of a miracle attributed to the saint. A German pilgrim was falsely accused of theft by a local girl after he had rebuffed her advances. After he was hanged on the gallows, his parents went to pay their last respects before continuing to Santiago. They found their son still breathing; Santo Domingo had saved his life, he claimed. So the parents went to see the judge to plead for his release. The judge, at his dinner table, was dismissive of their improbable story: their son was no more alive than the roasted chickens on his plate, he scoffed, whereupon the cock and the hen he was about to tuck into got up and crowed.

San Millán de la Cogolla

20km (12 1/2 miles) southeast of Santo Domingo de la Calzada on minor roads. Tourist information: in the courtyard of the Monasterio de Yuso. Tel: 94 137 3259.

Born in the nearby village of Berceo in 473, San Millán (St Emilian) 'of the Cowl' was a shepherd who became a cave hermit and lived to the ripe old age of 101. Many miracles were attributed to him after his death, and his tomb soon became an important place of pilgrimage.

A 10th-century church, **Monasterio de Suso**, with Visigothic and Mozarabic features, including some fine **horseshoe arches**, was subsequently hollowed out of the rock. At the time of writing it is undergoing restoration work and only a small part is accessible (*open: daily 1030–1330, 1600–1800, closed Mon in winter*). A second monastery, **Monasterio de Yuso** (*guided tours daily, 1000–1300, 1600–1800, closed Mon in winter; £*) was built further down in the valley. It contains the **first written example of the Castilian language**, by a 10th-century monk who lapsed into the vernacular in the footnotes of a Latin text.

> There will be miles where the soil looks like stripes of red lead or ochre, distances of sulphur and tin, the sharp colours of incineration, as if great areas of the kingdom had been raked out of a furnace …

V S Pritchett on travelling through Castile, *The Spanish Temper* **(1954)**

THE NORTH

Burgos

From 1037 until the unification of Spain in 1492, Burgos was the capital of the united kingdom of Castile and León. The city's most splendid sight is the glorious Gothic catedral *(open: daily 0930–1300, 1600–1900), the country's third largest after Sevilla and Toledo, and unlike the other two a stopover on the* Way of St James.

It was founded in 1221 and its construction continued over three centuries, involving some of the best architects and artists in Europe. Its twin lacy spires and the carved Puerta de la Coronería are its most distinctive exterior features. Inside, the Renaissance Golden Staircase is an indication of the slope on the site. Behind the altar is the Constable's Chapel, the tomb of the High Constable of Castile, and don't leave without looking up the middle of the church to see the star-shaped vaulting of the dome, beneath which El Cid and his wife lie buried.

Tip

The 11th-century warrior El Cid was born Rodrigo Díaz in 1043 in a town north of Burgos; his honorary name comes from the Arabic for 'lord'. The anonymous poem El Cantar del Mío Cid *(1180) turned him into the hero of the Christian Reconquest, but the truth is that at different times in his life he fought on both sides of the religious divide.*

Two magnificent religious houses stand a little way from the city centre. The Real Monasterio de las Huelgas (*Las Huelgas; tel: 94 720 1630; open: summer, Tue–Sat 1030–1315, 1530–1745, Sun 1030–1415, winter, Tue–Fri 1100–1315, 1600–1715, Sat 1100–1315, 1400–1745, Sun 1030–1415; £*) is a 12th-century Cistercian convent with Gothic and Romanesque cloisters and an interesting museum of medieval textiles; the Cartuja de Miraflores (*open: Mon–Sat 1015–1500, Sun 1120–1230, 1300–1500, 1600–1800*) is a monastery built by the Carthusian order in the 15th century. Its outstanding feature is a coloured altarpiece by Gil de Siloé which is supposedly covered with gold from the first shipment delivered from the New World.

Tourist information: Plaza de Alonso Martinez 7. Tel: 94 720 3125.

Covarrubias

40km (25 miles) southeast of Burgos, off the N234.

This charming old town on the Rio Arlanza shows off remnants of its 10th-century ramparts and several medieval half-timbered houses – see, in particular, the **Casa de Doña Sancha** – within a short walk of the Plaza Mayor. The main sight is the **Gothic collegiate church** (*open: Wed–Mon 1030–1330, 1630–1800, Sun 1000 1400, 1630–1830, to 1930 May–Sept; £*), which has a pleasant cloister, an unusual 17th-century organ and various art treasures in its museum. Another atmospheric town, 23km (14 miles) west of Covarrubias, is **Lerma**.

Monasterio de Santo Domingo de Silos

20km (12 miles) southeast of Covarrubias on a minor road. Open: Tue–Sat 1000–1300, 1630–1800; Sun–Mon 1630–1800.

This 12th-century monastery, named in honour of St Dominic, is much visited for its **elegant Romanesque cloisters**, considered among the finest in Spain. The capitals of the two-storey cloisters are carved into a variety of symbolic and realistic forms, drawing on a range of imaginative flora and bestiary; others illustrate Biblical scenes. In the old pharmacy, off the cloister, you can see an assortment of equipment, including 18th-century jars made in the ceramics town of Talavera de la Reina. The monks here regularly sing services in plainchant. In 1994 a recording of their singing became an international hit.

The coast of Cantabria

Castro Urdiales

40km (25 miles) northwest of Bilbao, on the A8. Tourist information: Avda de la Constitución 1. Tel: 94 287 1337.

This sturdy fishing port and summer resort sits on a rocky promontory overlooking the bay. Behind the harbour, narrow medieval streets lead up to the cathedral-like **Iglesia de Santa María de la Asunción** (*check opening times with tourist information*), perhaps the finest Gothic church in Cantabria. Beside the church, a ruined castle built by the Knights Templar now shelters a lighthouse. The seafront promenade here makes a delightful place to stroll, with glass-fronted houses, lively restaurants and bars, and fishing boats moored in the picturesque harbour.

Santander

Tourist information: Jardines de Pereda. Tel: 94 221 6120.

The point of arrival for ferry passengers from Britain is a mixture of modern provincial capital, fading *belle-époque* resort and busy ferry and fishing port. A massive fire in 1941 destroyed most of the city centre and the oldest remaining building is the **catedral** (*open: daily 1000–1300, 1600–1930*).

Santander's **Museo de Bellas Artes** (*Calle del Rubio; open: Mon–Fri 1030–1300, 1730–2000, Sat 1030–1300*) has collections of contemporary and Cantabrian paintings, the **Museo de Prehistoria** (*Calle Casimiro Sainz; open: Tue–Sat 1000–1300, 1600–1900, Sun 1100–1400*) contains exhibitions on Cantabrian archaeology and ancient history, and the **Museo Marítimo** (*Avda Luis Carrero Blanco; open: Tue–Sat 1000–1300, 1600–1800, Sun 1100–1400*) has on display a skeleton of a 24-m (79-ft) long whale.

The headland at the north end of Santander Bay is now the **Parque de la Magdalena** (*open: daily 0800–2000*), a popular playground with a beach, a tourist train circuit, a mini-zoo and a royal palace, now a prestigious international summer university. The El Sardinero beach, backed by elegant buildings including the recently restored Gran Casino, is particularly attractive.

THE NORTH

Santillana del Mar

30km (18¹/₂ miles) west of Santander, off the A67. Tourist information: Plaza Ramón Pelayo. Tel: 94 281 8251.

This village of golden stone houses is one of the prettiest in Spain. Two main streets of Renaissance mansions, with wrought-iron balconies, wooden galleries and coats of arms above the doors, converge at the **Colegiata** (*open: Oct–Jan and Mar–mid-June, Thu–Tue 1000–1300, 1500–1800, closed Wed and Feb, mid-June–Sept 1000–1300, 1600–2000 daily; £*), a 12th-century church built to house the relics of **St Juliana**, who was martyred in Asia Minor in the 6th century. Your ticket will also gain you entry to the **Museo Diocesano** (*same times as Colegiata*), a collection of sacred art in a former convent.

Las Cuevas de Altamira

Just outside Santillana del Mar.

The archaeologist **Marcelino de Sautuola** stumbled across this remarkable discovery in 1879 when his nine-year-old daughter pointed out some primitive rock paintings on the roof of a cave, but few were prepared to believe he had unearthed a treasure of palaeolithic art. The paintings date back to at least **12000 BC**, making them the most significant example of prehistoric art in Spain. Entry to the caves is restricted to a few visitors a day, but you can visit the accompanying museum (*tel: 94 281 8005; open: Tue–Sun 0930–1430; £*).

Comillas

20km (12¹/₂ miles) west of Santillana del Mar, on the C6316.

The town of Comillas was once the favoured resort of the Barcelona aristocracy and it is one of the few places outside Catalonia where you can see Modernista architecture – including **El Capricho**, a fantasy of a summer palace by Antoni Gaudí, now a restaurant, and the **Universidad Pontificia**, situated on a hill top.

THE NORTH

The Picos de Europa and Asturias

Picos de Europa

The Picos de Europa, one of Europe's biggest national parks, rise dramatically from sea level to over 2 600m (8 500 ft) in little more than 25km (15 miles). Deep gorges between the peaks add a further dimension to the landscape. The whole area is excellent for walking or wildflower hunting.

This great mountain chain is usually approached from the coast by car via two routes. The eastern of these (from the Cantabria side) is the **Desfiladero de la Hermida**, a gorge of towering walls of rock and cascading beds of scree. Halfway along the gorge is the **Iglesia de Lebeña** (*for opening times, check with the Unquera tourist information office on the main coastal road, the N623*), a rare and quaint example of Mozarabic architecture with horseshoe arches. The gorge at last opens out into the **Valle de Liebana**, which has a small wine industry producing a fiery spirit called *orujo*. From **Potes**, the main town on this side of the Picos, a road continues into the mountains past the **Monasterio de Santo Toribio** to come to an abrupt halt at the enormous semi-circular wall of rock of **Fuente Dé**. On clear days, a cable-car ferries sightseers to the breezy Balcón del Cable, a viewing platform and the starting-point of some good walks.

Tip

Of course there is an alternative way into the Picos, and that's through the middle – on foot. For a truly hair-raising walk, take the dramatic footpath along the **Desfiladero del Río Cares**, *and you'll find yourself negotiating rock ledges sometimes 1 000m (3 250ft) above the bottom of the gorge.*

The second approach, from the western, Asturian side, is through **Cangas de Onís** to the bustling shrine of **Covadonga**. The winding road continues to two beautiful high-altitude lakes, **Lago Enol** and **Lago de la Ercina**.

Oviedo

Tourist information: Plaza de la Catedral 6. Tel: 98 521 3385.

Asturias was one of the few areas of Spain to stay out of the hands of the Moors, and several very early, pre-Romanesque churches survive here, particularly in the area around Oviedo. Two such churches stand close together on Mount Naranco, a hillside a short way north of the city. The finest of them is **Santa María del Naranco** (*open: Mon–Sat 1000–1300, 1500–1700, to 1900 May–Oct, Sun mornings only; £*), built in the 9th century as a summer palace for Ramiro I; only later did it become a church. Further up the hill is **San Miguel de Lillo** (*same times*), which has carvings of acrobats and circus animal tamers on the door jamb. The largest of the pre-Romanesque churches is the 9th-century **San Julián dels Prados** (*open: May–Oct, Tue–Sun 1100–1300, 1630–1800, Nov–Apr, Tue–Sun 1200–1300; £*), northeast of Oviedo.

The city itself has a pleasing cluster of old buildings grouped around the Plaza Alfonso II, most notably the cathedral, built in a flamboyant Gothic style. Early Asturian carved stonework can be seen in the **Museo Arqueológico** (*open: Tue–Sat 1000–1330, 1600–1800, Sun 1100–1300*), and Asturian paintings from the 19th and 20th centuries in the **Museo de Bellas Artes** (*open: Tue–Fri 1030–1330, 1700–2000, Sat 1130–1400, 1700–2000, Sun 1130–1400*).

Costa Verde

Asturias's coast, between Ria de Ribadeo and Rio Deva, is a string of charming coves and beaches punctuated by low but sometimes spectacular cliffs. It is called the Costa Verde ('Green Coast') because of its lush vegetation; in places, pastures and trees reach down to the shore. **Luarca** and **Cudillero** – west of Asturias's largest city, **Gijón** – are both fishing ports in small coves and are delightful places to sit at a pavement café or take a stroll. **Ribadasella**, on an estuary, is another pretty town, and **Llanes** is an attractive seaside resort that can boast remnants of its old ramparts and castle.

THE NORTH

León and Galicia

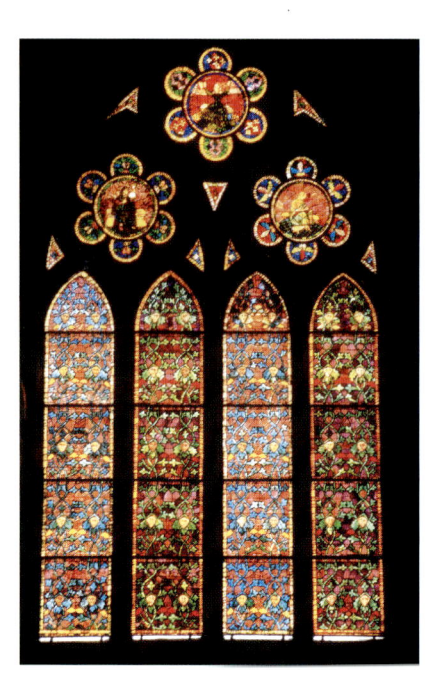

León

Tourist information: Plaza de la Regla 3. Tel: 98 723 7082.

Once capital of a medieval kingdom of the same name, the city of León preserves three outstanding monuments. The oldest of them is the **Real Colegiata de San Isidoro** (*open: 1000–1330, 1600–1830, Sun 1000–1330; guided tour only – the later times reflect last group entry; £*). The highlight of this cluster of rooms is the **Romanesque Panteón Real** where most of the kings of León were buried. It is covered with astonishing frescos.

Not far from the royal pantheon stands the Gothic **catedral** (*open: daily winter, 0830–1330, 1600–1900, summer, 0830–1330, 1600–2000*), famous for its 700-odd panes of stained glass and the 13th- to 14th-century cloister.

The other building of importance in León is the handsome **Hostal de San Marcos** (*Plaza de San Marcos 7; tel: 98 723 7300*), which stands beside the Rio Bernesga, a glory of Spanish Renaissance architecture. It is now a plush parador.

> *It is a saying amongst the inhabitants of Coruña, that in their town there is a street so clean that puchera [stew] may be eaten off it without the slightest inconvenience. This may certainly be the fact after one of those rains which so frequently drench Galicia.*

George Borrow, *The Bible in Spain* (1842)

THE NORTH

> *We buried him darkly at dead of night,*
> *The sods with our bayonets turning;*
> *By the struggling moonbeam's misty light*
> *And the lantern dimly burning.*

Charles Wolfe, *The Burial of Sir John Moore at Corunna* (1817)

A Coruña

Tourist information: Dársena de la Marina. Tel: 98 122 1822.

Felipe II's ill-fated Spanish Armada sailed out of this historic port in 1588; nowadays A Coruña (La Coruña) is an industrial town with an old quarter at the centre. Its pride, however, is the **Avenida de la Marina**, which is lined with banks of enclosed balconies (*galerías*), designed to give protection against sea winds.

The main square is a sober, monumental affair. In the middle of it stands a statue of María Pita, a local heroine after whom the square is named. The streets east of the main square comprise the Ciudad Vieja ('old town'). Wander around and you will come across two Romanesque churches: **Santa María del Campo** and **Iglesia de Santiago** (*open during services*).

On a headland just outside the city stands the **Torre de Hércules** (*open: Apr–June, Sept 1000–1900, Jul–Aug 1000–2100, Oct–Mar 1000–1800; £*), the only Roman lighthouse still in operation. The climb to the top is well worth the effort.

Pontevedra

Tourist information: General Mola 1. Tel: 98 685 0814.

Pontevedra was a port on a *ría* (an inlet of the sea) until the 18th century when the channel silted up. Since then it has expanded, but mercifully the old town, a handsome complex of stone streets and squares, has been left more or less intact. The prettiest square is the **Plaza de la Leña**; on it stands the **Museo Provincial** (*open: winter, Tue–Sat 1000–1330, 1630–1900, Sun 1100–1300, summer, Tue–Sat 1000–1415, 1700–2045*) housed in two 18th-century mansions, offering prehistoric collections, Celtic treasures and maritime exhibits.

The town's most important church is the **Basílica Menor de Santa María** (*open during services*), built in the 16th century with a Plateresque façade.

THE NORTH

Santiago de Compostela

*In medieval times the **Catedral de Santiago** was one of the most important shrines in Christendom, and even today it attracts thousands of visitors. It stands at the heart of a harmonious, mostly pedestrianised city centre full of venerable granite buildings.*

And it is worth taking a stroll around the cathedral to get your bearings before plunging into the interior. The effective centre of the ensemble is the **Praza do Obradoiro**, a vast square dominated by the cathedral's baroque west front. On one side of the square is the **Hostal de los Reyes Católicos**, built by Fernando and Isabel as a hospital for needy pilgrims, now a parador (*Praza do Obradoiro 1; tel: 98 158 2200*). Plateresque stonework crowds around its main door. And opposite the cathedral is the classical-style **Pazo de Raxoi**, now the town hall.

Working your way around the cathedral you come first to the Praza das Praterias, a square on to which the so-called **Goldsmiths' Doorway** (11th-century and sculpted with scenes from the Bible) opens. Next comes the **Praza da Quintana**, and to the east of this square is the **Convento de San Paio de Antealtares**, one of the oldest monasteries in the city, founded in the 9th century. To the north of the cathedral stands another large monastery, the **Convento de San Martiño Pinario** (*contact tourist information for opening times for monasteries*).

The **catedral** itself (*open: daily 0700–2100; museum open: daily June–Sept, 1030–1300, 1600–1830, Oct–May 1100–1300, 1600–1800*) is best entered from the Praza do Obradoiro. Climbing the steps like any good pilgrim you are greeted by the **Pórtico da Gloria**, the 'Doorway of Glory', a 12th-century construction

THE NORTH

> *In the venerable city of Santiago de Compostela, where the bones of the apostle Saint James are said to rest, they boast that it rains three hundred and sixty-five days a year – except in Leap Year, when the average is three hundred and sixty-six.*
>
> **Delano Ames, introduction to *Spain***

decorated with statues of prophets and apostles. St James himself sits on the central pillar, and it is traditional for arriving pilgrims to touch the carving below the saint – a depression has been worn into the stone here. The crypt under the altar is said to contain his relics.

One fixture which is not always on display is the **botafumeiro**, a giant censer which is brought out to be suspended from the ceiling and swung during important services.

Two further sights worth visiting are some way from the centre. The **Convento de Santo Domingo** east of the city centre is now a folk museum (*contact tourist information for opening times*), and the **Colegiata del Sar** (*open: Tue–Sat 1000–1300, 1600–1900, Sun 1000–1300; £*), to the south, a Romanesque church dating from the 12th century.

Tourist information: Rúa do Vilar 43. Tel: 98 158 4081.

Rías Baixas

Southwest of Santiago the coastline of Galicia is carved into *rías* ('inlets'). The hills in between these are covered with pine trees, making for some of the best scenery in Spain. The shores of the *rías* hide many good beaches, and a few towns, such as **Vilagarcía de Arousa**, have become thriving resorts.

There are several islands offshore too. One particularly attractive one, **Isla de la Toja**, is connected to the mainland at O Grove by a bridge, and you can go by boat to **Isla de Ons** (*from Sanxenxo, Portonovo or Marín, near Pontevedra; tel: 98 622 5272 or 98 673 1343*) and the **Islas Cíes** (*from either Baiona or Vigo; tel: Vigo tourist information office on 98 643 0577*), a nature reserve which admits a limited number of visitors per day.

And there are many other attractions to explore in the Rias Baixas, especially as it is one of Spain's up-and-coming wine regions. Even the local table wines are usually good here.

THE NORTH

Eating and drinking

Restaurants and bars

Altamira
Santillana del Mar. Calle Cantón 1. Tel: 94 281 8025. ££. This restored 17th-century mansion is now a charming hotel, whose restaurant has established a reputation as one of the best in town.

Arzak
San Sebastián. Alto de Miracruz 21. Tel: 94 327 8465. £££. The restaurant of the high priest of Basque cooking. If you can afford it, try the eight-course menu.

Bodega del Riojano
Santander. Calle Rio de la Pila 5. Tel: 94 221 6750. ££. The painted barrels are the best-known feature of this classic bodega, a dark old wine cellar where Riojan cuisine and *tapas* are served.

Café Iruña
Pamplona. Plaza del Castillo. A stylish art-nouveau coffee shop and popular meeting-place.

Casa Manolo
Santiago de Compostela. Rúa Traviesa 27. Tel: 98 158 2950. £. An inexpensive little restaurant packed with tables. It gets so crowded that you'll need to give your name and wait at the door for a table.

Casa Pardo
A Coruña. Novoa Santos 15. Tel: 98 128 0021. £££. Highly regarded Galician fish and seafood restaurant.

La Chistera
Pamplona. Calle San Nicolás 40. Tel: 94 821 0512. ££. Roast meat, especially lamb, is the thing to order at this popular restaurant just off the Plaza del Castillo.

Mesón del Pelegrino
Puente la Reina. Carretera Pamplona-Logroño. Tel: 94 834 0075. ££. This stone-built inn at the junction of the pilgrim routes has rustic charm and a reputation for excellent Navarrese cuisine.

Rianxo
Pontevedra. Plaza de la Lena 6. Tel: 98 685 5211. ££. The upstairs dining room of this restaurant looks out on to the prettiest square of Pontevedra.

Víctor Montes
Bilbao. Plaza Nueva 8. Tel: 94 415 5603. ££. This busy art-nouveau wine bar in the heart of the old town is one of the best places to try *pintxos*, Basque *tapas*. There is also a more formal restaurant specialising in seafood.

What to try

The north and northwest coast of Spain is rich in fish and seafood. The **Basque country** in particular has a cuisine held in high esteem in Spain. Try the cod dishes *bacalao al pil pil* and *bacalao a la bilbaina*, and the white tuna stew *marmitako*. In Navarra, roasted or grilled meat *al chilindrón* (red peppers) is prepared. The favourite dish of **Asturias** is a white bean stew called *fabada asturiana*, washed down with the local cider, poured from a height to give it a fizz. In **Galicia** there is an abundance of Atlantic seafood as well as excellent wines from Ribeiro and Rias Baixas.

Don't miss

Pamplona's Los Sanfermines fiesta, held from 6 to 14 July (*www.sanfermin.com*), has become a non-stop street party in which everyone eats and drinks a lot but sleeps little. Calle Estafeta, the main street on the bull-running route, has numerous *tapas* bars where *pintxos* are laid out on plates for you (try **Bodegon Sarria**, **La Estafeta** and **Ostatu Errategia**). The fiesta's international fame derives, of course, from the *encierro*, an event which lasts just 180 seconds each morning. During the *encierro*, bulls run through the streets to the bullring, accompanied by anyone brave or foolish enough to get in their way (joining in the *encierro* is not advised unless you know what you are doing). There are several injuries – sometimes deaths – each year and it's certainly safer to watch from behind a barricade. But whatever you do, don't blink or you'll miss the action.

THE NORTH

PROFILE

The Road to Santiago de Compostela

According to legend, the body of St James, one of Christ's apostles and the patron saint of Spain, was discovered at Santiago de Compostela in Galicia in the year 813. Soon after, people from all over Europe began to make their way to the shrine of the saint to pay homage to him, and Santiago became Christianity's most important place of pilgrimage after Jerusalem.

The main routes these medieval travellers took now comprise **El Camino de Santiago** ('The Way of St James'), which stretches for over 700km (440 miles). Thousands of latter-day tourists follow all or part of the route every year, the most dedicated of them on foot. Some make the journey for religious reasons, but many others do it to enjoy the wealth of **Romanesque architecture** that grew up along the route and the beautiful countryside through which it passes.

The two main branches of the Way of St James cross the Pyrenees at **Roncesvalles** (in Navarra) and **Somport** (in Aragón) and converge at

THE NORTH

Camino de Santiago

Itinerario Cultural Europeo

Puente la Reina to cross the Rio Arga via an ancient humpbacked bridge. Between here and Santiago de Compostela there is a succession of churches, cathedrals, *hospederías* (lodging houses for pilgrims) and historic cities and towns to encounter. The most important stops are to visit the cathedrals of **Burgos** and **León**. The route also passes by **Santo Domingo de la Calzada** (cathedral and pilgrim hospital), **Fromista** (Romanesque church), **Ponferrada** (medieval bridge and Templar castle) and **O Cebreiro** (9th-century church and ancient stone huts).

Pilgrims of old used to carry a staff with a gourd attached to it and wear a cape and a hat adorned with scallop-shells, the emblem of St James, and these are still the essential accessories of those making their way to Santiago. Nowadays, travellers along the Way are also likely to carry a 'passport' which they can get stamped at various stopping-points to chart their progress.

The end of the journey is the great cathedral at **Santiago de Compostela**. Pilgrims enter through the **Pórtico de la Gloria**, where it is traditional to touch the base of the column on which the figure of St James is carved, in thanksgiving for a safe journey.

THE NORTH

The Levant

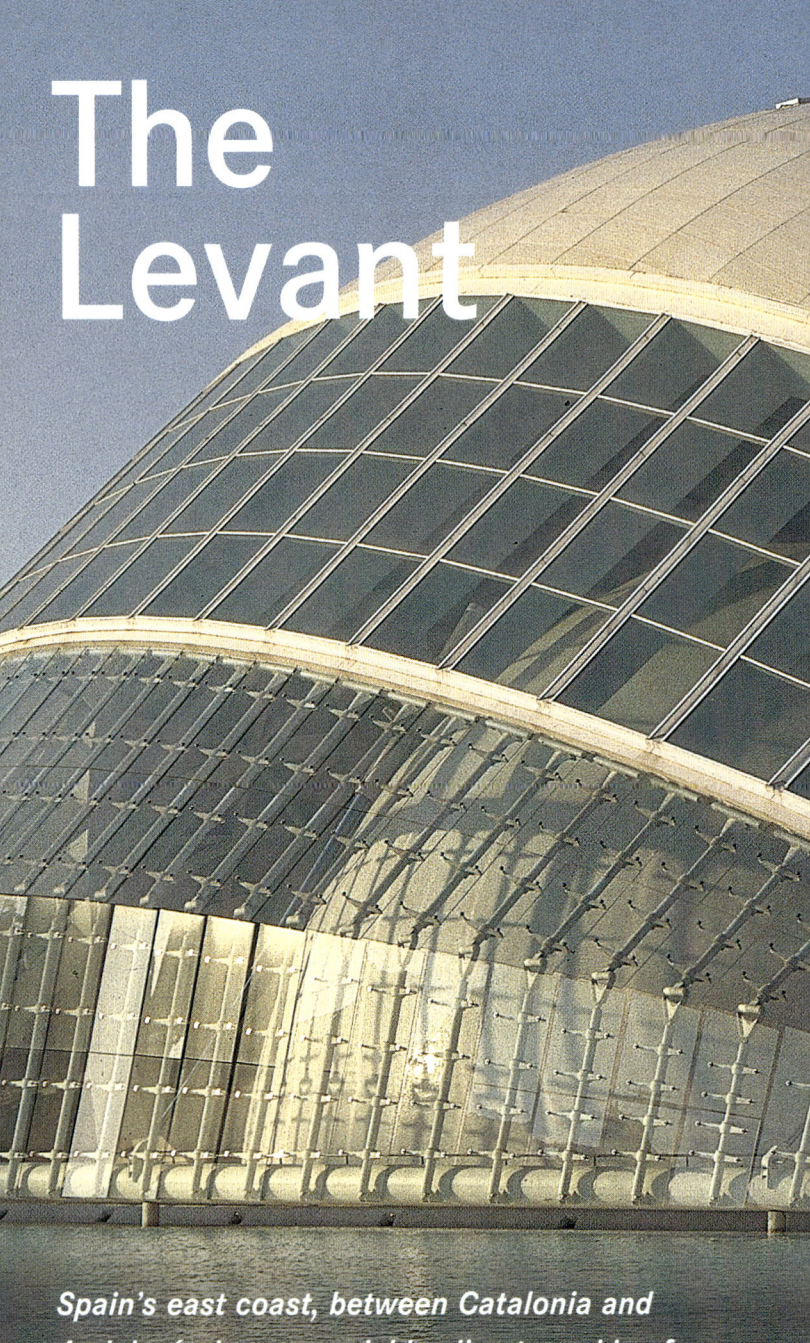

Spain's east coast, between Catalonia and Andalucía, has an enviable climate making for easy living. There's a string of great beaches, especially on the ever-popular Costa Blanca, few

THE LEVANT

of which are crowded or overdeveloped. In the middle of the coast sits the city of Valencia, which is at last getting the attention it deserves. See it now and beat the rush.

THE LEVANT

BEST OF
The Levant

Getting around: the Levant is a term used to describe the two east-coast regions of Valencia and Murcia. There are international airports at Alicante and Valencia, and a smaller one near the Mar Menor. The region divides into coast and mountain, with the coastal motorway (A7) and main road (N332) the principal arteries. Once you get into the hills behind the coast, the driving can be slow-going.

North

0 — 50 km
0 — 25 miles

Mora de Rubielos
Castellón de la Plana
Sagunt
La Albufera
MEDITERRANEAN SEA
Xàtiva
Gandía
Dénia
Xàbia
Guadalest
Calp
Altea
Benidorm
La Vila Joiosa
Elx
Santa Pola
Orihuela
Torrevieja
Mar Menor
Lorca
Cartagena

THE LEVANT

① Valencia

Spain's third city, the home of *paella*, has been undeservedly overlooked by many tourists in the past, but its new City of Arts and Sciences is likely to pull in the crowds. Its nightlife is also an attraction, as is its great March festival of fire. **Pages 166-7**

② Costa Blanca

The Costa Blanca avoids extremes. It's less hectic than the Costa del Sol and not as rugged as the Costa Brava. Most of its resorts have been kept to a manageable size. **Benidorm** is a special case, though – either you'll like it or you won't. **Pages 170-1**

③ Alicante

The port city of Alicante, capital of the Costa Blanca, is overlooked by the Castillo de Santa Bárbara from a 166m (545ft) summit reached by a lift from the seafront. **Page 172**

④ Murcia

A great cathedral is at the heart of the capital of this small region of Spain. Other historic towns and cities to visit include the ancient maritime base of **Cartagena**. **Page 174**

⑤ Peñíscola

See the impregnable seaside castle built by the Knights Templar which was occupied by a renegade pope in the 15th century. **Page 176**

⑥ Morella

This old walled hill town commands the **Maestrazgo**, a mountainous area few people bother to explore. A great chance to get off the main tourist track. **Page 177**

⑦ Teruel and Albarracín

Teruel is a rose-pink city of handsome Mudéjar (Moorish-Gothic) brick archictecture. The walled medieval town of Albarracin is of a similar hue, a delightful jumble of narrow streets and crooked houses. **Pages 178-9**

Tourist information

The main tourist information offices are in the regional capitals of **Valencia** (*Calle de la Paz 48; tel: 96 398 6422, www.comunidad-valenciana.com*) and **Murcia** (*Calle San Cristobál 5; tel: 96 836 6100, www.carm.es*), but there is also one in **Teruel** (*Calle Tomás Nogués 1; tel: 97 860 2279, www.aragon.es*).

THE LEVANT

Valencia

Valencia, Spain's third largest city, is blessed with an abundance of many delights. It is the capital of a prodigiously fertile plain, the huerta, *which grows orange trees and, to the south, the rice used to make Valencia's famous dish,* **paella**. *Much of the produce of the* huerta *ends up on the colourful stalls of the art-nouveau* **Mercado Central** *(Plaza del Mercado Central; open: Mon–Sat), a popular tourist attraction in its own right.*

> **All fiestas show you two things: how dissimilar we are and yet how similar.**
>
> **María Angeles Sánchez, authority on Spanish fiestas**

The first book in Spain was printed here in 1474, and the city's finest buildings date from the end of the Middle Ages. Opposite the central market is the old Gothic silk exchange, the **Lonja de la Seda** (*Plaza del Mercado 31; tel: 96 352 5478; open: Tue–Sat 0930–1400, 1700–1900, Sun 0930–1400*), decorated with carved gargoyles outside. Inside, the stellate-vaulting of the ceiling is supported on gracefully spiralling columns.

A network of narrow streets brings you to the **catedral** (*Plaza de la Virgen; open: daily*), built in a mixture of styles so that it has one Gothic, one baroque and one Romanesque doorway. A unique court meets outside the **Apostles Doorway** (the one leading into the Plaza de la Virgen) at noon each Thursday: the **Water Tribunal** meets in public in the open air and has been adjudicating on disputes over the use of water in the *huerta* for the last thousand years. In a chapel inside the cathedral is a gold and agate cup said to be the **Holy Grail**.

> **One of the noblest cities in all Spaine, situate in a large Vega or Valley … Here are the strongest silks, the sweetest wines, the excellentest almonds, the best oils and beautifullest Females, for the prime courtesans in Madrid and elsewhere are had hence … They commonly call it the second Italy, which made the Moors … to think that Paradise was in that part of the Heavens which hung over this City.**
>
> **James Howell on Valencia,** *Instructions for Forreine Travel* **(17th century)**

THE LEVANT

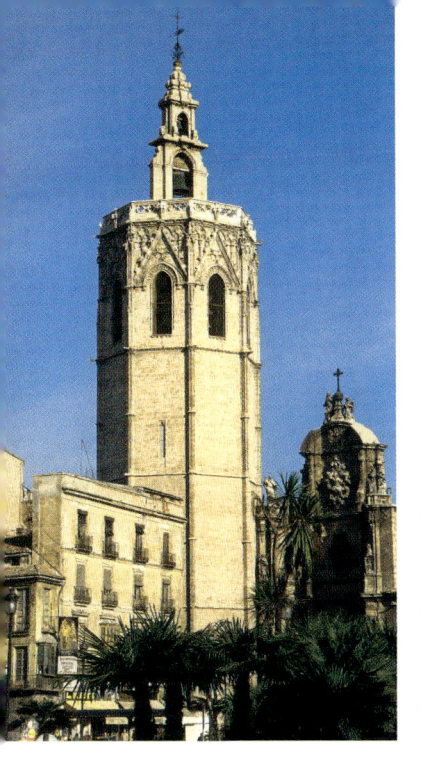

For a splendid view of the city, climb the cathedral's octagonal belltower, the **Miguelete**. The Miguelete is one of the city's two key landmarks; the other is the **Torres de Serrano**, a gateway which survived the destruction of the medieval walls in the 1870s.

Perhaps the best museum in Valencia is the **Museo Nacional de Cerámica** (*Poeta Querol; open: Tue–Sat 1000–1400, 1600–1800, Sun 1000–1400; £*), which is housed in the rococo palace of the Marqués de dos Aguas, designed by **Hipólito Rovira**. It houses a collection of 5 000 pieces of pottery, including works by **Picasso** and a complete traditional Valencian tiled kitchen. The fine arts museum **Museo de Sant Pius V** (*San Pio V 9; tel: 96 360 5793; open: Tue–Sat 1000–1400, 1600–1800, Sun 1000–1400; £*), across the dry bed of the Rio Turia (diverted to avoid flooding), is also worth a visit. It contains 15th-century altarpieces and a self-portrait by **Velázquez**.

If anything is going to put Valencia on the tourist map of Spain once and for all – if one discounts the appearance before tens of millions of viewers worldwide of the city's football team in the final of the European Champions League in 2000 – it will be the **Ciutat de les Arts i Ciencias** ('City of Arts and Sciences'; *tel: 90 210 0031, www.cac.es; check opening times before visiting*), a hugely ambitious project which, when it is complete, will include a science museum and an oceanographic park. The eye-shaped IMAX cinema, with a mechanically opening and closing 'eyelid', has already proved hugely popular.

In March, Valencia stages the extraordinary **Fallas** festival in which gigantic *papier-mâché* sculptures are burnt to the ground. Indeed, all year round the city has a renowned nightlife because of its equable climate.

Tourist information: Plaza del Ayuntamiento 1. Tel: 96 351 0417.

THE LEVANT

South of Valencia

La Albufera

15km (9 miles) south of Valencia, on the V15. Tourist information: Racó de L'Olla. Tel: 96 162 0172.

A short way south of Valencia is the freshwater lake of the Albufera, cut off from the sea by a sandbar and surrounded on the other three sides by paddy fields. One of Europe's prime wetlands, it's a good area for birdwatching: the lake, reed-beds and islands are a stopping-off point for around 260 species of birds including egrets and flamingos.

Although now declared a *parque natural* ('natural park'), the life of the Albufera is being threatened by industry, tourism and modern farming methods. But it remains a picturesque area, especially at sunset. You'll still see several of Valencia's traditional farmhouses – *barracas* – with their steeply pitched thatched roofs, and perhaps the odd *albuferenc*, a flat-bottomed boat traditionally used by rice farmers.

Xàtiva (Játiva)

60km (37 miles) southwest of Valencia, off the N340. Tourist information: Alameda de Jaume I 50. Tel: 96 273 3346.

This historic town founded by the Phoenicians has a magnificent ruined castle (*open: Tue–Sun 1030–1400, 1630–1900, to 1800 in winter*) running along the high ridge above it, once the most important fortress under the Crown of Aragón. Xàtiva was on the losing side, that of Archduke Charles of Austria, in the War of the Spanish Succession. In

Tip

The War of the Spanish Succession (1701–14) was triggered by Louis XIV's acceptance of the Spanish throne on behalf of his grandson, Felipe V of Spain, in the process breaking the Partition Treaty of 1700, which stipulated that the rightful heir was Archduke Charles of Austria. In addition to Spain, Austria and France, the long war involved the Netherlands, Portugal, Denmark and Britain. Peace was eventually agreed with the Treaties of Utrecht and Rastatt, Felipe V went on to found the Spanish branch of the Bourbon dynasty, and, as part of the deal, Britain was given Gibraltar.

THE LEVANT

revenge, the victor, Felipe V, burnt the town and renamed it San Felipe, and so it was called until the 19th century when it reclaimed its Moorish name and exacted its revenge in turn by hanging Felipe's portrait upside down upstairs in the **Museo Municipal** (*Carrer de la Corretgeria; open: Tue–Fri 1100–1400, 1600–1800, Sat–Sun 1100–1400; £*). Several ancient churches and numerous stately buildings have been preserved in the old town.

Gandía

60km (37 miles) south of Valencia, on the A7 or N332. Tourist information: Avda Marqués de Campo (opposite railway station). Tel: 96 287 7788.

Gandia was the home of the notorious **Borja** ('Borgia' in Italian) **family**. When Rodrigo Borja was elected Pope Alexander VI in 1492 he was already the father of several illegitimate children by a Roman woman, Giovanna Catenei ('Vanozza'), among them the notorious Cesare (1476–1507), who was suspected of murdering his elder brother, and Lucrezia (1480–1519), married three times to aid her father's ambitions and who is said to have committed incest with her father and her brother. As a result the Borja (or Borgia) name has become a byword for immorality.

Rodrigo's great grandson, however, born in Gandia in 1510, went some way towards redeeming the family name when he was canonised as **St Francis Borja** in 1671. After his wife died he had renounced worldly pleasures and joined the Jesuit order. The **Palacio Ducal** (*Santo Duque 1; tel: 96 287 1203; guided tours only: Mon–Sat 1000–1200, 1700–1900 on the hour, to 1800 in winter; £*), where he was born, is now a school run by the Jesuits. Visitors are shown the Gothic courtyard, the richly decorated chambers and the duke's private chapel.

THE LEVANT

Costa Blanca

The Costa Blanca, literally 'White Coast', starts in the north at Denia, originally a Greek colony. The modern town, beneath the castle, is a fishing and ferry port and a bustling holiday resort.

Xàbia (Jávea) is situated between the two capes of San Antonio and de la Nao, and separated from Denia by Mount Mongó. In the 1970s the council imposed a ban on buildings of more than three storeys so there are only three high-rise blocks along Xàbia's Arenales beach. The town centre is a short way inland, huddled around the 16th-century Iglesia de San Bartolomé (*for opening hours, contact Xàbia tourist information office, Plaça del Almirante Bastarreche 24; tel: 96 579 0736*), which was fortified against attack by fitting machicolations over the door from which boiling oil could be tipped over intruders. Much of the old town is built of *tosca* sandstone, which is also seen in country houses hereabouts, incorporated into *nayas*: wide, arcaded terraces, covered over to give areas of well-aired shade which were traditionally used to dry grapes into raisins.

Calp (Calpe) is dominated by a distinctive rocky peak, the Penyal d'Ifach, one of the Costa Blanca's most dramatic sights. It rises 382m (1 253ft) abruptly out of the sea and is now a nature reserve (*visitors' centre: Avda Ejércitos Españoles 66*), home to some 300 species of wild plants. Migrating

THE LEVANT

> *Spanish vitality is so great that it can digest the most awkward extraneous elements.*

V S Pritchett, *The Spanish Temper* (1954)

birds use it as a landmark. The views from the top are astonishing; on a clear day you can see Ibiza, about 90km (55 miles) away.

The old town of **Altea** clusters around a hill crowned by a blue-domed church, and is popular with artists; just 7km (4 miles) down the coast lies **Benidorm**, which can come as a shock to the system after Altea. The package-holiday resort of today resembles Manhattan more than the obscure fishing village it was in the 1950s. It is estimated that there is more accommodation in Benidorm than in any other resort on the Mediterranean. From the **Balcón del Mediterráneo**, a small park and viewpoint, you can see both Benidorm's beaches (**Levante** and **Poniente**) and its island shaped like a slice of cake diving into the sea. **Terra Mítica** (*tel: 90 202 0220, www.terramiticapark.com*), the biggest theme park on Spain's Mediterranean coast, has just opened outside Benidorm.

La Vila Joiosa, 11km (7 miles) south of Benidorm, has brightly painted houses along its river bank; it is said that they are like that so that fishermen can identify their own houses when out at sea.

South of Alicante, the Costa Blanca is less attractive, with the exception of the salt pans outside **Santa Pola**, where flamingos can be seen. The most commercially important salt pans in Europe are further down the coast at **Torrevieja**.

Tourist information: Explanada de España 2, Alacant (Alicante). Tel: 96 520 0000.

Guadalest

12km (7½ miles) inland from Benidorm on the CV755 via Callosa d'en Sarrià.

This pretty, unspoilt village within the walls of a Moorish fortress is a popular place of excursion for anyone spending their holidays in or near Benidorm. The entrance to the village is through a short sloping pedestrian tunnel cut into the rock over a thousand years ago. From the old castle there is a splendid view of the whole valley, shaped into terraced fields planted with almond trees. The church belfry is precariously and picturesquely sited by itself on an outcrop of rock.

THE LEVANT

Alicante and south

Alicante (Alacant)

Tourist information: Explanada de España 2. Tel: 96 520 0000.

Situated on a natural harbour with large beaches nearby, Alicante is both a commercial port and the tourist capital of the Costa Blanca. The Greeks called it *Akra Leuka* – the 'white citadel' (from which the title 'Costa Blanca' derives) – because of its sunny climate, and the Romans, *Lucentum* – the 'city of light'.

From the **Castillo de Santa Bárbara** (*Playa del Postiguet; open: daily Apr–Sept, 1000–2000, Oct–Mar, 1000–1900*), on the 166m (545ft) summit of Mount Benacantil, there are panoramic views over the city and its bay, including the Isla de Tabarca. You can get to the castle on foot (a long walk) or by car, or take the lift from Postiguet beach.

The *ayuntamiento* (town hall; *Plaza del Ayuntamiento; open: Mon–Fri 0900–1400*) is down below, as far down as it is possible to get, because a marker at the bottom of the stairs indicates the sea level by which all altitudes in Spain are judged. This 17th-century baroque building contains period paintings. Particularly worth seeing is the **Salón Azul**, with its mirrored gallery.

Elx (Elche)

25km (15½ miles) southwest of Alicante, on the A7 or N340. Tourist information: Parque Municipal. Tel: 96 545 2747.

In Spain, Elx is synonymous with its forest of palm trees, planted by the Carthaginians around 300 BC and watered by an irrigation system laid out in the 10th century. It is said that in the 18th century Elx had a million palm trees; now there are just over half that number, but Elx is still Europe's only date-producer. The **Huerto del Cura** (*Porta de la Morera 49; tel: 96 545 1936; open: Tue–Sun 0900–2030; £*) encloses an area of palm groves which is

THE LEVANT

also planted with citrus, carob, pomegranate trees and exotic plants and cacti. Some of the palms in it are more than 200 years old.

The Basílica de Santa María (*open: Tue–Sun 0700–1330, 1530–2100*) in the middle of town is a 17th-century baroque church which was built for a purpose: it is the auditorium in which a medieval miracle play, the Misteri d'Elx, is performed in August, complete with special effects.

Orihuela

35km (22 miles) southwest of Elx, off the A7. Tourist information: Francisco Die 25. Tel: 96 530 2747.

Orihuela, situated among orange and lemon groves and market gardens, was once a much richer city. In 1488 the 'Catholic Monarchs' Fernando and Isabel stopped here to collect men and money for the final struggle against the Moors defending Granada.

The catedral (*open: Mon–Fri 1030–1330, 1600–1800; £*), its finest building, has three doors: two Gothic (Cadenas and Loreto) and one Renaissance (Anunciación). There is also some ornamental grille work and a choir by Juan Bautista Borja, and a peaceful and picturesque Romanesque cloister outside, moved here from a convent that suffered damage in the Civil War. In the cathedral museum you can see one of Velázquez's most famous paintings, *The Temptation of St Thomas Aquinas*.

The Colegio de Santo Domingo is now a school, but it housed a university until the 18th century. The building has an interesting cloister and a refectory with 18th-century ornamental tiles from Manises (*ask permission to visit at the door*). Nearby is one of the old city gates, the Puerta de la Olma.

And why not visit the Museo de Semana Santa ('Easter Week Museum'; *Plaza de la Merced; open: Tue 1000–1300, 1630–1900, Sun 1000–1300*)? Among the gilded floats (by Salzillo and other artists) is the 'Diablesa', the image of a she-devil carved in 1688 by Fray Nicolás de Bussi. Until the museum was opened it had to be kept in the public library because no church would have such a profane object.

Murcia

Murcia

Tourist information: Plano de San Francisco. Tel: 96 821 9801.

Founded in the 9th century by the Moors, Murcia is now the capital of one of Spain's smaller autonomous regions. It took over from Cartagena in importance in the 13th century when the coast was plagued by pirate attacks.

The **catedral** (*open: daily 1000–1300, 1700–1900*) is the city's essential sight. It was originally built in the 14th century but has a largely Renaissance and baroque exterior. The **Capilla de los Vélez** inside is sumptuously late Gothic. The tomb of Alfonso X is in the Capilla Mayor, and the museum (*open: daily 1000–1300, 1700–1900; £*) contains a splendid **Gothic altarpiece**.

On Calle de la Trapería is the **Casino** (*open: daily 0900–2300, closed July and Aug; £*), a gentlemen's club rather than a gambling den. It is lavishly decorated; see especially the **Arab Patio**, the **ladies' cloakroom** (which has a painted ceiling) and the **romantic ballroom**.

Murcia's most famous sons are the statesman **Count of Floridablanca**, who helped stabilise the Spanish economy in the late 18th century, and the sculptor **Francisco Salzillo**. The latter is remembered in the **Museo Salzillo** (*San Andrés 1; open Tue–Sat 0930–1300, 1600–1900, Sun 1100–1300; £*), which contains several of his polychromed religious images.

Lorca

50km (31 miles) southwest of Murcia, on the N340. Tourist information: Palacio de los Guevara, Calle Lope de Gisbert. Tel: 96 846 6157.

Lorca, something of an oasis among arid sierras, was a frontier town in the time of the Romans and the Moors. It prospered in the 17th century, when many fine buildings were erected. In the Plaza Mayor are several buildings with baroque façades, notably the town hall, built in two parts between 1677 and 1739 and later connected by an arch that spans the street. On the other side of the square is the 16th-century **Colegiata de San Patricio** (*contact tourist*

THE LEVANT

information office for opening hours), the only church in Spain dedicated to St Patrick. Its interior is mainly baroque. The **Palacio de los Guevara** has a splendid carved doorway.

The Roman **Columna Milenaria**, on the corner between Calle Corredera and Plaza San Vicente, marked the distance between Lorca and Cartagena on the *Via Heraclea*.

Cartagena

Tourist information: Plaza del Almirante Bastarreche. Tel: 96 850 6483.

> " New Carthage is by far the most powerful of all the cities in this country ... "
>
> **Strabo, Greek geographer (c 60 BC–AD 20)**

This ancient port was founded in 223 BC by the Carthaginians, after whom it is named. It is now an important naval base, as well as a commercial port. Near the harbour stands **El Submarino Peral**, an early craft launched in 1888 – just too late to be a first. The **Museo Nacional de Arqueología Submarina** (*Carretera Faro de Navidad; open: Tue–Sun 1000–1500; £*) has an interesting collection of underwater finds, mainly Greek and Roman jars. And there is a most unusual monument for Spain here too: the **Muralla Bizantina** (*Calle Nueva; open: Tue–Sat 1100–1300, 1730–2100*), a Byzantine wall built between AD 589 and 590.

You can get a good view of Cartagena from **Castillo de la Concepción**, an ancient fort set in public gardens. Nearby are the ruins of the old Romanesque cathedral destroyed in the Civil War.

Mar Menor

20km (12½ miles) northeast of Cartagena.

The Mar Menor is a large saltwater lagoon all but cut off from the Mediterranean by a long sandy strip, La Manga, along which stride the high-rise buildings of a tourist resort. The landward side of the Mar Menor, however, is pretty. **Santiago de la Ribera**, for instance, has delightful painted wooden jetties, and from here you can take a trip to two of the six islands in the lagoon (*for details, contact the tourist information office in Santiago de la Ribera*).

THE LEVANT

North of Valencia

Sagunt (Sagunto)

25km (15 1/2 miles) north of Valencia, on the A7 or N340. Tourist information: Plaza Cronista Chabret. Tel: 96 266 2213.

The old Roman town of *Saguntum* unwillingly played a key role in Spain's ancient history when the Carthaginian general Hannibal – of elephants fame – sacked the town, thus provoking the wrath of Rome. The incident sparked off the Second Punic War, which ended in Rome's colonisation of the Iberian peninsula. The town's chief Roman remain is the **Teatro Romano** (*open: Tue–Sat 1000–1400, 1600–1900, to 1800 in winter, Sun 1000–1400; £*), in a natural depression on the hillside. Above it is a ruined castle, an accumulation of Iberian, Carthaginian, Roman and Moorish remains.

Peñíscola

70km (43 1/2 miles) northwest of Castellón, on the A7 or N340. Tourist information: Paseo Marítimo. Tel: 96 448 9392.

The old town of Peñíscola clusters around the base of an impregnable castle, the **Castell del Papa Luna** (*Calle Castillo; open: daily; £*), built in the 13th century on a promontory surrounded on three sides by the sea. It is thought to be the work of the **Knights Templar**, and is now well restored.

The fortress was the residence of the rebellious 15th-century pope Benedict XIII, also known as Pope Luna, whose study is in one tower. Benedict was born Pedro de Luna and elected pope during the Great Schism that split the Christian Church. He was branded an anti-pope in 1409 and withdrew from Avignon to Peñíscola to await a summons that never came. He died here, in 1422, a nonagenarian, obstinate to the last and even naming his own successor as pope.

Part of the film ***El Cid*** was shot here, on the long beach to the north with the castle – fitted with fake battlements – in the background.

THE LEVANT

Morella

65km (40 miles) inland, northwest of Vinaròs, on the N232. Tourist information: Plaza de San Miguel 3. Tel: 96 417 3032.

Some 1 000m (3 300ft) up, surging out of the landscape on its own rocky outcrop and protected by an unbroken ring of medieval walls, Morella cuts a dramatic profile. It's even better when you get up close: within the wall are endless steps and tapering alleys overhung by projecting half-timbered first storeys and lined with solid 15th- and 16th-century **Gothic mansions**.

In Calle de la Virgen, parallel to the main street, a plaque on the wall tells the story of a miracle. The plaque marks the house in which St Vincent Ferrer reconstituted a boy who had been chopped up and put in the cooking pot by his mother, who had no other meat to offer the saint for supper. St Vincent restored the boy to life, except for one little finger which his mother had eaten to see if it was well salted.

At the end of this street is the **Basílica de Santa María la Mayor**, which has a raised choir-loft reached by a magnificently carved **stone spiral staircase**. The castle (*open: daily May–Aug, 1030–1930, Sept–Apr, 1030–1830; £*) at the very top of the town is an impregnable fortress which exploits numerous caves as extra chambers. Go up to the battlements that crown the hill; from there you get a good overview of the countryside around Morella. This is the **Maestrazgo**, an upland area spread between the provinces of Castellón and Teruel that has been dubbed the 'Gothic Mountain' for its wealth of medieval architecture.

Tip

In Spain, there is a saint to serve every human need. Every trade has its own patron saint and every person has his or her 'saint's day'. There is a saint to help you find a partner, one who gives good milk to breast-feeding mothers, and another who, apart from making your business prosper, will, in return for a small offering, help you to scoop the lottery jackpot.

THE LEVANT

Teruel

Teruel is an inland city, almost 1 000m (3 300ft) up on the meseta *('plateau'). In the Civil War it was the site of a crucial battle during which freezing temperatures contributed to heavy casualties on both sides, but its main claim to fame is its* **Mudéjar brick architecture**. *The city has several towers of ornamental brickwork decorated with white and green tiles, with arches at street level, built between the 12th and 16th centuries; the two most appealing are* **San Martín** *(Plaza Perez Prado) and* **San Salvador** *(Calle El Salvador).*

The **catedral** (*open: daily; £*) combines Romanesque and Islamic elements. It has a coffered ceiling decorated with Gothic paintings, a 13th-century tower and a lantern dome with glazed tiles.

In the **Iglesia de San Pedro** (*open: Tue–Sun 1000–1300, 1600–2000; £*) are the tombs of the **Lovers of Teruel**, who lie on display below marble statues (designed by Juan de Avalos) the hands of which reach out for each other but do not quite meet. There are many versions of their legend, but the essence is as follows. Isabel de Segura, a beautiful girl from a wealthy family, falls in love with Diego de Marcilla, a second son from a humble background. Isabel's father forbids the match, but Diego begs Isabel to give him five years to make his fortune. She agrees to wait for him, so Diego goes off to fight the Moors.

Five years pass with no news, so Isabel succumbs to family pressure and weds a man of her class. Diego arrives back in Teruel just after the wedding, rich but mortally wounded from his last battle. He steals into the the newly weds'

THE LEVANT

> *Los Amantes de Teruel: tonta ella y tonto el! ('The Lovers of Teruel: silly him and silly her!')*
>
> **Spanish popular saying**

bedroom, wakes Isabel and asks her for a last kiss. She refuses him, and he collapses and dies. The next day at Diego's funeral, Isabel, dressed in black, flings herself on Diego's body, kissing his lips and thereby complying with his last request; she then dies on the spot of grief and remorse, with her arms wrapped around him. Her family realise what has happened and decide to bury the lovers together.

Tourist information: Tomás Nogués 1. Tel: 97 860 2279.

Mora de Rubielos

40km (25 miles) southeast of Teruel, on the A232.

This restored monumental town in the Lower Maestrazgo is dominated by one of the best-preserved castles in Aragón (*contact the tourist information office on Calle Diputación for opening hours – summer only*). It was built in the 13th and 14th centuries but effectively rebuilt in the 15th century. In the fortified **Colegiata** (*open for services*) you can see chapels decorated with tiles from Manises, and nearby there is an elegant black fountain depicting playing dolphins.

Some 10km (6 miles) to the southeast you will find **Rubielos de Mora**, worth exploring for its stone and timber buildings and balconied houses.

Albarracín

40km (25 miles) northwest of Teruel, on a minor road.

This walled medieval town, a cluster of pink buildings, stands on a cliff above the Río Guadalaviar, at the edge of the unfrequented Montes Universales. With its alleys and small squares, it is a picturesque place to stroll around. The Moorish ramparts that surround it date from the 11th century or earlier, and the 16th-century cathedral has a handsome belfry and inside a Renaissance wooden altarpiece carved with scenes from the life of St Peter. There are many picturesque corners of the town and details to observe, but look out especially for the wedge-shaped, slightly unbalanced **Juliana's House**, which stands beside a gateway.

THE LEVANT

Eating and drinking

Restaurants

Dársena
Alicante. Marina Deportiva Muelle. Tel: 96 520 7589. ££. An excellent restaurant on the seafront with a magnificent selection of rice dishes as well as fish and seafood.

Los Habaneros
Cartagena. San Diego 60. Tel: 96 850 5250. ££. In a well-known hotel, this restaurant serves local delicacies such as fine green asparagus and *tarta de sesos* (literally 'brain pie').

L'Obrer
Benimantell. Carretera de Alcoi. Tel: 96 588 5088. ££. This family restaurant, in a small village adjacent to Guadalest (inland from Benidorm), serves good hearty mountain food, based on local meats and vegetables.

La Pepica
Valencia. Avenida Neptuno 6. Tel: 96 371 0366. ££. One of the oldest of the line of traditional *paella* restaurants along Valencia's Las Arenas beachfront. It gets busy at weekends as extended families and big groups of friends descend on it for a lingering lunch. It is essential to order your *paella* in advance (specifying how many it is for), which will give you time for a stroll along the promenade or a swim to build up your appetite. Try also **La Rosa** (*Avenida Neptuno 70; tel: 96 371 2076; ££*), and **L'Estimat** (*Avenida Neptuno 16; tel: 96 371 1018; ££*).

El Poblet
Denia. Carretera Las Marinas. Tel: 96 578 4179. ££. Good Valencian cooking, with rice dishes, prawns and other seafood.

Rincón de Pepe
Murcia. Apóstoles 34. Tel: 96 821 2239. ££. Restaurant of national fame specialising in the regional cuisine of Murcia. In summer there are numerous cafés with tables outside on Avda Alfonso X El Sabio.

Paella

Paella *is served all over Spain but it comes originally from Valencia, and this is where you can try the real thing. The traditional* paella *is* paella valenciana *(made with chicken, rabbit and snails), and* paella de mariscos *(with seafood) is also an authentic dish;* paella mixta *is a combination of the two, however, and true* valencianos *will shun this and other careless imitations. The best restaurants – such as La Pepica, listed above – will cook your* paella *to order so that you can eat it the moment it is finished cooking. Other rice specialities of Valencia include* arroz a banda *(rice cooked in fish stock),* arroz negro *(in squid ink) and* arroz al horno *(baked rice).* Fideua *is like seafood* paella *with noodles replacing the rice.*

THE LEVANT

Shopping

What to buy

The souvenir to take home from Valencia is **ceramics**. Manises (near the airport) is famous for its tile manufacturers. **Lladró**, the manufacturer of fine porcelain figures which has devoted fans around the world, has its factory near Valencia.

In Gata de Gorgos, on the Costa Blanca, there is a wide choice of **baskets**, *esparto products* and **crafts** in general, and you can get **glassware** at good prices in Olleria. And if you're going to buy some *jamón serrano*, buy it in Teruel, which has just the right climate and produces some of Spain's best cured ham.

Nightlife

Valencia has a reputation for its carefree nightlife. The balmy climate makes it easy to drift from bar to bar, staying out until dawn or even later. Most of the action is in what the Spanish call *pubs* – fashionable bars with loud music and few seats. In the centre of the city, the old **Barrio del Carmen** is a good hunting-ground for bars where you can hear contemporary music and dance. If you want somewhere more peaceful, the **Cervecería Madrid** (*Abadia de San Martín 10*) is a tranquil, labyrinthine old bar adorned with old posters and a collection of naïve paintings.

In summer, you'll find most of the action moves out to the **Malvarrosa** or **Cabanyal** beaches, or further still to out-of-town discos, the in-places changing every year. On the **Costa Blanca**, most of the nightlife is concentrated in Benidorm and Alicante. **Penelope** and **Star Garden** (*Carretera Alicante-Valencia*) are two of Benidorm's largest discos, standing together on the ring road on the edge of town.

THE LEVANT

PROFILE
Fiestas

Barely a day goes by in Spain without a fiesta going on somewhere. Even the smallest village annually honours its patron saint or the Virgin with a procession or mass pilgrimage, bull-running event, firework display or some bizarre ancestral rite. These traditional celebrations are remarkable spectacles, but they also serve a vital social purpose, reaffirming local identities and giving the populace an annual chance to down tools and let off steam.

The dates of most fiestas in the first half of the year move with Easter. **Carnival**, in February or March, is a time of uninhibited revelry, best seen in **Cádiz**. Soon after, on the night of 19 March, the people of **Valencia** set fire to gigantic monuments, *fallas*, in squares and streets while fire-fighters hose down windows to prevent their panes from cracking with the heat.

THE LEVANT

During Easter Week penitents wearing conical hats push or carry great baroque floats in procession up and down Spain, particularly in **Sevilla**, **Valladolid** and **Murcia**. Straight after Easter, **Sevilla** stages its glitzy **April Fair**, a celebration of horses, flamenco music and all things Andalucian. In **Alcoi**, near the Costa Blanca, meanwhile, they re-enact the battles between Moors and Christians by firing antiquated firearms into the air.

At **Whitsun** (May or June), the hamlet of **El Rocío**, next to the Doñana national park, is besieged by great numbers of people who have travelled in decorated carts to honour a famous image of the Virgin Mary. **Corpus Christi** (also in May or June) sees yet more religious processions, at their best in **Valencia** and **Toledo**.

But most fiestas take place during the high summer months. In **Pamplona's Sanfermines** (*see page 144*), in early July, bulls are let loose in the cordoned-off streets each morning. At the end of August, **Buñol** stages its **Tomatina**, a free-for-all tomato fight involving thousands of people.

Autumn sees the grape harvest celebrations in **La Rioja** and other wine-producing areas, and the rituals in honour of the dead around 1 November. The last festival of the year is New Year's Eve, when all Spaniards focus on the **Puerta del Sol** in Madrid (*see page 24*) and try to swallow a grape each time the clock there strikes the hour, for good luck in the new year.

THE LEVANT

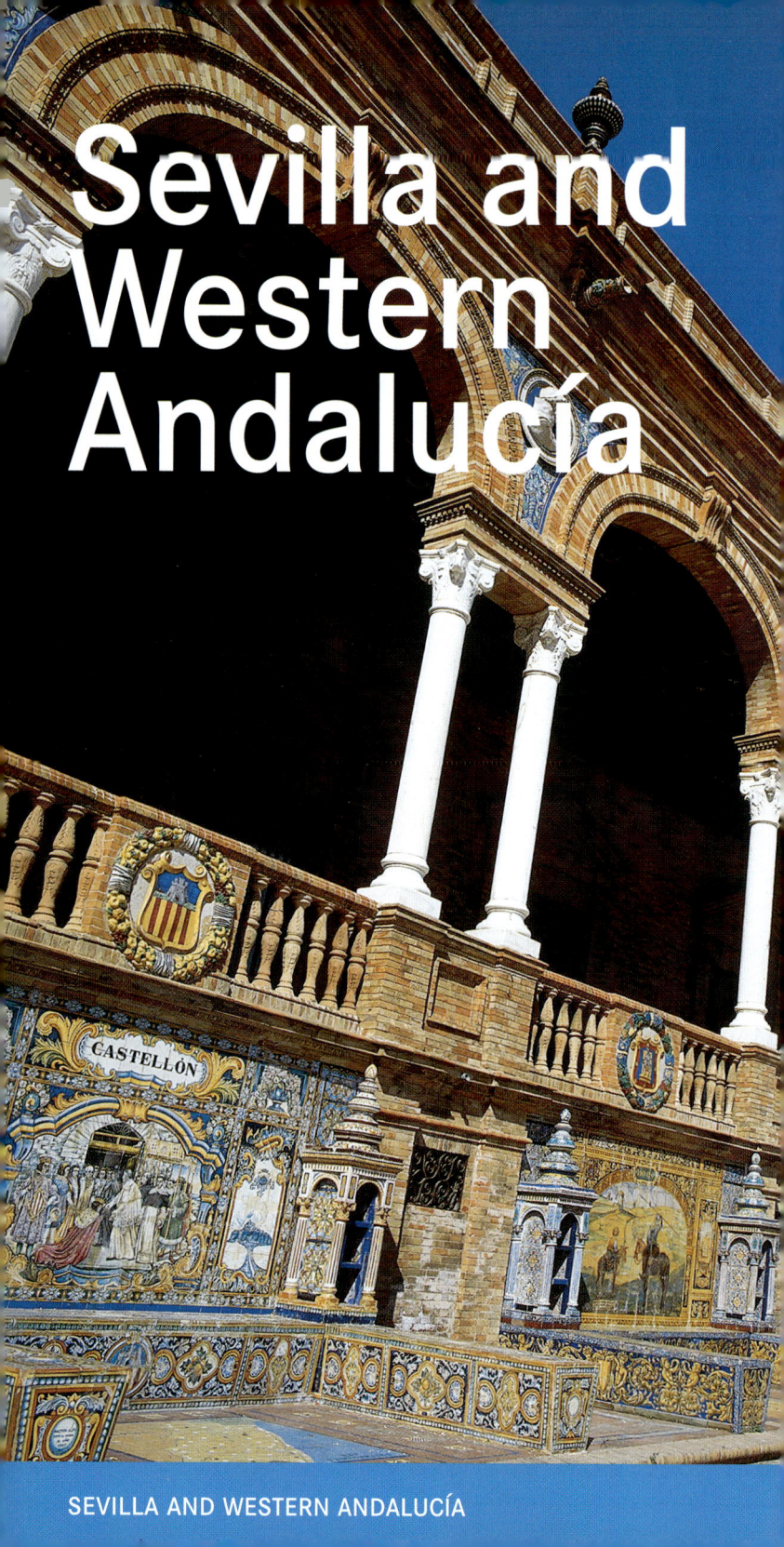

Sevilla and Western Andalucía

SEVILLA AND WESTERN ANDALUCÍA

Many visitors barely venture beyond the two greatest sights of the Andalucían capital, Sevilla: the Reales Alcázares *and the* catedral. *Yet if they do they find a prodigious zest for life on the streets and in the bars. From the city it is but a short hop to one of Europe's best national parks and the immaculate white hill towns of Andalucía.*

SEVILLA AND WESTERN ANDALUCÍA

BEST OF
Sevilla and Western Andalucía

*Getting around: Sevilla has no **metro**, and it doesn't need one. Almost all the main sights lie within a short walk of each other, and on foot is often the fastest way to travel between two points (see street plan on inside back cover). One of the pleasures of the city is to wander aimlessly around such an area – taking sensible precautions against opportunist pickpockets, as you would in any city. Should you need them, there are always buses and taxis.*

SEVILLA AND WESTERN ANDALUCÍA

① Plaza de Toros de la Real Maestranza

Sevilla's bullring is the most famous in the world, usually packed out on days when there is a *corrida*. Take a seat in the sun or shade if you want to see a fight, or visit it at another time if you don't want to see blood being spilled. **Page 188**

② Torre del Oro

There's not much to see, but see it you must. The 'Tower of Gold' on the banks of the Rio Guadalquivir is emblematic of the city. **Page 188**

③ Catedral and La Giralda

A climb to the top of the cathedral's tower, La Giralda, originally a minaret, is obligatory during a stay in Sevilla. The cathedral itself is massive, packed with art and history, and contains the tomb of explorer **Christopher Columbus**. **Page 189**

④ Reales Alcázares

Dating from the 10th century, this is the oldest palace in Europe still in use and one of the two essential sights of Sevilla. Inside are stunningly decorated royal quarters; outside are Renaissance and Romantic gardens. **Pages 190–1**

⑤ Parque Nacional de Doñana

One of Europe's prime national parks covers the marshes at the mouth of the Rio Guadalquivir, southwest of Sevilla. These wetlands are home to rich birdlife which can be observed from hides or on guided 4-wheel-drive tours. **Pages 196–7**

⑥ Jerez de la Frontera

Go sherry-tasting in the bodegas where the stuff is painstakingly made. The city is also famous for its **performing horses**. **Page 198**

⑦ Los Pueblos Blancos

One of the archetypal images of Andalucia is its brilliant white towns clustered on steep mountainsides, their narrow streets full of details and the window sills of houses adorned with flowers. Places such as **Arcos de la Frontera**, **Grazalema** and **Zahara de la Sierra** live up to this reputation. **Page 199**

Tourist information

Paseo de las Delicias 9, Sevilla; tel: 95 423 4465; www.sevilla.org.

Travel tip

For leisurely sightseeing in Sevilla, there is a special tourist bus *which does the rounds of the main sights. More exclusively, you can hire a* horse-drawn carriage *near the Giralda. Beyond the city,* coaches *will take you to larger places such as Cádiz and Jerez de la Frontera, but for the smaller places, for example, the White Towns, you will need to hire a car. Several motorways sprout from Sevilla, the most useful being the A4 to Cádiz (and the White Towns) and the NIV to Carmona, which continues to Córdoba.*

SEVILLA AND WESTERN ANDALUCÍA

Sevilla: the riverside and the cathedral

Plaza de Toros de la Real Maestranza

Paseo de Cristóbal Colón. Tel: 95 422 4577. Open: daily 0930–1400, 1500–1900; on days of bullfights 1000–1500. £.

Sevilla's bullring is easily the world's most famous and quite possibly the most beautiful. The vast ochre and white structure near the river was completed in the last half of the 18th century for the Real Maestranza de Caballería (Royal Equestrian Society) and became Spain's leading venue for bullfighting in the early 19th century. Bizet made it world famous in his opera **Carmen**. The immense ring seats 14,000 people and is generally full at every *corrida*.

The 20-minute tour of the bullring and its associated museum bears a strong resemblance to official tours of old churches, with reverential viewing of faded costumes, dramatic oil paintings and the heads of bulls. You will also see the *enfermería,* where wounded matadors are treated, and the poignant chapel, where they pray before fights.

Torre del Oro

Open: Tue–Fri 1000–1400; Sat–Sun 1100–1400. £.

This tower located on the riverbank north of **Puente de San Telmo** was built in 1220 by the Almohads as part of the walled defences of the city, linking up with the **Reales Alcázares**. Its name, 'Tower of Gold', possibly referred to the gilded tiles that used to clad its walls, or to the treasures brought from the Americas, which used to be unloaded here.

SEVILLA AND WESTERN ANDALUCÍA

> *The Spaniard sometimes appears to be indifferent to suffering of all kinds, his own included. But if you see an especially thin horse you will notice that its owner is equally thin. You may think too many hungry cats prowl the streets of Spanish villages. The reason for this is that Spaniards refuse to kill them. Where we drown unwanted kittens the Spaniard lets them fend for themselves, feeling that everything has a right to live – if it can …*

Delano Ames, introduction to *Spain*

Catedral and La Giralda

Plaza Virgen de los Reyes. Open: Mon–Sat 1100–1700; Sun 1400–1800. £.

Sevilla's cathedral was completed in 1507 on the site of the main Almohad mosque. It measures a massive 160m by 140m (525ft by 460ft) – only St Peter's in Rome and St Paul's in London have more floor space.

> *It is recorded that those who planned Seville Cathedral said: 'We shall build so mighty an edifice that future generations will marvel and think us mad'.*

Delano Ames, introduction to *Spain*

The cathedral's five naves and innumerable chapels are a **treasure trove** of art and history. On the north side, the Capilla de San Antonio has an image of the saint by **Murillo**, before which young women often pray for boyfriends; **Columbus** and other explorers often prayed in the Capilla de la Virgen de la Antigua on the south side before embarking on their voyages. The explorer's tomb stands nearby. The Gothic *retablo* ('altarpiece') on the main altar is believed to be the largest in the world, with more than a thousand Biblical figures in carved, gilded and polychromed wood.

The 90m (295ft) brick tower on the east side of the cathedral, **La Giralda**, was originally the minaret of the mosque. Its elegant proportions and fine detailing stand out from the cathedral. It is one of Sevilla's most prized monuments, and the bronze weathervane representing faith, *El Giraldillo*, has *de facto* become the civic symbol. Ramps permit an easy climb to the belltower for views of the city and a bird's-eye perspective on the cathedral itself.

SEVILLA AND WESTERN ANDALUCÍA

Sevilla: around the Reales Alcázares

Archivo de las Indias

Plaza Triunfo. Open: Mon–Fri 1000–1300.

The 'Archive of the Indies' was built between 1584 and 1598 and stands testament to the pre-eminent role Sevilla played in the colonisation and exploitation of the Americas. It is the work of **Juan de Herrera**, the architect of El Escorial (*see page 50*), and it was originally a commercial exchange.

It was Carlos III who, in 1785, collected together all documents relating to the New World. The millions of written pages and maps in the archives include letters from **Christopher Columbus**, the *conquistador* **Hernan Cortés** and the author of *Don Quixote*, **Miguel de Cervantes**.

Reales Alcázares (or Alcázar)

Open: Mon–Sat 0930–1900; Sun 0930–1700; closed Mon in winter. £.

Since the king of Spain stays here when he visits Sevilla, the Alcázar can claim to be the oldest palace in Europe still in use. The original fort was constructed by the Moors in the 10th century, with palaces added as the region prospered. After 1248, the Alcázar became the primary residence of several Spanish monarchs, including **Fernando III**, who recaptured Sevilla, and his son, **Alfonso X**, who constructed the Gothic chambers now called the **Salones de Carlos V**.

The palace is one of the defining works of the **Mudéjar (Moorish-Gothic) style**, synthesising 400 years of Iberian Muslim architectural tradition. Visitors enter through the **Patio del León**, part of the garrison of the 11th-century Moorish palace, which leads into the larger **Patio de la Montería**, central to the entire complex. This courtyard serves as an anteroom for admiring the façade of the **Palacio de Don Pedro** directly ahead. The most spectacular of the public rooms of the palace is the **Salón de Embajadores** ('Hall of the Ambassadors'). The centre of the private quarters, the small **Patio de las Muñecas**, is adorned with filigree carving.

On another side of the Patio de la Montería are two 15th-century palace additions: the **Salón del Almirante**, hung with **Goya tapestries**, and the **Sala de Audiencias**, which displays a model of Columbus's flagship, the ***Santa María***, and the famous 16th-century altarpiece ***Virgen de los Navegantes***. To one side of the Alcázar are extensive gardens in both Renaissance and Romantic styles.

Hospital de los Venerables

Plaza Venerables Sacerdotes. Open: daily 1000–1400, 1600–2000. £.

Recently restored as a cultural centre, this 17th-century building was originally a home for elderly priests. From the central sunken patio, stairs lead to the upper floor which is used as an exhibition gallery, along with the infirmary and the cellar. The hospital church contains a wealth of baroque treasures and splendid frescos by **Juan Valdés Leal** and his son **Lucas Valdés**, including a very effective *trompe-l'oeil* in the sacristy depicting *The Triumph of the Cross* (by Valdés senior).

SEVILLA AND WESTERN ANDALUCÍA

Sevilla: Santa Cruz and Triana

Barrio de Santa Cruz

After the reconquest of Sevilla, Fernando III brought in Jews to help administer the royal palace. They settled in the maze of streets that spread out from the cathedral and Alcázar. Although the streets nearest the cathedral are lined with restaurants and shops, the old *barrio* (or 'quarter') still retains a certain charm with its whitewashed houses with potted geraniums hanging in windows and from roof ledges along the narrow, twisting streets.

Specific sites within the *barrio* include the **Museo de Murillo** (*Santa Teresa 8; open: Tue–Sat 1000–1400, 1700–2000, Sun 1000–1400*), the house where the painter **Bartolomé Murillo** (1617–82) lived at the end of his life, and the **Hospital de los Venerables** (*see page 191*).

Casa de Pilatos

Plaza de Pilatos. Open: daily 0900–1300, 1700–1900. £–££.

One of the city's finest mansions, on the edge of Barrio Santa Cruz, was commissioned by the governor of Andalucia, Don Pedro Enriquez, after his son, the **Marqués de Tarifa**, made a pilgrimage to Jerusalem in 1519. The Marqués made measurements of the path Jesus took from Pilate's house to Golgotha, then made similar marks in Sevilla that are still followed by the religious brotherhoods on their penitential processions during Semana Santa ('Easter Week'). The family palace, naturally, stands in for Pilate's residence.

The house is a fabulous hybrid of Gothic, Renaissance and Mudéjar styles. After the Civil War the Medinaceli ducal family reclaimed this ancestral home and restored it to its original splendour. Family members still occupy some chambers of the upper level, so tours of that section are strictly guided. There are beautiful Renaissance gardens too.

SEVILLA AND WESTERN ANDALUCÍA

Calle de la Sierpes

The pedestrianised Calle de la Sierpes, reputedly named after its serpentine course, is the commercial heart of Sevilla. Many of its shops sell more expensive souvenir items, such as mantillas, flamenco costumes, painted fans and castanets, and it is dotted with small booths authorised to sell tickets for bullfights. There are only plaques to mark two significant sites: the jail where **Cervantes** is thought to have conceived *Don Quixote* while locked up for embezzling tax revenues, and the erstwhile gardens of **Nicolás Monardes** where the first tomatoes, potatoes, tobacco and castor-bean plants from the New World were grown. The district also boasts a wonderful **baroque town hall** on Plaza de San Francisco.

Barrio de Triana

Southwest of the city centre, across the Río Guadalquivir, Triana is the traditional gypsy quarter, one of the birthplaces of **flamenco** and the cradle of many great bullfighters. It is now principally a working-class district distinguished by its workshops making decorative tiles. These *alfarerías* are concentrated along Calle San Jorge and surrounding streets, where tailors producing flamenco garb are also found.

The ceramics industry is more than 2 000 years old, originally producing amphorae to transport oil and wine in Roman times. The ceramic tradition continued to flourish during the Moorish centuries, when decorative tiles in blue, white, green and black came to be known as *azulejos*. The interiors of most buildings in Triana (indeed, throughout Sevilla) are abundantly lined with these tiles. The painted tiles depicting scenes and religious images are an 18th-century development.

The riverfront at the foot of **Puente Isabel II**, the so-called 'Puerto de Triana', has a concentration of *cervecerías* (bars serving beer) and *marisquerías* (bars serving seafood) that set up tables all along the river wall during warm weather. Further east along the river, approaching **Puente de San Telmo**, the banks are occupied by the terraced gardens of restaurants offering great views back across the river. Halfway between these two bridges, a small chapel houses the image of the **Esperanza de Triana**, a representation of the Virgin which during Sevilla's Easter Week processions becomes a rival to another holy statue, the **Virgen de la Esperanza Macarena**.

SEVILLA AND WESTERN ANDALUCÍA

Sevilla: beyond the city centre

Isla de la Cartuja

The island of Cartuja, between two branches of the Río Guadalquivir, encompasses large parts of the old city, including **Triana** (*see page 193*), but 'La Cartuja' generally refers to the northern lobe that was the site of **Expo 92**, a world fair. Many modern buildings were constructed for the fair but have failed to win the hearts of *sevillanos*. A portion of the fairground is occupied by the **Isla Mágica** (*tel: 95 446 1493; open: mid-June–mid-Sept, 1100–2300, call for off-season hours; £££*), an amusement park which opened in 1997.

The most promising development in 'La Cartuja' is the recent installation of the **Centro Andaluz de Arte Contemporáneo** (*open: Tue–Sat 1000–2000, Sun 1000–1500; £*) in the Conjunto Monumental de la Cartuja, a 15th-century monastery that was one of many that provided shelter to **Columbus** during his lifetime and actually held his remains between 1509 and 1536. When the monks were expelled in the 19th century, Englishman Charles Pickman converted the complex to a porcelain factory that remained in operation until 1982. Now the beautiful courtyards and Mudéjar chapels serve as galleries for changing exhibitions of contemporary art.

> " *His bones rattled back and forth across the Caribbean almost as much in death as in life. First interred among the Franciscans of Valladolid, [Columbus's remains were] transferred in 1509 to the family mausoleum his son had founded in Seville. A change of heart by Don Diego caused them to be removed after his death to the sanctuary of the cathedral of Santo Domingo. In 1795 … they were transferred again to the decency of Spanish soil in Havana, until the 'liberation' of Cuba in the war of 1898 made it seem proper to send them back to Spain, where they were buried under a suitably pompous monument in Seville Cathedral. With each removal, the possibilities of some mistake multiplied …* "

Felipe Fernández-Armesto, *Columbus* **(1991)**

SEVILLA AND WESTERN ANDALUCÍA

Parque de María Luisa

The core gardens of this extensive park system south of the cathedral were donated to Sevilla in 1893 by the **Duchess of Montpensier**, and much of the surrounding park was the gift of **Princess María Luisa de Borbón** in 1914. This lush green oasis has a rich variety of trees, shrubs and flowers, but seems appropriately dominated by orange trees.

In 1929, the park and surrounding areas were built up as the site for the **Exposición Ibero-Americana**. Former colonies mounted stunning neo-Mudéjar buildings, many of which still serve as national consulates, and Spain went all out building the Plaza de España and the Plaza de América as showcases. Alas, in 1929 the world plunged into a depression and the fair was a flop, but the legacy of buildings and parkland has served Sevilla well.

The **Plaza de España**, on the northeast side of the park, has been converted into government offices. This 200-m (655-ft) diameter semicircular plaza is an architectural extravagance that bends the Renaissance arcade, anchors it with baroque towers and encrusts all the lower levels with *azulejos* (decorative coloured tiles). Surrounded by a canal (rowing on it is a popular Sunday family activity) are 54 tiled enclosures depicting scenes from Spain's provinces.

The southeast flank, **Plaza de América**, is filled with families on outings and white pigeons. On one side, the Renaissance-style **Museo Arqueológico** (*open: Tue 1500–2000, Wed–Sat 0900–2000, Sun 0900–1430; £*) chronicles the succession of Andalucian cultures. The most stunning exhibit is the **Tesoro Carambola**, a collection comprising one Tartessan man's gold jewellery. Facing the museum is the former Palacio Mudéjar of the 1929 fair, now the **Museo de Artes y Costumbres Populares** (*open: Tue 1500–2000, Wed–Sat 0900–2000, Sun 0900–1430; £*). The museum is worth a visit just to see the old *feria* posters, flamenco costumes and *azulejos*.

SEVILLA AND WESTERN ANDALUCÍA

Around Sevilla

Carmona

40km (25 miles) northeast of Sevilla, on the NIV. Tourist information: Arco de la Puerta de Sevilla. Tel: 95 419 0080.

Commanding the fertile Guadalquivir valley, Carmona – an old city still contained within walls – was founded by Carthaginians and rose to prominence under the Romans. The **Necrópolis Romana** (*Avda Jorge Bonsor 9; open: mid-June–mid-Sept, Tue–Sat 0900–1400, Sun 1000–1400, rest of year, Tue–Sat 1000–1400, 1600–1800, Sun 1000–1400; £*) is one of the most extensive Roman burial sites outside Italy, with more than 250 tombs. The ruins of a **Roman amphitheatre** stand nearby. One of the main gates is the **Puerta de Sevilla**.

Itálica

Santiponce, just a few kilometres north of Sevilla, off the N630. Open: Tue–Sat 0900–2000, Sun 1000–1600. £.

Itálica was founded in 206 BC as the first major Roman settlement outside Italy. Within 400 years it became a splendid city, the birthplace of **Trajan** and **Hadrian**. Much of Itálica still lies beneath the suburb of Santiponce, but a portion has been excavated, notably the amphitheatre and baths.

> " *… according to the Greek historian Polybius, between 206 and 198 BC Rome received 6 316 Roman pounds of gold bullion and 311,622 pounds of silver from Spain …* "
>
> **Juan Lalaguna, *A Traveller's History of Spain* (1990)**

Parque Nacional de Doñana

Once a hunting preserve of dukes, kings and sherry barons, the Coto de Doñana is now one of Europe's most important national parks, comprising three main ecological zones: dunes, woods and wetlands.

The dunes and wet inter-dune valleys (*corrales*) are made up of waves of shifting sand steadily blown and washed inland from the Atlantic. The wild camels that once wandered these dunes recently died out. A narrow stripe of evergreen woodland with a substantial deer population separates the dunes from the wetlands. Most of the park consists of *marismas*, shallow seasonal marshes that flood each spring and turn to salty dry plain in the summer, where hundreds of thousands of waterfowl, from ducks to flamingos, take refuge in the winter and late spring. Due to its critical location on the Europe–North Africa flyway, more than half of Europe's migratory birds depend on Doñana.

There are two easy options for casual visitors to sample Doñana. Storks nest atop the visitor centre at **El Acebuche** (*A483, km26; tel: 95 944 8711; open: daily 0800–2000; displays on Doñana ecosystems, AV presentation, souvenir shop, information desk, reservation desk for guided tours*), where a boardwalk trail leads to hides where waterfowl can be observed. This is the departure point for guided 4-wheel-drive tours to the interior reserves.

The **Arroyo de la Rocina** protected area is traversed by a 3 $^1/_2$-km (2-mile) path along reedy marshes and then a 7-km (4$^1/_2$-mile) path through pine forest and heather to **Palacio El Acebrón** (*A483, km16; tel: 95 944 2340; open: daily 1000–1900*), which has audio-visual displays on the relationship that local peoples have always had with the marsh.

The village of **El Rocío**, home to one of Spain's holiest pilgrimage sites, sits on the edge of the park.

Costa de la Luz

The Costa de la Luz stretches along the 90-km (56-mile) coastline between Cádiz and Tarifa, Europe's southernmost point, only 8km (5 miles) from Africa. Cooler and windier than the nearby Costa del Sol, the Costa de la Luz is far less built up and its clean, white-sand swimming and bathing beaches are some of the finest in the world. Its landscape remains, for the most part, wild, windblown and starkly untamed, and the towns retain their character as fishing villages. From **Algeciras** ferries depart for **Tangier** in Morocco and **Ceuta**, a Spanish colony on the Moroccan coast.

The province of Cádiz

Jerez de la Frontera

Tourist information: Larga 39. Tel: 95 633 1150.

Jerez, a medieval city at its heart, is the capital of sherry production and the largest and most prosperous of the wine-producing cities. It is worth visiting the **barrio viejo** ('old quarter') west of Calle Larga, and the small **Alcázar**, or fortress (*Alameda Vieja; tel: 95 631 9798; open: daily summer, 1000–2000, winter, 1000–1800; £–££*).

But sherry is the main attraction, and bodegas making the stuff riddle the city. The most interesting ones to visit are **González Byass** (*Manuel González 12; tel: 95 635 7016; open: Mon–Fri 1000–1300, 1630, 1730, Sat 1000–1300, tours on the hour; ££*) and **Domecq** (*San Ildefonso; tel: 95 615 1500; open: Mon–Fri 0900–1300, Sat–Sun 1000–1300; ££*). These two bodegas are near each other, west of the Alcázar.

The **Real Escuela Andaluza de Arte Ecuestre** (*Avda Duque de Abrantes; tel: 95 631 1111*) offers training sessions and puts on performances where horses and riders are trained in formal show styles and dressage.

Cádiz

Tourist information: Calderón de la Barca 1. Tel: 95 621 1313.

Cádiz was founded 3 100 years ago as the Phoenician port of *Gadir*. Its commanding position at the tip of a peninsula guarding the Atlantic coast has made the city a prize for every major power since. In 1755 an earthquake obliterated most of its past, so today it is a sophisticated 18th-century city with an intense intellectual history and an enviable legacy of music and poetry.

The **catedral** (*open: Tue–Sat 1000–1230; services Sat 1830 and Sun 1200; £*) is a baroque and neo-classical church completed in 1853 to replace an older building destroyed by fire in 1596. Of main interest are the **carved choir stalls** topped with busts of saints and musicians. The cathedral museum has a towering **silver monstrance** said to be adorned with a million jewels.

One of Andalucía's best museums is the **Museo de Cádiz** (*Plaza Mina; tel: 95 621 2281; open: Tue 1430–2000, Wed–Sat 0900–2000, Sun 0930–1430; £*), housed in a handsome mansion and boasting some of the best archaeological collections in the Mediterranean, as well as some superb fine art displays. The **Oratorio de San Felipe Neri** (*Santa Inés; open: daily 0830–1000, 1930–2200; £*), a shrine to liberalism since 1812 when Spain's first liberal constitution was declared here, is worth a look too.

And if you're hungry, the **Barrio de la Viña** ('fishermen's quarter'), with its small and narrow low-rise houses, is a good place to eat seafood.

Los Pueblos Blancos

The 'White Towns' of the Sierra de Grazalema are often built below fortifications which once marked the shifting border between Muslim and Christian territories. While **Arcos de la Frontera** is a ducal town of many churches and monuments, most of the White Towns are simple agricultural villages surrounded by beautiful landscapes.

This is undoubtedly a region for leisurely exploration. The area around the White Towns holds some of Spain's best trout fishing, and the villages produce some surprisingly good table wines, cured meats and cheeses. Some towns have special attractions: **Ubrique**, for instance, is known for its leather industry, and **Gaucín** offers fantastic views over the Mediterranean and the Atlantic. The charming **Grazalema** has the highest rainfall in Spain but is nonetheless a good base for hiking trips. Also worth visiting are **Ronda la Vieja Setenil de la Bodegas** and **Zahara de la Sierra**

> *I must own that, in spite of everything, Spain does amuse me. Every day with perfect regularity a sky so blue that one can scoop it out with a spoon.*
>
> **Henry Adams (1838–1918)**

SEVILLA AND WESTERN ANDALUCÍA

Eating and drinking

Restaurants

In Sevilla itself, casual outdoor dining is at its best in the **Barrio Santa Cruz**, in the **Plaza Catalina Ribera**, and in the adjacent streets where Calle Santa María la Blanca meets Avenida Mendez Pelayo.

El Convento
Arcos de la Frontera. Calle Marqués de Torresoto 7. Tel: 95 670 3222. £££. Very attractive dining room offers local game in various presentations.

Mesón Don Raimundo
Sevilla. Argote de Molina 26. Tel: 95 422 3355. £££. This restaurant in a 14th-century Santa Cruz monastery has an emphasis on Andalucian entrées and Mozarabic desserts.

La Parra Vieja
Jerez. San Miguel 9. Tel: 95 633 5390. ££. You can't miss this place, with its great tile murals out front. Inside, the walls are covered with *azulejos* and there's a big wooden bar. Specialises in meats, local fish and shellfish, all grilled on a wood fire.

Restaurante El Faro
Cádiz. Calle San Felix 15. Tel: 95 621 1068. £££. This elegant fish restaurant in the Barrio de la Viña is one of the best known in the city. The *menu del día* (*££*) is a good way to sample its style, or try the *tapas* in the bar.

El Rinconcillo
Sevilla. Plaza Terceros. Tel: 95 422 3183. £–££. The city's oldest tavern, established in 1670.

Festivals

Semana Santa
('Easter Week'), Sevilla. *Tel: 95 423 4465.* Daily processions are staged by the city's 57 brotherhoods.

Feria de Abril
Sevilla. *Tel: 95 423 4465.* Held in April at El Real de la Feria in Los Remedios. Features horse promenades and signals the start of the bullfighting season.

Feria del Caballo
Jerez. *Tel: 95 633 1150.* The early-May horse fair is one of the biggest festivals in Andalucia, with music, dance and horse parades.

Carnaval de Cádiz
Tel: 95 624 1001. February or March. Considered the most exuberant carnival in mainland Spain. The city's flamboyant gay community is very much in evidence, giving Cádiz an air of Rio de Janeiro.

Shopping

Bullfighting and *feria* posters, castanets, flamenco gear and music, handpainted silk scarves and shawls, decorated fans, and ceramics from the **Barrio de Triana** are among the most popular souvenirs from Sevilla. In **Jerez** you can buy sherry and horse gear, and **Ubrique**, one of the White Towns, is a good source of leather wallets, boots and cases.

Allegro
Sevilla. Dos de Mayo 38. Wide selection of Spanish classical, popular and flamenco music on cassette and CD.

La Casa del Jerez
Jerez. Divina Pastora 1. Tel: 95 633 5184. Tourist-oriented shop near the Real Escuela Andaluza de Arte Ecuestre which offers the opportunity to sample wines from a variety of makers and purchase other souvenirs.

Cerámica Santa Ana
Sevilla. Calle San Jorge 31. One of the largest of Triana's ceramics factories. Will ship purchases.

Felix
Sevilla. Avda Constitución 26. The place to invest in a vintage poster of a *feria* or *corrida*.

Le Portier Didier
Sevilla. Ximénez de Enciso. Tel: 95 421 4532. Small shop in Santa Cruz selling handpainted fans, silk scarves and shawls.

Flamenco in Sevilla

To see a flamenco show, you can visit any of the *tablaos* offering flamenco performances geared to tourists: **El Arenal** (*Calle Rodo 7; tel: 95 421 6492*), **El Patio Sevillano** (*Paseo Cristóbal Colón 11A; tel: 95 422 2068*) and **Los Gallos** (*Plaza Santa Cruz; tel: 95 421 6981*). The **Biennial of Flamenco** (*tel: 95 423 4165*), held during September in even-numbered years, is one of Spain's major festivals of the art.

SEVILLA AND WESTERN ANDALUCÍA

PROFILE

Flamenco

Flamenco is the song and the dance of southern Spain, of Andalucía. It originated in the gypsy community but to some extent has become part of Andalucían culture as a whole and is popular in the rest of Spain and abroad.

Its roots are difficult to trace, but it probably combines several historical influences. The gypsies must have brought songs with them from the East when they arrived in Spain in the 15th century. These may have been fused with forms of Arabic music and Jewish liturgical chants, but practioners of flamenco will tell you that it is not something to be analysed and defined. It is a way of life, a way of expressing emotions, pleasant and unpleasant. All the emotions are there, and even if you don't understand the words you will pick up on the sentiments behind them: joy, desperation, hatred, love – the whole gamut of human feelings.

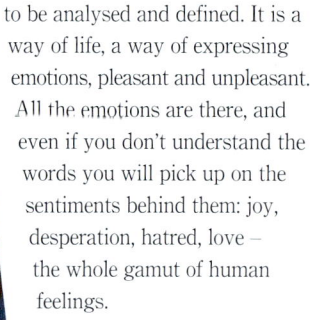

The essence of flamenco is song, *el cante*, performed unaccompanied or together with the strumming of a guitar, and sometimes handclapping. There are more than 70 kinds of flamenco song. The singer is usually a man; a deep, rough voice, far from being a hindrance, is considered necessary to perform *cante jondo* (literally 'deep song'),

SEVILLA AND WESTERN ANDALUCÍA

which expresses the darker emotions of the human condition, such as sorrow and torment.

With the song goes the dance. Flamenco dance expresses the same emotions as the words of the song, but through the body, principally the arms and legs. Its movements are free, but at the same time the dancer remains planted on the earth, symbolising his or her attachment to life, however much pain is being suffered. The rapid rhythm created with the heels is called *zapateado*; together with the *palmas* (clapping) it marks the *compás* (the rhythm pattern that is the basis of the song).

The best flamenco is to be seen in Andalucía, where summer *ferias* are particularly atmospheric, but authentic flamenco is also performed in venues in Madrid and Barcelona.

SEVILLA AND WESTERN ANDALUCÍA

Granada, Córdoba and the Costa del Sol

Andalucía could claim to have the best of everything – and the climate to go with it. Granada and Córdoba have the two finest Moorish buildings in Spain. There are the two showpiece Renaissance towns of Baeza and Úbeda, and wildlife aplenty in the nature reserve of Cazorla. And there's an endless choice of beaches along the coast, from the teeming resorts of the Costa del Sol to the discreet coves of Almería.

GRANADA, CÓRDOBA AND THE COSTA DEL SOL

Best of Granada, Córdoba and the Costa del Sol

Getting around: Málaga is by far the busiest airport in this area, but Almería is more appropriate if you are going to be staying in the east. There are motorways between most major cities, but there are still glaring gaps in the network (notably along the coast between Málaga and Almería) and it can be better to go around a longer way rather than crawl along a main road which passes through every town.

GRANADA, CÓRDOBA AND THE COSTA DEL SOL

① Costa del Sol

Love it or hate it, you'll find plenty of action between Marbella and Estepona. **Torremolinos** is one of the coast's throbbing high-rise package-holiday resorts; **Marbella** and **San Pedro de Alcántara** are more manageable. If you want to see how the rich spend their leisure time, hang out on the quayside of Puerto Banús. **Pages 208–9**

② Ronda

The Puente Nuevo, spanning a narrow gorge 120m (395ft) above the river, is one of the most familiar images of Andalucía. This old Moorish town is a gateway to the Pueblos Blancos ('White Towns'). **Page 210**

③ Granada and the Alhambra

Granada attracts visitors as if it were a centre of cultural pilgrimage. There is something compelling about the Islamic civilisation that occupied Spain for centuries, and here it lingered the longest, leaving behind it the stunning fortress-palace which overlooks Granada, the Alhambra. **Pages 212–15**

④ Córdoba

Moorish Spain's other great legacy is **La Mezquita**, the mosque at Córdoba which could hold 40,000 worshippers among its forest of columns and arches. A walk around the atmospheric **Judería**, the Jewish Quarter beside the mosque, is also essential. **Pages 216–17**

⑤ Baeza and Ubeda

Discover the 'Renaissance triangle' of inland Andalucia, comprising these two towns and the provincial capital city of Jaén. **Pages 218–19**

⑥ Desierto de Tabernas

The desert of Almeria province proved to be the perfect place for film-maker Sergio Leone to shoot 'spaghetti westerns' in the 1960s and 1970s. The old film sets are now a tourist attraction, and Almeria itself has interesting places to explore. **Page 220**

Tourist information

Málaga, **Granada** and **Córdoba** all have main tourist offices, as do the other provincial capitals here, **Jaén** and **Almería** (*see relevant entries*), but the best source of information is the website: *www.andalucia.org*.

GRANADA, CÓRDOBA AND THE COSTA DEL SOL

Costa del Sol

The 85-km (53-mile) stretch of Mediterranean coast west of Málaga to Estepona is Spain's famed Costa del Sol. The region boasts 325 sunny days per year, striking vistas where mountains tower just inland from the sea, and a nearly continuous strand of clean beaches, including 15 with EU Blue Flags.

Although the Costa del Sol has some of Spain's densest development, it is not just a concrete jungle. It certainly offers high-density resorts on the east end in **Torremolinos**, **Benalmádena Costa** and **Fuengirola**, but it also has a luxurious middle belt centred on **Marbella**, with **Puerto Banús** acting as a chic and ostentatious marina. And there is a more contemplative western segment anchored by **Estepona**, more popular with families. **San Pedro de Alcántara** is another quieter and smarter resort with a modern marina.

The towns follow a pattern: delightful beaches flanked by a fishing fleet and a yacht marina, the core of an old town, and a modern commercial centre. Extensive hotel renovations and improved roads, landscaping, seafront promenades and litter control have given this venerable resort area new legs.

GRANADA, CÓRDOBA AND THE COSTA DEL SOL

Málaga

Tourist information: Casa del Jardinero-Park, Avda Cervantes 1. Tel: 95 260 4410.

Málaga, Andalucia's second largest city and the capital of the Costa del Sol, is a vibrant urban centre with beautiful buildings, green parks, historic sites, chic shops and sandy beaches.

Unlike the typical Andalucian Moorish fortress, Málaga's **Alcazaba** (*open: Wed–Mon 0930–2000*) does not dominate the highest point of the city, ceding that place of honour to the **Castillo de Gibralfaro** (*open: daily 0930–2000*), but it still occupies a good vantage point for watching the Bay of Málaga. Another fine building in the city is the **catedral** (*Molina Lario; open: Mon–Sat 0900–1845; £*). Built on the site of Málaga's former main mosque, it was begun in the 16th century but never finished because of lack of funds. Only one of two planned towers was ever completed, so the cathedral was dubbed 'La Manquita', or 'one-armed lady'.

The **Casa Natal de Picasso** (*Plaza Merced 15; open: Mon–Sat 1100–1400, 1700–2000, Sun 1100–1400*), the house where the painter was born and spent his early years, is now an art gallery with an interesting collection of photographs and works on paper and ceramics. The city has another two main fine arts museums, but both are still undergoing renovation. The **Museo de Picasso** will contain major works donated by the artist's daughter-in-law Christine Ruiz-Picasso, and the **Museo de Bellas Artes** will house a collection of works by *malagueño* artists, including Picasso's first tutor, **Muñoz Degrain** (*contact tourist information for opening dates*).

Marbella

Tourist information: Glorieta Fontanilla. Tel: 95 277 1442.

Marbella is the most stylish resort of the Costa del Sol, visited by royalty, Gulf oil millionaires and film stars, all of whom frequent the **Paseo Marítimo**, the golden promenade of the Costa del Sol.

Within the pedestrian old town (*casco antiguo*), partially walled and set back from the ocean, a 16th-century convent hospital houses the excellent **Museo del Grabado Contemporáneo** (*Hospital Bazán; tel: 95 282 5035; open: Mon 1100–1400, Tue–Fri 1100–1400, 1730–2015, Sun 1130–1415; £*), with a permanent collection that includes works by **Picasso**, **Miró** and **Dalí**.

Inland from Málaga

Ronda

Tourist information: Plaza España 1. Tel: 95 287 1272.

Pliny the Elder called Ronda 'the glorious' two millennia ago, and the description still holds. The white city crouches on a limestone shelf cleft by the precipitous El Tajo gorge, cut by the Río Guadalevin. Of three bridges that cross the river, the most impressive is the 1793 **Puente Nuevo** at the top of the gorge, 120m (395ft) above the river.

The chief Moorish remains of Ronda are the **Baños Arabes** (*below Puente Viejo; open: Tue 1500–1730, Wed–Sat 1000–1400, 1500–1730, Sun 1000–1400*), a superb 13th-century example of public architecture with barrel vaults, horseshoe arches and brick columns.

The **Palacio del Marqués de Salvatierra** (*Calle Marqués de Salvatierra; open for guided tours: 1100–1400, 1600–1900, closed Thu and Sun afternoons; £*) offers the rare opportunity to tour a home where the same aristocratic family has lived since 1485. Across the street, the **Casa del Rey Moro** (*Cuesta de Santo Domingo 17; open: daily 1000–1900; £*) has lovely gardens opening on to the gorge and an underground stairway that goes down to the river.

The **Palacio de Mondragón** (*Plaza Mondragón; open: Mon–Fri 1000–1800, Sat–Sun 1000–1500; £*) is Ronda's city museum, but its best parts are the courtyards, largely unchanged since the days of Fernando and Isabel, who lodged here when they visited Ronda. Another museum worth a visit is the **Plaza de Toros y Museo Taurino** (*Plaza Teniente Arce; tel: 95 287 4132; open: daily 1000–1900; £*), which pays homage to the legendary bullfighter **Pedro Romero**, reputed to have killed over 6 000 bulls.

GRANADA, CÓRDOBA AND THE COSTA DEL SOL

Garganta del Chorro

60km (37 miles) northwest of Málaga. Tourist information: Camping El Chorro. Tel: 95 249 8380.

Southwest of Antequera and northwest of Alora, the El Chorro gorge is the top rock-climbing destination in Andalucia. The Rio Guadalhorce has cut rocky labyrinths with 300-m (980-ft) vertical cliffs in the soft limestone, and climbers have affixed permanent bolts and rings in many of the rock walls, turning dangerous free-climbs into somewhat safer sport-climbs.

The main defile is crossed by the sometime footpath **El Camino del Rey**, purportedly so called because Alfonso XIII walked it to dedicate a railroad tunnel in the 1920s. It is now officially closed because it is considered too dangerous to use. The drops are truly stomach-wrenching, but many foolhardy hikers are not deterred.

Antequera

Tourist information: Plaza San Sebastian. Tel: 95 270 2505.

The Roman city of Antequera was also a Moorish fortress-town defending Granada during the Reconquest. When the Moors were deported, the Christians began a building spurt that lasted for the next two centuries.

The 16th-century Arco de los Gigantes makes for a ceremonial entry to the **Alcazaba** (*open: Tue–Sun 1000–1400*), where the **Torre Papabellotas** offers good views. In the Barrio del Coso Viejo, the Arabic quarter, stands the former ducal Palacio de Nájera, now the **Museo Municipal** (*Plaza Coso Viejo; open: Tue–Fri 1000–1330, 1600–1800, Sat–Sun 1100–1330; £, guided tour only*), which has a beautiful **Roman bronze of a boy**.

Antequera also has many churches. It is worth visiting the **Iglesia de Nuestra Señora del Carmen** (*Plaza Carmen; open: Tue–Sun 1000–1400; £*) and the **Real Colegiata de Santa María la Mayor** (*Plaza Santa María; open: Tue–Sun 1000–1400*). Also have a look at the prehistoric **Dólmenes de Menga**, **Viera** and **El Romeral** (*open: Tue 1500–1730, Wed–Sat 1000–1400, 1500–1730, Sun 1000–1400*), three neolithic tombs probably housing chieftains who would have been buried with their weapons and treasures.

Just outside Antequera, don't miss **El Torcal**, an area of extraordinary rock formations.

GRANADA, CÓRDOBA AND THE COSTA DEL SOL

Granada

Granada is a tantalising ghost of what might have been. The palaces and gardens of the Alhambra (see page 214) represent the final flowering of al-Andalus, an Islamic world extinguished in the name of a Christian god and a united Spanish crown. But Granada is more than just the fabled fortress of the Nasrid kings.

When the Nasrid court moved into the Alhambra in the 13th century, the old residential town, **El Albaicín**, stayed behind on the opposite bank of the Río Darro to admire the glories of the new palace on the facing hill. The Muslim past is palpable here; the Albaicin's jasmine-scented streets follow an organic logic of their own. The neighbourhood's original mosques have been converted to churches that maintain only bits and pieces of their origins. **El Bañuelo** (*Carrera Darro 31; open: Tue 1500–2000, Wed–Sat 0900–2000, Sun 0900–1430*) are 11th-century Arabic baths with four vaulted chambers. Nearby is the Casa de Castril, a striking 16th-century palace housing the **Museo Arqueológico** (*Carrera Darro 41; open: Tue 1500–2000, Wed–Sat 0900–2000, Sun 0900–1430; £*).

Granada's **catedral** (*Gran Vía Colón; open: Mon–Sat 1045–1330, 1600–1900, Sun 1600–1900; £*) began to rise in 1521 on the site of the main mosque. Left unfinished, it has a Renaissance plainness that contrasts with the elaborate façades of the city's Moorish monuments. The most notable side chapel depicts **St James (Santiago) the Moorslayer** on horseback, and similar images of **St Michael** throughout the building drive home the point of Christian triumph at swordpoint.

The **Capilla Real** (*Oficios 12; open: Mon–Sat 1030–1300, 1600–1900, Sun 1100–1300, 1600–1900; £*) stands as an exuberant late Gothic tribute to **Fernando and Isabel**, whose coffins lie in an underground crypt with their daughter Juana la Loca ('Juana the Mad') and her husband, Felipe el Hermoso ('Philip the Handsome'). The sacristy contains Isabel's crown and sceptre, Fernando's sword and Isabel's personal collection of Flemish art.

GRANADA, CÓRDOBA AND THE COSTA DEL SOL

Federico García Lorca's spirit haunts much of Granada. The **Huerta de San Vicente (Casa-Museo Federico García Lorca)** (*Virgen Blanca; open: May–July, Tue–Sun 1000–1300, 1600–1900, Aug, Tue–Sun 1000–1400, Sept–Apr, Tue–Sun 1000–1300, 1700–2000; £*) sits in the middle of a rather new and splendid park of roses – an extravagant gesture of which Lorca would have approved. The half-hour guided tours in Spanish show the famous poet and playwright's writing-desk, his piano, portraits of friends and family members, and some of his sketches for theatrical productions. The house now lies well within the busy city, about a 15-minute walk from the cathedral.

Granada's large gypsy population used to be concentrated in the caves of **Sacromonte** above El Albaicin. Once a poor neighbourhood, it's now showing signs of gentrification to take advantage of the unusual lodgings (many of the houses along the Camino de Sacromonte are dug into the side of the hill) and extraordinary views. A number of flamenco-ish shows and disco-bars now hold forth in some of the larger 'caves' in the first half-kilometre of this road. The *barrio* is no more dangerous than any urban neighbourhood, but visitors should be careful of their belongings. For a pleasant opportunity to visit a traditional dwelling, walk up in the afternoon to the **Museo de Zambra de María 'La Canastera'** (*Camino del Sacromonte; tel: 95 812 1183; open: Mon–Fri 1600–1900, Sat–Sun 1200–1500*).

Tourist information: Corral del Carbón, Calle Mariana Pineda. Tel: 95 822 5990; www.granadainfo.com.

GRANADA, CÓRDOBA AND THE COSTA DEL SOL

Granada: La Alhambra and El Generalife

Open: daily 0830–2000. Evening visits to palaces only: Tue, Thu and Sat 2200–2300 (tickets can be reserved three days in advance; call 95 822 0912 or fax 95 821 0584). ££. Tickets may also be purchased Mon–Fri 0900–1400 at Banco BBV in Plaza Isabel la Católica.

As the outlying reaches of al-Andalus fell to the Christian Reconquest in the 13th century, Islamic Spain became increasingly concentrated in the kingdom of Granada, where the Nasrid dynasty held on for 250 years until 1492, when Granada was the last Muslim city to fall. By that time the Nasrid kings had drawn on the best architects and finest artisans of al-Andalus to build a palace city atop the hill, one that still casts a spell over everyone who sees it (travellers often come to Granada as pilgrims; once they have walked the halls and grounds of the Alhambra, they are content to leave). Touring the complex takes at least three hours, and savouring it can stretch the experience to a full day.

The oldest extant portion is the **Alcazaba**, which dates from the 13th century and was built on the ruins of earlier fortifications. Napoleon's troops destroyed much of the fort, but surviving ramparts and watchtowers provide a feel for how the hill was guarded. Views from the **Torre del Vela**, the highest point of the Alhambra, are stunning.

GRANADA, CÓRDOBA AND THE COSTA DEL SOL

The **Palacio Nazaries (Casa Real)** is undoubtedly the brightest jewel of the complex. Built primarily during the rule of Mohammed V (1354–91), its restrained and simple exterior in no way prepares visitors for the richness of the internal decor. Every surface is adorned with **carved plaster** in lacy and delicate abstract patterns and Arabic inscriptions. Ponds and fountains provide both the sound and sight of water in virtually every chamber, and light and shade are patterned in ways that continually delight the eye. The third section of the palace is the **Harem**, or private apartments, but the **Patio de los Leones** is the most memorable and photographed: an elegant courtyard where the pool's central fountain rests on the backs of a dozen carved stone lions.

American storyteller **Washington Irving** lived here in the 1820s. His *Tales of the Alhambra* proved instrumental in saving the old palaces, which had been used as barracks by Napoleon's troops and were left to decay. The appreciation of such Romantic-era writers as Irving led to the Alhambra being declared a national monument in 1870, and it was subsequently heavily restored.

From the lovely **El Partal** gardens, the paths lead either to El Generalife or to the **Palacio de Carlos V**, built by the Holy Roman Emperor who was also King Carlos I of Spain. He demolished a large section of the Casa Real to build his own palace, which was begun in 1526 and never finished. Much of it has been turned over to the **Museo de la Alhambra** (*open: Tue–Sat 0900–1430*), which explores the artistry of the Muslim era with objects found at the Alhambra and elsewhere in Granada and Córdoba.

Tip

Just outside Granada there is a hill called El Suspiro del Moro ('The Moor's Sigh'). Legend says that the last Moorish king of Spain, Boabdil, sat down there to look for the last time at his beloved Granada, and wept. When his mother saw him she reproached him: 'Cry as a woman over what you couldn't defend like a man.'

The Renaissance palace may have an elegant symmetry, but it is an alien building for life in Granada's swelter. The **Generalife**, the summer palace of the Muslim rulers, on the other hand, belongs to the land and climate. Sitting on the slopes of the Cerro del Sol facing the Casa Real, the palace buildings off in one corner almost seem an afterthought to the beautifully laid-out courtyards filled with pools and fountains.

GRANADA, CÓRDOBA AND THE COSTA DEL SOL

Córdoba

Córdoba reached its apogee in the 10th and 11th centuries as the fabled capital of western Islam, a cosmopolitan centre of art, science and scholarship that ranked among the great cities of the world. Nearly a millennium later, the bare bones of that eminence remain in the largest mezquita ('mosque') and most intact medieval Arabic city layout in Europe. A walk around the Judería, the Jewish quarter – situated to the west of the mosque and little altered since the 13th century – is the surest way to find the beating heart of this ancient world.

Córdoba's mosque, **La Mezquita** (*open: Mon–Sat 1000–1930, Sun mornings for worship services and 1400–1930; £*), stands testament to the inescapable stamp of Moorish culture on the city even after seven centuries of Christian rule. The mosque, which could hold 40,000 worshippers facing Mecca, was begun during the reign of Abd ar-Rahman (AD 756–88) on the site of a Visigothic church which had been built, in turn, over a Roman temple. In the 11th century it was the second largest mosque in the Islamic world and the grandest of western Islam. In particular, look out for splendidly ornamented *mihrab* (prayer niches). The Patio de los Naranjos, originally the area of ritual ablutions before prayer, remains a retreat from the hubbub.

There are several museums worth seeing. The **Torre de la Calahorra** (*Puente Romano; open: daily May–Sept, 1000–1400, 1630–2030, Oct–Apr, 1000–1800; £*) should be

Tip

Manuel Rodríguez Sanchez, universally known as 'Manolete', is considered one of the best matadors ever to have lived. A hero of Franco's Spain, he was born in Córdoba in 1917 and gored to death on 28 August 1947 in Linares, a village near Jaén. You can see the hide of the bull, Islero*, that killed him in the Museo Municipal Taurino.*

every first-time visitor's initial stop in the city. It tells the history of Córdoba, a city where Christian, Jew and Muslim lived together in harmony and produced wonders of art and science, the like of which Europe would not see again for another five centuries.

Another interesting museum is the Palacio-Museo de Viana (*Rejas Don Gome 2; open: Mon–Tue, Thu–Sat 1000–1300, 1600–1800, Sun 1000–1400; £*), a magnificent 15th-century villa where the rooms chronicle the lifestyle of the various marquesses of Viana. The 14 courtyards constitute a spectacular overview of Córdoban patio gardening, each garden constructed to highlight certain plants or gardening techniques.

The Museo Municipal Taurino (*Plaza Maimónides 5; open: Tue–Sat 1000–1400, 1800–2000, Sun 0930–1500; £*) is evidence of Córdoba's passion for bullfighting. The city has in fact produced some of Spain's most famous matadors. The palace which belonged to the Catholic Monarchs, the Alcázar de los Reyes Cristianos (*Campo Santo de los Mártires; open: Tue–Sat 1000–1400, 1800–2000, Sun 0930–1500; £*), is also worth a quick visit to see the Roman mosaics in the throne room, the Moorish baths and the serene gardens.

Tourist information: Torrijos 10. Tel: 95 747 1235.

Medina Azahara

Ctra. Palma del Río, 7km (4½ miles) northwest of Córdoba. Open: Tue–Sat 1000–1400, 1800–2030; Sun 1000–1400. £.

This palatial city was built during Córdoba's golden age, but enjoyed only fleeting glory. Caliph Abd ar-Rahman III started building his showpiece palace in AD 936 and spared no expense, but it was destroyed 74 years later by the Berbers. The fraction of the site that has been excavated evokes the melancholic spirit of a lost time and place.

GRANADA, CÓRDOBA AND THE COSTA DEL SOL

The province of Jaén

Jaén

Tourist information: Maestra 18. Tel: 95 323 7422.

Settled by the Romans and expanded by the Moors as a convenient stopover for caravan routes, Jaén has an impressive hilltop castle, the **Castillo de Santa Catalina** (*open: 15 June–15 Sept, Mon–Tue and Thu–Sun 1030–1330, rest of year, 1000–1400*). With Ubeda and Baeza it now forms the so-called 'triangle' of the Renaissance cities.

The 16th-century **catedral** (*Plaza Santa María; open: daily 0830–1300, 1700–2000*) is the greatest work of **Andrés de Vandelvira**; the extraordinary carvings and statuary on the main façade are by **Pedro Roldán**. And Jaén's 11th-century **Baños Arabes** are the largest Arab baths remaining in Spain. They are now part of a museum complex in the **Centro Cultural Palacio de Villardompardo** (*Plaza Santa Luisa Marillac; open: Tue–Sat 0900–2000, Sun 0900–1500*).

Baeza

50km (31 miles) northeast of Jaén, on the N321. Tourist information: Plaza del Pópulo. Tel: 95 374 0444.

The heart of the modern town is **Plaza de España**, at the head of Paseo de la Constitución, the highlight of which is the **Torre de los Aliatares**. At the other end of the *paseo*, **Fuente de los Leones** is the centrepiece of Plaza del Pópulo. Steps behind this fountain lead up to the 'Zona Monumental' which, with the exception of the Moorish-Gothic **Iglesia de Santa Cruz** (*open during services*), is dominated by Renaissance architecture, mostly designed by Vandelvira. The **Catedral de Santa María** (*open: daily 1000–1300, 1700–1900*) underwent a 16th-century reconstruction and its 13th–14th-century Mudéjar features are now obscured.

GRANADA, CÓRDOBA AND THE COSTA DEL SOL

Ubeda

10km (6 miles) northeast of Baeza, on the N321. Tourist information: Avda Cristo Rey 2. Tel: 95 375 0897.

Many of Ubeda's finest buildings are concentrated in the **Plaza de Vázquez de Molina**, in which stands a statue of Andrés de Vandelvira, the 16th-century architect who built many of them. The **Parador de Condestable Dávalos** is a noble mansion converted to a parador (*tel: 95 375 0345*); the **Palacio de las Cadenas** now houses the Ayuntamiento (town hall); the **Capilla del Salvador** (*open: daily 1000–1400, 1630–1900; £*) fuses Vandelvira's artistry with the power and ego of its patron, Francisco de los Cobos. Vandelvira's other major masterwork in Ubeda is the magnificent **Hospital de Santiago** (*Avda Cristo Rey; open: Mon–Sat 0800–1500, 1530–2200*), now a cultural centre.

> "The town's reputation for remoteness is reflected in the popular expression 'to wander off on the hills of Ubeda' (irse por los cerros de Ubeda), meaning to 'wander off the point' or 'to be distracted'."
>
> **Michael Jacobs, *A Guide to Andalusia* (1990)**

The **Museo de Ubeda** (*Cervantes 6; open: Tue 1500–2000, Wed–Sat 0900–2000, Sun 0900–1500; £*), in the 14th-century **Casa Mudéjar** relates the region's long past, and the **Museo de Alfarería** (*Plaza Vázquez Molina, side entry of Palacio de la Cadenas; open: Tue–Sat 1030–1430, 1630–1900, Sun 1030–1400; £*) displays traditional pottery from throughout Spain.

Cazorla

50km (31 miles) southeast of Ubeda, on the A319. Tourist information: Paseo del Santo Cristo (in the Casa de Cultura by the park). Tel: 95 371 0102.

Cazorla, nestled beneath the Peña de los Halcones, or 'Falcon Peak', serves primarily as a base camp for excursions into the adjacent **Parque Natural de Cazorla**, which has some of Europe's densest forest and more than a hundred species of resident bird, including the golden eagle and griffon vulture. The oval Renaissance square of **Plaza Corredera** is dominated by a 17th-century convent converted to house the town hall. In **Plaza de Santa María**, the immense ruins of **Iglesia de Santa María**, designed by Vandelvira and destroyed by Napoleon's troops, serve as an outdoor concert and theatrical venue (*contact tourist information office for details*). Above the square stands the **Castillo de la Yedra**.

GRANADA, CÓRDOBA AND THE COSTA DEL SOL

Eastern Andalucía

Almería

Tourist information: Parque Nicolás Salmerón at Martínez Campos. Tel: 95 027 4355.

Almería's colossal 10th-century **Alcazaba** (*open: mid-June–Sept, 1000–1400, 1700–1930, rest of year, 0930–1330, 1530–1900; £*), the largest in Andalucía, was begun in AD 955 by Córdoba caliph Abd al-Rahman III, and it rivalled the splendour of the Alhambra. It affords great views of the city, the harbour and the surrounding hills.

The plain exterior belies the ornate interior of the fortress-like **catedral** (*open: Mon–Fri 1000–1700, Sat 1000–1300; £*), built on the site of a mosque destroyed in a 1522 earthquake.

Worth seeing too is the gypsy/fisherman district of **Barrio de Chanca**, an area of cave dwellers where many doors are brightly decorated with tiles and mosaic patterns.

Desierto de Tabernas

The Desierto de Tabernas, just 24km (15 miles) inland from Almería, is a rare example of true desert in western Europe. The rugged mountains, multi-coloured sands and sparse vegetation of succulents and cacti attracted moviemakers in the 1960s and 1970s, most notably the *auteur* of the 'spaghetti western', **Sergio Leone**. Local residents were given parts as Indians, outlaws and US cavalry riders. Some of the old sets are now entertainment centres. One of them is **Mini Hollywood** (*N340, km364; tel: 95 036 5236; open: daily 1000–2100, closed Mon in winter; western shows at 1200, 1700, 2000 mid-June–mid-Sept; £££*), a set used for *A Fistful of Dollars*, *The Magnificent Seven* and *The Good, the Bad and the Ugly*, among others.

Mojácar

Tourist information: Plaza Nueva. Tel: 95 047 5162.

Mojácar is an Arabic mirage sprouting from the rock of a hilltop 2km (1¼ miles) inland. Its beaches are long, clean and unshadowed by high-rise development, and the arid

GRANADA, CÓRDOBA AND THE COSTA DEL SOL

climate guarantees maximum sunshine most of the year. In the 1960s, faced with a town where whole *barrios* were deserted, the mayor came up with a novel idea to reverse its decline: he gave away houses to artists. As is often the case, the artists made the charming village fashionable, and real-estate developers and speculators followed on their heels, gutting medieval quarters and installing modern conveniences.

Las Alpujarras

West of Almería and south of Granada over the 3 000m (10,000ft) peaks of the Sierra Nevada lie the green valleys of Las Alpujarras (the Granada side far more picturesque), isolated until the mid-20th century by poor roads. The Alpujarras remained a stronghold of Moorish culture into the early 17th century, when their inhabitants were expelled and the area was repopulated with northern Europeans. The villages retain a striking similarity to Berber settlements of North Africa, with terraced vineyards, olive groves and wild mulberry trees. Above Órgiva, the three stunning mountain villages of **Pampaneira**, **Bubión** and **Capileira** squat like white birds' nests along the east wall of the Barranco de Poqueira ravine.

Parque Natural de Cabo de Gata

Tourist information: Centro de Interpretación Las Almoladeras, Crta Almería. Open: Easter and July–Aug, Tue–Sun 1000–1400, 1700–2100; rest of year, Tue–Sun 0930–1530.

This natural park comprises three distinct geographic regions: the **Estepa Litoral** (stretching east of Almería), the small but ecologically critical district of **Las Salinas** (salt marshes and flats declared a waterfowl preserve, mostly to protect the flamingos) and the black-rock landscape of the **Sierra de Cabo de Gata** mountain range, formed by now-extinct volcanos. Its unusual flora is characterised by Europe's only native palm, the **dwarf fan palm**, which grows no more than a metre tall, and the thorny **jujube bush**. Some 170 species of resident and migratory bird are found here, among them the flamingo, griffon vulture and avocet.

GRANADA, CÓRDOBA AND THE COSTA DEL SOL

Eating and drinking

Restaurants and bars

Gazpacho andaluz, a cold summer soup made from fresh raw ingredients, and *pescaíto frito* ('fried fish') are common items on menus in Andalucía, especially on the coast.

Bodegas Campos
Córdoba. Los Lineros 32. Tel: 95 749 7643. ££. An ancient bar-cum-restaurant in a wine cellar, which serves well-prepared dishes drawing on typical *Cordobesa* cuisine.

Bodega El Picadero
Ronda. Calle Nueva 21. Tel: 95 287 2113. £. Simple and honest food in a small, friendly bar-restaurant with flamenco memorabilia in one room and bullfighting items in the other.

Café-Pastelería López Mezquita
Granada. Reyes Católicos 39. Tel: 95 822 1205. ££. This café has been serving tasty *tapas* and pastries since 1862. Its only shortcoming is that it closes early for Spain, at 2100.

Corral del Carbón
Granada. Mariana Pineda 8. Tel: 95 822 3810. ££. Grilled meats, especially lamb and sausages, are served in this restaurant redolent of old Granada, down to the signed photo of Federico García Lorca at one end of the bar.

El Churrasco Restaurante
Córdoba. Romero 16. Tel: 95 729 0819. ££. Restaurant with bustling, traditional patio and attractive dining rooms. Specialises in grilled meats.

Marbella Patio
Marbella. Virgen de los Dolores 4. Tel: 95 277 5429. ££. In the *casco antiguo* with patio and terrace dining. The ovens are the feature here, with superb roasted fish, suckling pig and lamb.

Mesón Gabino
Ubeda. Fuente Seca. Tel: 95 375 4207. ££. Seemingly carved into one of the city's old walls, this restaurant has a good bar for *tapas*.

Valentin
Almeria. Tenor Iribarne 2. Tel: 95 026 4475. £. A formal, excellent fish restaurant a street away from the Paseo de Almeria.

Bars and *tapas*

The best *tapas* in Málaga can be found in three bars on Calle Moreno Monroy, a small alleyway off Calle Marques de Larios: **Candiles**, **Orellana** and **Chinitas** (*tel: 95 221 0972*), which is the best bet for a sit-down meal. You could also try **Antigua Casa de Guardia** (*Alameda Principal 18; tel: 95 221 4680; £*), a wine bar that seems little changed since its founding in 1840. Customers stand at a long wooden bar, watching bartenders drawing Málaga wine *dulce* ('sweet') or *seco* ('dry') from barrels and chalking up the tab on the bar. Even Picasso tossed back a few here. In Granada, a good selection of riverside cafés and bars can be found along **Paseo Padre Manjón**, north of the Museo Arqueológico, at the edge of the Albaicín.

Nightlife

Bar Málaga Siempre
Málaga. Pasaje Chinitas 7. Live flamenco music every Thursday and Saturday, starting around 2300.

Jardines Neptuno
Granada. Arabial. Tel: 95 852 2533. £££. The best *tablaos* ('flamenco shows') in town. Many shows are held in the 'gypsy caves' of Sacromonte for the benefit of the tourists, making up in atmosphere what they might lack in polish or authenticity. Show up around 2200 and be prepared to spend plenty for drinks.

Marcelo's Café
Málaga. Paseo de la Farola 1. Tel: 95 222 2742. Live music on Thursday and Saturday nights, usually alternating between blues and flamenco fusion.

Tablao Cardenal
Córdoba. Torrijos 10. Tel: 95 748 3112. Flamenco shows almost every evening.

Shopping

What to buy in Granada

Granada is a great place for souvenir hunting. Good shops can be found along the riverside edge of the Albaicín and behind the cathedral. **Artesanía Corral Carbón** (*Mariana Pineda*), artists' studios which share with the tourist office the oldest surviving Moorish building in Granada, just a block from the cathedral, sells a wide range of arts and crafts. *Guitarrerías* ('guitar shops') can be found along **Cuesta Gomérez**, including the shop of the composer and guitarist Antonio Morales (*No 9*).

GRANADA, CÓRDOBA AND THE COSTA DEL SOL

PROFILE

The Moors

In AD 711 a Berber army led by Tariq, the governor of Tangier, landed at Gibraltar and soon afterwards defeated the Visigoth rulers of Spain at the battle of Guadalete. The Islamic 'occupation' of Spain endured, in places, for almost 800 years and left behind it lasting monuments and traditions.

The Islamic inhabitants are usually called the Moors, although this term hides the complexity of this stage of Spanish history. In reality there were several stages of Islamic incursion and 'Moorish' Spain was never one homogenous place.

Many ancient towns and cities bear witness to the presence of the Moors. They built castles in high defensive locations and laid out mazes of shady narrow streets that taper suddenly, dodge round corners and disappear unexpectedly down steps. Their houses were austere from the outside but mini-paradises within, often gathering around luxuriant gardens and patios. The Albaicín quarter of Granada, especially, still preserves its authentic Arab flavour.

The Moors were also skilled farmers and gardeners who knew how to exploit the land to a maximum. They carved the mountains into the distinctive terraces that we can still see today, laid out ingenious irrigation systems and introduced many new plants and animals. They also spread their expert knowledge of falconry, pigeon-keeping and horseriding.

But the civilisation of the Moors was not to last. Almost as soon as Spain had been conquered, the Christians began the Reconquest in the name of their God. Ousting the Moors was a long, slow process, but in 1492 King Boabdil, the last, ill-fated ruler of the Moors of Granada, was forced to surrender to the triumphant 'Catholic Monarchs', Fernando and Isabel. The defeated Moors were at first granted religious toleration

GRANADA, CÓRDOBA AND THE COSTA DEL SOL

by the victors, but later they were forced to choose between conversion to Christianity, expulsion from the realm or facing the Spanish Inquisition. Many of them fled to North Africa, but some became nominal Christians.

Their skills and knowledge were, as a result, mainly lost, despised or forgotten. Nevertheless, the influence of the Moors is still tangible in the fields they first cultivated and irrigated, the castles they built, the labyrinthine towns they laid out and in the towers of churches adapted from minarets.

GRANADA, CÓRDOBA AND THE COSTA DEL SOL

Lifestyles

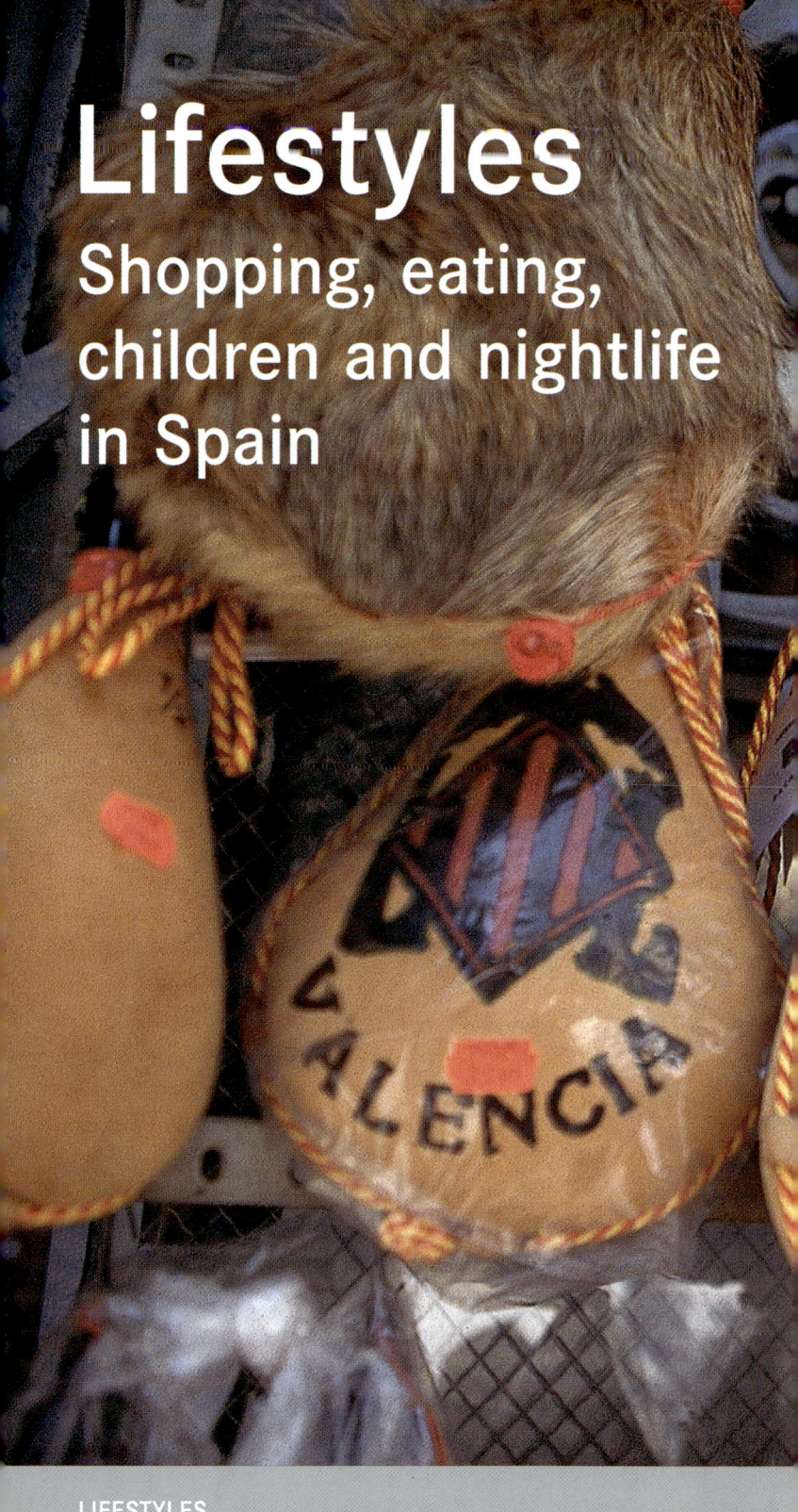

Shopping, eating, children and nightlife in Spain

LIFESTYLES

Shopping

Spain still has many small shops despite the invasion of chain stores and international brands. While prices may not compete with hypermarkets, you will get personal service and probably a more specialist stock to choose from. The main kinds of shops are:

carnicería: butcher's

charcutería: shop selling cold meats and cheese, often combined with other types of shop

droguería: soap and household goods

estanco: tobacconist, which also sells stamps, bus passes and phone cards

farmacía: chemist

ferretería: hardware, tools, DIY supplies

frutería: fruit and vegetable shop

kiosko: news-stand, usually also selling bus passes and phone cards

librería: bookshop

panadería (or **horno**): bakery

papelería: stationer's

pastelería: cake shop

ultramarinos (or **tienda de comestibles**): grocer's, general food provisions

Department stores and hypermarkets

Spain's biggest and best-known department store, **El Corte Inglés**, has branches in all the main Spanish cities. Hypermarkets (*hipermercados*), such as **Continente**, **PRYCA** or **Alcampo**, are located outside towns but usually have bus services to get to them. If you are driving follow the signs for *centro comercial*.

Food

Shopping for food in Spain can be a way of getting to know the people in their everyday lives. Don't be afraid to ask questions of a shopkeeper before buying. Your interest in the unfamiliar commodities on the shelves will probably be enough to get him or her talking, explaining the best way to prepare them. And you may be offered a small sample of cheese, ham or whatever to help you make up your mind.

LIFESTYLES

If you prefer to serve yourself, branches of **El Corte Inglés** have supermarkets which are a cut above the average.

Some regions specialise in a particular food. Andalucia, for instance, is renowned for its olives and olive oil.

Spain is especially good for its **cold, cured meats**. You'll see legs of ham hanging in shops and bars wherever you go. The most popular sandwich ingredient in Spain is cured **jamón serrano** – literally 'mountain ham'. If you want to try the very best (significantly more expensive) you should ask for **jamón iberico de bellota**, which is made from a particular species of pig fed on a pure diet of grass and acorns. Cooked ham is *jamón de york*.

No pork product is wasted, and there are a great many other cold meats to try. After ham comes *chorizo*, which can be roughly divided into two types: one needs cooking but the other can be eaten as it is.

As for **cheeses** (*queso*), if Spain has no internationally well-known cheeses it is no reflection on their quality. There are seven regions with a *denominación de origen* producing a variety of cheeses from cow's, sheep's and goat's milk. The most common Spanish cheese is **queso manchego**, a sheep's-milk cheese from La Mancha. If you like blue cheeses look for **cabrales**, which is made from a mixture of cow's, sheep's and goat's milk in the Picos de Europa.

Wine is available from supermarkets, specialist wine shops and – best of all – from the producers themselves. In any wine region you will be able to take your own bottles to fill up in the local co-operative.

LIFESTYLES

Fashion

In Madrid and Barcelona, look out for clothes by top Spanish and Catalan designers such as **Adolfo Domínguez** and **Antonio Miró**. Mid-range fashion chain stores can be found in any city centre.

Leather and shoes

Spanish leather is no longer the bargain it was, but the quality is good and prices are reasonable if you shop around. Better still, go where the goods are made. Shoes, for instance, are made in **Elda** and other towns around Alicante, and some of the best leather goods are made in **Ubrique**, one of the Pueblos Blancos ('White Towns') in Andalucia.

Crafts

Every region has its particular crafts although some turn up everywhere, such as guitars, flamenco shoes, leather drinking-bottles and fans. Shop with discretion and you will be able to tell the real article from the stuff made solely for tourists.

Spanish **pottery** is always good value. It ranges from simple brown-glazed cooking-pots to elaborate Moorish designs. Some pieces can be bought at ridiculously low prices at street markets. **Paterna** and **Manises**, near Valencia, and **Talavera de la Reina**, near Toledo, are well known for their ceramics.

Music, books and maps

Fnac and **El Corte Inglés** have branches in the main cities with their own music, book and map departments. They are particularly well stocked with CDs featuring Spanish folk musicians, flamenco performers and contemporary Spanish rock acts, as well as Cuban and Latin American dance music, all at reasonable prices.

LIFESTYLES

and 1630 to 2000. Some shops close on Saturday afternoons, especially in summer, though this custom is gradually dying out. The tradition of taking a lunchtime siesta is still very much alive, though this too is under threat from the growing number of department stores and shopping malls which open from 1000 to 2130 six days a week. The majority of shops are also closed on Sundays, except during the run-up to Christmas. Markets start around 0800 and are usually closed by 1400, though some of the larger markets reopen in the evenings.

Markets and flea markets

Visiting a market in Spain can be a wonderful experience, even if you are not shopping. You'll find stalls piled high with fresh produce and local delicacies. Fish markets in coastal towns can be particularly interesting. Every large town has a covered, permanent market, sometimes a beautiful old building in its own right, and most towns – even the smallest – will have a weekly **mercadillo** – a temporary, open-air market in the streets or main square where you will be able to buy a little of everything at reasonable prices. The biggest flea market is Madrid's **Rastro** on Sunday mornings (*see page 27*).

Opening hours

Most shops are open Monday to Saturday from around 1000 to 1400 If you are looking for bargains, many stores hold their **annual sales** (*rebajas*) in late January and February, and again in July and August.

How to pay

Department stores will accept **credit cards** but smaller shops will prefer **cash**, and almost no shop at all will accept a **cheque**. The prices on display generally include a **sales tax** (IVA) of 16 per cent. Visitors from European Union countries must pay this tax, but are exempt from customs duty on their return home; travellers from non-EU countries may claim a tax rebate on purchases above a set limit, currently 15,000 pesetas. This is usually given in the form of a cheque at customs, but if you shop at a store displaying the **'Tax Free Shopping' logo** you may be able to claim an immediate refund on your credit card.

LIFESTYLES

Eating out

Spain has thousands of bars, cafés and restaurants to choose from where you can eat anything from a hasty snack to a banquet. If you can't find what you want on the menu you can always ask. Spanish waiters usually take pride in keeping the customer satisfied.

Where to eat

Several restaurants describe themselves as *asador* or *horno de asar*, indicating that they roast meats in a wood-fired oven. *Posada*, *mesón* and *tasca* are all antiquated words for an 'inn', and they can feature in the name of any establishment, from a simple bar to an expensive restaurant. Other types of restaurant include: **arrocería** (rice restaurant), **casa de comidas** ('a place to eat' – without gourmet pretensions) and **marisquería** (restaurant or bar specialising in seafood). A **bodega** is a bar serving mostly wine and little in the way of *tapas*, but you can usually get something to eat anywhere describing itself as a bar or café, as most of them will serve snacks or sandwiches (*bocadillos*).

Eating hours

The lateness of Spanish mealtimes comes as a shock to visitors from northern Europe and America. **Breakfast** is a casual affair, usually a milky coffee and a croissant or sandwich at any time up to about 1200. Very few restaurants serve **lunch** before 1300 or **dinner** before 2100, and it is quite normal to see people sitting down to dinner at 2300, especially at weekends. If you can't wait so long, you can always have *tapas* at any hour of the day. Most restaurants are closed for one day a week, usually Sunday or Monday, and the majority are closed on Sunday evenings.

The *menú del día*

If you are on a budget, or just don't know what to order, choose the *menú del día* ('menu of the day'), which is offered by most restaurants on weekday lunchtimes and sometimes in the evening. This will usually comprise **three courses** with a limited choice for each. A bottle of the house wine (or water) and bread may or may not be included in the price, and there will be a basic choice of desserts – probably fresh fruit or *flan* (crème caramel). If you order coffee, an aperitif or anything else extra it will be added to the bill.

All restaurant prices are subject to 7 per cent VAT (IVA), which is not normally included on the prices you see on the menu outside the restaurant. The price of a *menú del día*, however, may be given as a round figure, including IVA.

LIFESTYLES

Special requirements

Vegetarians should be able to find something to eat in any bar or restaurant, even if it is only that great standby *tortilla de patata* (potato omelette). Almost every big city now has at least one dedicated vegetarian restaurant.

Few restaurants in Spain specifically cater for **people in wheelchairs**. The staff may have a ramp to cope with entrance steps, but it is rare to find a toilet adapted for disabled

LIFESTYLES

people. However, the Spanish are generally so accommodating that if the first restaurant you go into doesn't offer to lift your wheelchair in and shuffle tables round to make you comfortable, you should class it as an exception, give it a miss and try elsewhere.

Spain is behind the times when it comes to **smoking/non-smoking areas** and there are few places where you can get away from the fumes. Restaurants do not, as a rule, have no-smoking sections and the best you can do is ask to be reseated next to an open window.

Formal dress is not necessary except at the very smartest restaurants, but the Spanish do like to look their best and smart casuals are the norm.

Regional cuisines of Spain

Spain is a country of many different cuisines. In larger cities you'll find a choice of food available, but in smaller, more remote places there may be nothing more on the menu than local dishes. These can tell you something about the people: the food served in ordinary restaurants up and down Spain is the culmination of centuries of tradition, reflecting the ingredients available (usually fresh and sometimes homegrown) and methods of preparation handed down through the generations, although some parts of Spain have richer culinary traditions than others. **Coastal areas** have an abundance of seafood, and in **Mediterranean regions** the markets burst with fresh fruit, but in much of **central Spain** – Madrid excepted – you may find the same few dishes repeated over and over again on menus.

What to drink

Any half-decent restaurant will serve a good selection of Spanish wines. The locals tend to drink red wine whatever they are eating, or occasionally *rosé* in summer. The top Spanish wines are the oak-aged

LIFESTYLES

reds from **Rioja** and **Ribera del Duero**, though Catalonia also produces some excellent wines in its **Penedès**, **Costers del Segre** and **Priorat** regions. Penedès white wines are excellent, and other recognised *blancos* come from **Rías Baixas** (on the coast of Galicia) and **Rueda**.

Cava, the sparkling wine from the Penedès region, makes an inexpensive treat. It goes down well with early-evening *tapas*, as does **fino** (chilled dry sherry) and **txakoli** (fizzy white wine from the Basque country).

In the summer months, cheap wine is often combined with other ingredients to make refreshing drinks. Red wine is mixed with the Spanish equivalent of lemonade, *gaseosa*, to make **vino con gaseosa** (or *tinto de verano*).

Most of the beer (*cerveza*) drunk in Spain is lager (popular brands are **San Miguel** and **Cruzcampo**), but some bars, *cervecerías* especially, will also serve darker beers (*cerveza negra*).

As for spirits, Spain makes good **brandy**. Other spirits to try include **pacharán** (made from sloes and served with ice) and **anís** (a strong grape spirit tasting of aniseed). **Orujo** is often served as an after-dinner digestive – the variety flavoured with herbs is less strong than the straight *orujo blanco*.

Cocktails such as **gin-tonic** and **cuba-libre** (rum and Coke) are also popular.

The tap water in Spain is safe to drink. It can be more prudent, however, to stick to bottled water if you are on a short break – *agua sin gas* is still mineral water, *con gas* is sparkling.

Coffee has its own mystique in Spain and it's worth learning about the varieties available before you click your fingers at the bar staff. Ask for **café solo** if you want a strong black coffee (espresso), **café con leche** if you want white coffee. A popular variation is **café cortado**: a black coffee with a dash of milk. Spanish coffee is invariably strong; ask for **un americano** if you want a diluted espresso coffee, or **descafeinado** if you prefer decaffeinated. In the summer, a **café con hielo** makes a refreshing change: you'll get a black coffee and a glass of ice cubes to pour it over.

Tea is not widely drunk. Mostly you will be given a run-of-the-mill tea-bag to steep in a cup of hot water. If you want to steer clear of caffeine you could order a **manzanilla** (chamomile tea), **menta** or **poleo** (both types of mint tea). **Hot chocolate** can be drunk at any time of day or night. It is normal to dunk *churros* (sugared sticks of batter) into it.

235

LIFESTYLES

Spain with children

Spain could be a country made for kids. It's not just that the sunshine allows them to play out of doors all year round. Here, people – almost everyone – love children, and they are welcomed almost everywhere, although there are rarely any special provisions for them. Most restaurants, for example, except the most formal, will happily accept children, but there is not usually a special children's menu and no allowance will be made for their fussy dining habits: they will be expected to eat squid rings rather than fish fingers and chips.

However, most places will serve half-portions on request; if they won't, try elsewhere. Special facilities, such as baby-changing rooms and pushchair ramps, are still extremely rare in Spain; children are simply expected to fit into ordinary life. Spanish parents do not think twice about taking very young children out dining with them late into the night, so you may want to emulate them and not bother with baby-sitters.

On the plus side of provisions for youngsters, all parks have children's play areas and some lay on special activities on Sunday mornings. Many museums have hands-on activities and children's events at weekends, and the busiest beaches will be child-friendly, with lifeguards, safe swimming, playgrounds and level promenades.

Don't fight it: if your children are happy, so are you. Here are some recipes for family bliss.

Beach holidays

The brasher the resort the better as far as kids are concerned. Don't go anywhere with any pretensions to culture. Megaresorts like Torremolinos on the Costa del Sol, Benidorm on the Costa Blanca and Salou on the Costa Brava know all about keeping kids amused with funfairs, shops full of cheap souvenirs, go-karts and other adrenalin sports for older kids – and a road train to ride about on.

Water parks

Near any beach resort of any size there will be a water park – a glorified swimming-pool complex

LIFESTYLES

with enough slides, swimming-pools, scary rides and things to climb on to keep any hyperactive youngster amused for hours.

Theme parks and fun fairs

Port Aventura
10km (6 miles) southwest of Tarragona, off the A7 or N340. Tel: 90 220 2220; www.portaventura.es. Open: daily Mar–mid-June and mid-Sept–Nov, 1000–2000; daily mid-June–mid-Sept, 1000–2400. ££.
This vast theme park is divided into five areas dominated by the thrilling roller-coaster **Dragon Khan**. There is too much to do in a single day; buy a two-day ticket so that you don't have to rush.

Terra Mítica
Tel: 90 202 0220; www.terramiticapark.com. Port Aventura now has a rival down the coast near Benidorm. Terra Mitica, which opened its doors in summer 2000, claims to be the largest theme park on the Mediterranean coast with the second-largest roller-coaster in the world.

Isla Mágica: *see Sevilla, page 194.*
Mini Hollywood: *see Desierto de Tabernas, page 220.*
Tibidabo: *see Barcelona, page 107.*

Train rides

Several old-fashioned trains operate in Spain. The **Limón Expres** runs along the Costa Blanca from Benidorm to Gata de Gorgos; the **Strawberry Train** connects Madrid and Aranjuez; and in the Pyrenees there is **La Cremallera**, a cog-railway between Ribes de Freser and Núria.

Boat trips

You can take a boat trip along the coast from almost every sizeable resort – the Costa Brava is particularly good for this – or you can hire your own canoe or other boat and paddle around off the beach. Madrid's **Parque del Retiro** (*see page 39*) is a tame place to go for a row in between museums, and you have the added advantage of street entertainers performing around the lake at weekends.

LIFESTYLES

After dark

You shouldn't ever get bored in Spain, a country where there is plenty of organised entertainment and where there always seems to be something going on in every square and around every street corner. But you will need to pace yourself to stay the course, especially when most events happen in the cool of the evening or at night.

Theatre and cinema productions rarely start before 2200, **jazz and rock concerts** may kick off at midnight or after, and **clubs** start to fill up around 0100 and stay busy until breakfast time. Exhausted foreign tourists often stumble back to their hotels shortly before midnight wondering what all the fuss was about, then find out next morning to their horror that they simply went out too early and missed the fun. In such conditions the lazy **siesta** after lunch is more than a cliché or an unnecessary indulgence: you'll enjoy yourself more if you slow down, get some rest during the afternoon, go out when the Spanish do and generally prepare yourself for long waits before anything happens.

Madrid and Barcelona

The best choice of entertainment is to be found in Madrid and Barcelona, except in August when Spanish cities virtually close down and there is more going on in coastal resorts. In both these cities you can get 'what's on' listings guides in English, but they will not be as complete as their Spanish-language counterparts. Madrid, Barcelona and the other major cities have cinemas showing **original-version films** – elsewhere, and on TV, films are invariably dubbed into Spanish.

Bars and clubs

The distinction between cafés, bars and clubs is blurred, although it is usually clear whether a place is a daytime place to eat and likely to wind down in the evening or a night-time place to drink in which the atmosphere is dead until around midnight.

Bares de copas (sometimes called *pubs* – bars to drink rather than eat in) will have few seats and loud music playing. They don't usually charge admission, even at weekends, though some may turn into discos for the night. Every town usually has its street of bars, which you can walk down during the day without noticing because everything is shut up. You may have to ask around to find the hippest place.

LIFESTYLES

The evening usually starts in places like this, then groups of friends will move on to **discos** or **clubs** to dance. These tend to be located out of town where the noise and comings and goings outside won't disturb anyone. Some of these clubs, where you will have to pay admission, are truly colossal, their music and lighting systems on an industrial scale. In holiday resorts you won't have to look for the clubs because they will come looking for you: their representatives often cruise the streets in novelty cars offering a free ride to the door.

Flamenco

Andalucía is the home of flamenco, but even the best practitioners will tell you that it has become something of a national phenomenon, and good flamenco can be seen not only in Sevilla but also in Barcelona and Madrid. If you want to see authentic flamenco rather than a show put on for tourists, it's best to ask the locals where to go. A National Flamenco Competition is held in **Córdoba** in May every third year (2001, 2004 etc) and a biennial flamenco festival in **Sevilla** in the September of even years only (*see page 202*).

Bullfighting

It is something you either love or hate, but bullfighting is part of Spanish culture. Most towns have a bullring, and fights are reported in the papers and shown on television. Bullfighting is considered more an art form than a sport. There are, of course, animal-rights activists who would like to do away with *corridas*, but they have yet to sway public opinion. If you do want to see a fight, it is best to ask an *aficionado* to accompany you or you might not understand what is going on. Seats in the bullring are either **sol** (in the sun) or **sombra** (in the shade). Informal bull-running – when bulls chase people in the streets and hopefully neither human nor animal is hurt – is a fairly common ingredient of fiestas in some regions (*see page 144*).

Arts and music festivals

Spain has a packed calendar of arts and music events. Some are small scale, but none the less well worth attending. Many events take place out of doors and some are held in historic buildings. The most important cultural festivals of the year include:

Festival of Ancient Music (Sevilla, end of January)

Grec Arts Festival (Barcelona, June and July)

Granada International Festival of Music and Dance (Granada, June and July, with some events being put on in the Alhambra and the Generalife)

Guitar Festival (Córdoba, July)

International Jazz Festivals (San Sebastián and Vitoria, both July)

National Classical Theatre Festival (in the Golden Age theatre of Almagro, July)

Classical Theatre Festival (in the Roman theatre at Mérida, July–August)

International Festival of Santander (music, dance and theatre, July–August)

San Sebastián Film Festival (September)

Fiestas

If you don't mind crowds and you have the patience to stay up all hours, look out for the nearest fiesta, which will offer hours of free entertainment (*see page 182*). Some fiestas are little more than a big street party, but many preserve curious and ancient traditions. Be sensitive to what is going on and don't join in activities such as bull-running unless you are sure you know what you are doing. It's always worth asking in a tourist information office if anything special is about to take place. Some of the best fiestas for spectators are:

Fallas, Valencia. Arrive a day or two before 19 March and get up early to see the *fallas* (satirical *papier-mâché* sculptures) before they are burnt. On the night itself it may be more rewarding to watch one of the smaller, suburban *fallas* burning rather than the one in the crowded main square.

April Fair, Sevilla. You'll get the atmosphere by being there, but the best part of the fair is reserved for the private clubs, *casetas*.

Semana Santa. There are processions almost everywhere during Easter Week and you don't have to brave the frenetic streets of Sevilla, Valladolid or Murcia to get the flavour.

LIFESTYLES

Moors and Christians, Alcoi.
The first day, 22 April, is the best to see the showy costumes of the two armies; the last, 24 April, if you prefer action.

Sanfermines, Pamplona.
See page 159.

Els Castellers, provinces of Tarragona and Barcelona.
These teams of daredevil human-tower builders perform in many places. Find the highest vantage point you can.

241

LIFESTYLES

Practical information

PRACTICAL INFORMATION

PRACTICAL INFORMATION

Practical information

Accommodation

As well as conventional hotels, Spain has other types of accommodation to choose from. **Paradors** are upmarket hotels which belong to a state-run chain. Many of them are renovated old buildings (castles, monasteries, and so on), which makes for an atmospheric stay. As a sightseer you are always free to wander round those parts of the parador not reserved for guests, or to have a drink in the bar.

At the other end of the price band, there is now an enormous number of bed and breakfasts, or *casas rurales*, in country areas. Some of them are village or farm houses of great character. Tourist offices can usually provide lists of *casas rurales* in the area.

Airlines, airports and ferries

Most visitors get to Spain from the UK by air. **Air Europe**, **British Airways**, **GB Airways**, **British Midland**, **Debonair Airways**, **Easyjet**, **Era**, **Go**, **Iberia**, **Monarch** and **Virgin Express** all operate regular flights between British and Spanish airports. The main airports for international scheduled flights are **Madrid** (*Barajas; tel: 91 305 8343*) and **Barcelona** (*El Prat de Llobregat; tel: 93 298 3838*).

A more leisurely way to travel is by sea: **Brittany Ferries** (*tel in UK: 0990 360 360, www.brittany-ferries.com*) and **P&O European Ferries** (*tel in UK: 0990 980 555, www.poportsmouth.com*) run services from Britain to northern Spain.

Climate

Spain is a large country and the climate can vary from one place to another. In northern Spain summers are warm but it can be rainy, although it is rarely cold. Rainfall is highest in Galicia, Asturias and Cantabria, the so-called 'Green Spain'.

Central Spain's continental climate means there are very hot summers and very cold winters, with heavy

PRACTICAL INFORMATION

snowfalls on high ground and biting winds. The climate of Mediterranean Spain guarantees sunshine in summer and mild winter days, when it is often warm enough to eat lunch out of doors by the sea.

Currency

Spain's currency is the **peseta (pta)**, issued in coins from 1 to 500 ptas and banknotes from 1 000 to 10,000 ptas. The practically worthless one-peseta coin is rarely seen these days and most bills are rounded down to the nearest 5 ptas. On 1 July 2002, the peseta will be replaced by the **euro**, and it is already common to see prices displayed in both currencies. Euro coins and notes will be issued in January 2002, and this will be followed by a six-month period during which both pesetas and euros will be in circulation.

Major credit cards are widely accepted, and travellers' cheques and foreign currency can be changed at banks, exchange bureaux and hotels. You will need to show your passport when changing travellers' cheques. Cash can also be obtained from ATMs (automated teller machines) using a credit card. Your bank will make a charge for this, but it may compare favourably with the commission charged by Spanish banks for changing foreign currency.

Customs regulations

Visitors arriving from other European Union countries may bring in any amount of goods provided they are for personal use and tax has already been paid. The limits for travellers arriving from outside the EU are 1 litre of spirits, 2 litres of wine, 200 cigarettes and 50g of perfume.

Disabled travellers

After a slow start, facilities for disabled people are improving rapidly in Spain, and all new public buildings have to be equipped with wheelchair access. The best advice is to ring before your visit so that your needs can be accommodated as far as possible. **Public transport** is not yet fully accessible, though more and more metro stations are introducing lifts and ramps, and adapted buses run on some routes. For the latest information, contact any of the main organisations who deal with the needs of disabled people: **ONCE** (*Calle Prado 24, Madrid; tel: 91 589 4600*), **COCEMFE** (*Calle Eugenio Salazar 2,*

PRACTICAL INFORMATION

Madrid; tel: 91 413 8001) and the Spanish Red Cross, **Cruz Roja Española** (*Calle Rafael Villa s/n, El Plantio, Madrid; tel: 91 335 4444*).

Electricity

Electrical appliances run on 220 225 volts AC, using standard European round-pinned plugs. Visitors from the UK will require an **adaptor** and US visitors may need a **transformer** for appliances operating on 100–120 volts. If you have forgotten to bring these, they are usually available from **El Corte Inglés** department stores.

Entry formalities

Citizens of European Union countries may visit Spain without restrictions, provided they hold a valid passport or national identity card. All other visitors require a passport. Citizens of the USA, Canada, Australia and New Zealand do not need a visa for visits of less than 90 days. Citizens of South Africa and some other countries require a visa, issued by their nearest Spanish embassy or consulate.

Health and insurance

There are no major health hazards in Spain, though it is important to ensure that you are covered by adequate health insurance. Citizens of European Union countries should take **form E111**, which entitles them to free basic health care within the Spanish social security system. In most cases it will

PRACTICAL INFORMATION

be easier to use **private health insurance**, included on a comprehensive travel insurance policy along with cover for accidents, theft and personal liability. This is advisable for everybody, and essential for visitors from outside the European Union.

The biggest health hazard is usually the **sun**. It is important to protect your skin with a strong sunscreen and to avoid the intense heat of the early afternoon, at least until your body has acclimatised. Drink plenty of water, and remember that small children are particularly vulnerable. Tap water is safe to drink, but mineral water is widely available.

Pharmacies can easily be identified by a large flashing red or green cross displayed on the street. Outside normal hours, a notice on the door of each pharmacy saying *Farmacia de guardia* gives the address of the nearest duty chemist.

Information

The tourist information office in the main cities and towns (for addresses, see relevant chapters) are a source of information on sites, opening hours (which frequently change in Spain), accommodation and restaurants. For information on the latest shows and exhibitions, consult the local media, which publishes listings of events as well as what's on at cinemas, theatres and concerts. For information on Spain before your trip, contact the **Spanish Tourist Office** (*see page 17*).

Opening times

For shop opening times *see page 231*, and for restaurants *see page 232*.

Banks are open Monday to Friday from around 0900 to 1400, and on Saturday mornings between October and April. Outside these hours you can change money at hotels and private exchange bureaux. There are also out-of-hours currency-exchange services at the main airports and railway stations.

Post offices are open from around 0830 to 1400 Monday to Friday and 0930 to 1300 on Saturdays, though stamps can be bought at tobacconists' outside these times.

Museums are usually closed on Mondays and on Sunday afternoons, but check the hours of individual entries in this book.

Churches are usually open for mass in the morning and the evening, and closed at midday, although the main churches and cathedrals will stay open longer hours.

Tourist offices have a wide range of opening times, but they are normally open between 1000–1300 and 1500–1900.

Petrol stations on the main roads don't usually close at lunchtime and are open until late. Some are open 24 hours, but don't rely on them and try to keep your tank full whenever you know you are going far from a motorway or a main road.

PRACTICAL INFORMATION

PRACTICAL INFORMATION

Public holidays

Apart from national holidays, which are taken across Spain, there are others that apply only to each region (*comunidad autónoma*). The majority of shops, banks and offices will be closed on these days, and museums and public transport facilities tend to keep Sunday hours. If a holiday falls on a Saturday or Sunday, many businesses will close on the following Monday instead; if it falls on a Tuesday or Thursday, it is traditionally extended over a long weekend, a device known as a *puente*, or bridge. The following are the main public holidays in the whole of the country:

1 January	New Year's Day
6 January	Epiphany
Thursday before Easter	Maundy Thursday
Friday before Easter	Good Friday
Monday after Easter	Easter Monday
1 May	Labour Day
15 August	Assumption of the Virgin
12 October	Día de la Hispanidad (Spanish National Day)
1 November	All Saints' Day
6 December	Día de la Constitución (Constitution Day)
8 December	Feast of the Immaculate Conception
25 December	Christmas Day

Safety and security

Like most countries, Spain has its share of crime, though this mostly takes the form of petty annoyances rather than serious danger. The biggest problems are **bag-snatchers** and **pickpockets**, so it pays to take a few common-sense precautions. Leave your passport, money and valuables in the hotel safe, and never carry around more cash than you need. In crowded places, keep your handbag firmly closed and avoid having a wallet in your back pocket. If you put down your bag or coat, leave it where you can see it, preferably on your lap, rather than slung over a chair in the street. There is no need to be paranoid, but it pays to be alert and aware of your surroundings and possessions at all times.

If you are unlucky enough to be the victim of a crime, you will need to report it, if only for insurance purposes. Your first point of contact will usually be the **Policía Nacional**, who are responsible for dealing with serious crimes. They can be recognised on the street by their dark-blue combat-style fatigues. A second police force, the **Policía Municipal**, wear navy jackets and pale blue shirts and are responsible for urban traffic and enforcing law and order. In an emergency, you can contact the Policia Nacional on **091**.

Telephones

In most Spanish cities there are a number of public telephones on the street, although in rural areas sometimes it is not so easy to find one. Phone booths have instructions in several languages. Most will accept coins, telephone cards and major credit cards. For international calls, the easiest option is to buy a **phonecard** (*tarjeta telefónica*), available in units of 1 000 or 2 000 ptas from post offices, newsstands and tobacconists. These same outlets also sell a growing range of

PRACTICAL INFORMATION

PRACTICAL INFORMATION

pre-paid calling cards, where you dial a toll-free number and enter a PIN (personal identification number) before making your call, which often works out cheaper. The cheap rate for international calls is from 2200 to 0800 on weekdays, after 1400 on Saturday and all day Sunday. Calls made from your hotel room are normally subject to a heavy surcharge.

The area code (which starts with a 9) must be dialled for all phone numbers, even if you are calling next door. To make an international call from Spain, dial 00 followed by the code of the country you are calling (UK = 44, Ireland = 353, USA/Canada = 1) and then the area code, omitting the first zero in calls to the UK. To call Spain from abroad, dial the international access code (00 from the UK, 011 from the USA) followed by 34 for Spain and then the number listed in this book. A series of long tones means that the phone is ringing; short, rapid tones mean it is engaged. The usual greeting is *dígame* ('speak to me').

Time

Spain is one hour ahead of GMT (Greenwich mean time) in winter and two hours ahead in summer, from the

PRACTICAL INFORMATION

last Sunday in March to the last Sunday in October. The harmonisation of summer time across the European Union means that Spain is always one hour ahead of the UK.

Tipping

Most restaurant bills include a **service charge**, but it is usual to leave a small extra tip of around 5 per cent for good service. In bars, you usually pay for all the food and drink when you leave, not as you order it, and it is customary to leave some small change on the counter. Taxi drivers expect around 10 per cent, and hotel porters, chambermaids and toilet attendants are always happy to receive a modest tip.

Toilets

A shortage of public toilets means that the easiest solution is usually to go into the nearest bar, where the price of a cup of coffee will save any potential embarrassment. Other good standbys are museums and department stores. If you need to ask for the toilet, the word is *los servicios*. The ideograms on the doors are usually self-explanatory, but if you are in any doubt the words are *caballeros* for men and *señoras* for women.

Index

A
accommodation 244
airlines 14, 244
Alarcón 79
Albarracín 165, 179
Alcalá de Henares 62
Alcalá del Júcar 71, 80
Alicante 165, 172
Altea 171
Andorra 125, 131
Aranjuez 71, 72–3
Ávila 49, 56–7

B
Baeza 207, 218
Barcelona 18, 90–111
    Barri Gòtic 18, 93, 94
    Catedral 93, 94
    L'Eixample 102–3
    festivals 240, 241
    Monestir de Pedralbes 32, 93, 106
    Montjuïc 104
    Museu Nacional d'Art de Catalunya 93, 105
    Museo Picasso 96–7
    museums 96–7, 100, 101, 105
    nightlife 239
    Parc de la Ciutadella 100–1
    Parc Güell 106–7, 111
    Poble Espanyol 93, 104–5
    Las Ramblas 93, 98–9
    La Sagrada Família 93, 103, 111
    Tibidabo 107
Belmonte 79
Benidorm 165
Bilbao (Bilbo) 137, 138–9
    Museo Guggenheim 138
bullfighting 13, 73, 239
Burgos 137, 148, 161

C
Cáceres 71, 82
Cádiz 198
Calp 170
car hire 16
Cartagena 165, 175
Castillo de Olite 67
castles 54–5, 66–7, 79, 128, 179
Castro Urdiales 150
Catalan Pyrenees 124–5
Cervantes 10
children 236–7
Chinchón 73
climate 244–5
coach travel 14
Córdoba 18, 207, 216–17
    festivals 240
    La Mezquita 18, 216–17
Costa Blanca 6, 165, 170–1, 236
Costa Brava 6, 115, 120–1, 236
Costa Daurada 6, 117
Costa de la Luz 6, 197
Costa del Sol 6, 207, 208–9, 236
Costa Verde 6, 153
Cuenca 69, 71, 78–9
Cuidad Rodrigo 57
cultural festivals 240
culture 12
currency 245–6
customs 246

D
Dalí, Salvador 121, 122–3
Desierto de Tabernas 207, 220
disabled travellers 246–7
Don Quixote 88–9
drink 234–5
driving 16–17

E
eating out 8, 24, 42, 64, 86, 108, 130, 158, 159, 180, 200, 222, 232–5, 236
El Escorial 18, 49, 50–1
El Greco 10, 71, 76–7
electricity 247
entry formalities 247
Extremadura 69

F
ferries 244
fiestas 63, 65, 141, 144, 159, 167, 182–3, 200, 240–1
Figueres, Teatre-Museu Dalí 115, 122–3
flamenco 201, 202–3, 222, 239
food 228–9
Franco, General Francisco 11, 51

G
Gandia 169
Gaudí, Antoni 103, 106, 110–11
getting around 14–16, 22, 48, 70, 92, 114, 136, 164, 186, 206
Girona 123
Goya, Francisco de 34, 37
Granada 207, 212–15, 224
    festivals 240
    La Alhambra and El Generalife 18, 67, 207, 214–15
Guadalajara 63
Guernika-Lumo (Guernica) 139

H
health 247–8
history 10–11

J
Jaén 218
Jerez de la Frontera 187, 198
Jerez de los Caballeros 85

L
La Mancha 69, 71, 80, 88–9

La Rioja 146–7, 183
La Vila Joiosa 171
language 8
Las Alpujarras 221
Las Cuevas de Altamira 137, 151
León 137, 154, 161
Los Pueblos Blancos ('White Towns') 187, 199, 207, 230

M

Madrid 22–43, 183
    Café Gijón 30–1, 42
    Centro de Arte Reina Sofía 19, 23, 31, 38–9, 139
    El Rastro 23, 27
    Museo del Prado 19–20, 23, 31, 34–7
    Museo Thyssen-Bornemisza 18, 23, 31, 32–3
    nightlife 238
    Palacio Real 23, 28
    Paseo de la Castellana 40
    Plaza Mayor 23, 26
    Puerta del Sol 23, 24
Málaga 66, 209
maps 17
Marbella 209
markets 109, 231
Mérida 71, 84–5
metro 16, 22
Miró, Joan 38, 98, 105
Monasterio de Guadalupe 71, 83
Monasterio de San Juan de la Peña 115, 126
Monestir de Santa Maria de Poblet 115, 117
Montserrat 18, 115, 119
Moors 10, 224–5
Mora de Rubielos 179
Morella 165, 177
Murcia 165, 174, 183

N

nightlife 43, 109, 131, 181, 238–9

O

opening hours 231, 232, 248

P

paella 166, 180
Pamplona (Iruña) 144, 183
Parque Nacional de Doñana 187, 196–7
Parque Nacional de Ordesa 115, 126
Parque Natural de Monfrague 83
Peñiscola 165, 176
Picasso, Pablo 23, 33, 36, 38, 108
Picos de Europa 19, 137, 152
public holidays 250

R

rail travel 15, 237
Rías Baixas 6, 137, 157
Ronda 207, 210

S

safety 250
Salamanca 19, 49, 58–9, 65

San Millán de la Cogolla 147
San Sebastián 137, 140–1
    festivals 240
Sant Sadurní d'Anoia 118–19
Santa Pola 171
Santander 150
    festivals 240
Santiago de Compostela 19, 137, 156–7, 160–1
    Praza do Obradoiro 19
Santillana del Mar 137, 151
Santo Domingo de la Calzada 146
Segovia 49, 52–3, 67
    Alcázar 49, 52–3
    Castillo de Coca 49, 55, 67
    Castillo de la Mota 49, 55
    La Granja de San Ildefonso 49, 53
    Pedraza de la Sierra 54
Sevilla 19, 186–95
    Catedral and La Giralda 187, 188
    festivals 183, 240
    Plaza de Toros de la Real Maestranza 187, 188
    Reales Alcázares 187, 190
    Torre del Oro 187, 188
    shopping 43, 65, 87, 109, 118, 131, 181, 201, 223, 228–31
Sierra de Gredos 57
Sigüenza 63
Sitges 118

T

tapas 44–5
Tarragona 115, 116–17
taxis 15–16
telephones 250, 252
Teruel 165, 178–9
time 252–3
tipping 253
toilets 253
Toledo 19, 67, 69, 71, 74–5, 183
    Mudéjar Toledo 77
Tordesillas, Convento de Santa Clara 49, 61
Torrevieja 171
tourist information 17, 23, 48, 70, 93, 114, 115, 137, 165, 187, 206, 248

U

Úbeda 207, 219

V

Valencia 165, 166–7, 182
    fiestas 240
Valladolid 61, 183
Valle de los Caídos 51
Velázquez, Diego de 10, 18, 34, 35, 36

W

wildlife 132–3

Z

Zafra 85
Zamora 60
Zaragoza 128–9

INDEX

Editorial, design and production credits

Project management: Dial House Publishing Services
Series editor: Christopher Catling
Proof-reader: Gill Colver

Series and cover design: Trickett & Webb Limited
Cover artwork: Wenham Arts
Text layout: Wenham Arts
Cartography: Polly Senior Cartography

Repro and image setting: Z2 Repro, Thetford, Norfolk, UK
Printed and bound by: Artes Graficas ELKAR S. Coop., Bilbao, Spain

Acknowledgements

We would like to thank Nick Inman for the photographs used in this book, to whom the copyright belongs, with the exception of the following:

Michael Busselle: pages 62 and 73

Government of Andorra, Ministry of Tourism and Culture: page 130

Patricia Harris: pages 188, 201 and 225

David Lyon: pages 15, 191, 192, 197, 203, 214, 216 and 218

Museo del Prado, Madrid: page 36

Museo Thyssen-Bornemisza, Madrid: page 33

Neil Setchfield: pages 44, 45, 90, 94, 96, 100, 103, 104, 106, 109, 110, 111, 138, 140 and 242

Spanish Tourist Board: pages 124, 127 and 147

Spectrum Colour Library: pages 34, 39, 50, 51, 184 and 195.

The author would like to thank the following for their invaluable assistance:

Genoveva Martín Aliste	Mark Little
Jon Bilbao	Juan Carlos Murillo
Miguel Angel Colino Blanco	Klaas Schenk
Josefina Fernández	Puri Villanueva

CREDITS